The 'Vindication' of Remi De Roo

The Lacey Land Saga

Political Sea-change in the Catholic Church

The 'Vindication' of Remi De Roo

The Lacey Land Saga

Political Sea-change in the Catholic Church

Patrick Jamieson

National Library of Canada Cataloguing in Publication Data

Jamieson, Patrick
        The 'Vindication' of Remi De Roo
        The Lacey Land Saga   –   Political Sea-change in the
        Catholic Church

        Includes bibliographical references and index.

        ISBN 978-0-9865254-6-9

    1.   De Roo, Remi J.   2. Catholic Church – British Columbia –
        Victoria   3. Politics in the Roman Catholic Church – Victo-
        ria Diocese 4. Controversial Land Investments

    I.   Title

© Patrick Jamieson, 2010

Typesetting and layout: Louise Beinhauer, Word Works
Editor assistance: Marnie Berger
Cover design: Sarah Roland

Published in 2010 by:
SMHN Editions of SAMARHANOR Press
204 – 4383 W. Saanich Road
Victoria, BC V8Z 3E8

DEDICATION

Two prophets in their own right.
To Bernice Levitz Packford, 1915 – 2010,
   a woman of valour and courage; and
My father, James Easton Jamieson,
   Founder of St. Andrew Refugee Association, Victoria.

THE CONDITION OF FOLLOWING CHRIST

"Then, speaking to all, he said: If anyone wants to be a follower of mine, let him renounce himself and take up his cross every day and follow me. Anyone who wants to save his life, will lose it; but anyone who loses his life for my sake, will save it.

What benefit is it to anyone to win the whole world and forfeit or lose his very self?

But while everyone was full of admiration for all he did, he said to his disciples. 'For your part, you must have these words constantly in mind: The Son of man is going to be delivered into the power of men.' But they did not understand what he said; it was hidden from them so that they should not see the meaning of it, and they were afraid to ask him about it."

Gospel of Luke, Chapter 9 verses 23-26, 43-45.

Contents

The 'Vindication' of Remi De Roo

Preface – In Praise of Unconventional Wisdom

The need for this book came home to me a few years ago. I was at a meeting at a progressive Roman Catholic parish in Victoria, populated largely by university educated and somewhat theologically literate professionals, ones who had recently and publicly demonstrated their acumen in these areas.

We were waiting for the meeting to begin and somehow the conversation turned to the recent financial scandal saga of the post-Remi De Roo era. Remi De Roo of Swan Lake, Manitoba had been bishop of Victoria for nearly thirty-eight years between October 31, 1962 when he was appointed at age 38, to February 24, 1999 when he was retired at the mandatory age of 75.

All the usually held conventional wisdom was aired, that obviously Bishop De Roo had been at best a poor financial administrator, that he had foolishly and scandalously invested in race horses, that he had been bilked by his business partner who was held to be a shyster American lawyer on the make, that De Roo had been primarily if not personally responsible for all the huge financial losses and that his successor, a noble and admirable man, had done his level best by putting together a team of experts to make the best of a bad situation, clearly not of their own making.

As the reader will discover in the pages of this book, I don't believe that any of the above five 'facts' happen to be true. But the really shocking thing to my sensibility after 25 years in Victoria doing Catholic church journalism is that people who might have been expected to know better (or to at least exercise some critical reflective judgment as imparted in their experience of Bishop De Roo) had transparently swallowed whole the five most (in)famous myths about the man.

It would have been just then that the need for such a book manifested itself permanently in my consciousness, or perhaps

v

my unconscious. Anyway, I was getting tired of swimming against the stream, a stream of patent ignorance and non-reflective non-analysis as far as I could make out. Conventional wisdom seemed to have won the day.

It may be time to try to create a new day. Sometimes a book can help to do that. The newspaper I was associated with had done a steady stream of critical journalism attempting to expose these falsehoods and this book is a collection of those articles along with some other pertinent material. It is all framed by an analysis that obviously leads to some specific conclusions.

2.

The meeting I attended when I had the start of this revelation (or at least resolution) was at a parish, Holy Cross, in the upper middle class area of the city adjacent to the university, which had just undergone a huge public scandal of its own, one publicized daily in the pages of the local newspaper of record throughout the early months of 2007. This happened to be the time of my mother's death. Our last conscious acts together were sorting through the story in the pages of the morning paper hours before she slipped into her final coma.

It was an odd story really, one only too typical of what the Catholic Church was starting to go through consistently. The bishop of the day, the second since De Roo left office, had been caught blatantly trying to put the parish back in line with his version of Catholic orthodoxy. Ordering his parish priest to fire the parish administrator on the basis of the administrator's alleged sexual orientation, he had been caught out when the pastor refused to co-operate and went public with the facts of the situation.

To its great credit, the parish rose up in shock, indignation and anger and held the bishop to account at public meetings. It seems fair to say that the bishop barely escaped without his mitre removed from both above and below. Certainly his integrity and style and moral character were given a public airing.

The meeting was part of the follow-up process instigated by the parish leaders who had confronted the bishop. Its purpose was to make certain the parish did not go off the rails again in this sullen direction.

With such a radicalization in their experience, I had almost assumed that the participants might now be exercising second thoughts about this earlier episode in the diocese that was, as it was clear, instigated by the same protagonists as the recent debacle. This was a group who unsuccessfully attempted to control and over-influence the new bishop's agenda to rectify the Catholic Church to traditionalist moorings.

Holy Cross had been established in the 1970s as a thorough-going Post Vatican II parish and this galled some of its more 'conservative' well-heeled members. This 2007 episode had been their effort to bring it back in line with their style of Roman orthodoxy.

3.

Another preliminary item that should be mentioned at this juncture was the original document issued by the man who followed Remi De Roo into office, Bishop Raymond Roussin in February 2000, the one that announced the entire crisis that was inevitably blamed on De Roo. It was written and designed in such a way that it patently revealed the whole problem of the political realignment of the Catholic church worldwide.

Upon close scrutiny it demonstrates how Roussin was being steered, how he did not have a grasp of the details of the financial situation himself and was forced to rely on advisors with their own agendas. He was not really ready or suited for the job of bishop, something he readily enough admitted during several interviews with the *Island Catholic News* editor Marnie Butler.

He was certainly unsuited to the acrimonious politics that had always surrounded the progressive prelate De Roo and which coloured this case. He seemed to me the sort of Catholic leader who might hold the view petty politics has no place in true Christianity.

Unfortunately when one holds this view, the snake of ugly politics often sneaks up from behind and stings badly from the anterior position.

Raymond Roussin had told editor Butler often enough how his dream had been to remain a simple brother in his order, and not even necessarily be ordained to the priesthood, never mind be elevated to the level of Bishop, a job which he stated held no appeal. He was doing it out of duty and he got caught out.

A breakdown here, following an automobile accident and subsequent psychological difficulties when he was Archbishop of Vancouver demonstrated this more eloquently than his words could. He was later prepared to be featured in a front page story in the *Vancouver Sun* newspaper candidly discussing his clinical depression, the roots of which transparently dated back to the dilemma he found himself in when in Victoria.

The momentous nature of the accusations and decisions in the 'Lacey Land Saga' required fine judgment and a clear capacity for independence of mind. All the chaos and confusion that followed his opening volley could only be avoided by a clear thinking leader with the gifts necessary for the brinkmanship required at that level of leadership.

From the start he allowed himself to be surrounded and ultimately, fatally controlled, by a group with an extreme right-wing theology and business perspective who had long been at odds with De Roo's program of reform as it arose out of the Second Vatican Council. Roussin could not have known this history unless he had initially consulted more broadly than he did. This deficit and his own naive predisposition manufactured the situation that was to ensue disastrously.

4.

It lead to disastrous effects, perhaps the least of which is the damaging of Bishop De Roo's name and reputation. The future of the church is the far more serious issue at stake. The diocese was basically spiritually and financially bankrupted by decisions deliberately taken by this group of 'advisors'.

Even from a cursory glance at the statement issued February 27, 2000, (**reprinted in Appendix**) from its tone and structure, it is clear that it is the start of a blame operation. It is rare, in my experience, to find one bishop going after another in that way within the structure of the Catholic Church, especially the Canadian Catholic Church. It seemed to augur a political sea change. Conventionally, unity and solidarity were the norm. Usually they bent over backwards to avoid being seen to be at odds, even at some personal and professional sacrifice.

For example, as the saga unfolded, Bishop De Roo refused to go anywhere near fighting back or blaming any decisions on his succeeding bishop. Many people felt he should have at least come out with an objectively stated version of the facts from his point of view. No one could have blamed him for that. Instead, he almost became an obstacle by this attitude when we were trying to get at the deeper truth of what was going on with the issue.

The structure of this statement that started the whole publicly-aired mess was that of a lawyer not a bishop seeking pastoral stability. Upon closer reading of the document which is included in the appendix of this book, as published in the *Island Catholic News* of March 2000, it seems clear that the bishop/author did not have a clear grasp of the issues at stake. He was not exercising independence of mind as the situation required, but rather was being steered by the actual authors and their advisors. He was steered this way until the day he left the diocese for higher office in Vancouver four years later.

In that four years all the damage was done, probably irreparably, to the financial affairs of the diocese and to the reputation of Bishop De Roo. More importantly to the nearly forty years of pastoral work done under Bishop De Roo's aegis, and that, it seems to me, was the real purpose of the exercise, to get back under the strict control of a certain theology, a geographical area of the church that had dared to exercise a refreshing libation if not liberation.

The usual and normal thing in such a situation for the Catholic Church would be to call in the previous administrator and the previous bishop and behind closed doors work out the situation. This is what would have been done under the previous more pastoral era.

Instead, there was an incessant condemnatory flow of information directly to the local media – previously unheard of in my now thirty-five years in Canadian Catholic journalism – which changed the tone from pastoral reconciliation and rectification to sensationalist journalism, legalist confrontation and forensic accounting in the pages of the newspaper for six months.

Thirty times in six months there were banner headlines to fuel the fire. Intentionally or not, this was a political attack and the incontrovertible evidence of a major political sea change in the direction and style of the Catholic Church with Victoria Diocese as a perfectly exemplary case study.

Remi De Roo, 75, and Raymond Roussin, 59, at the Diocesan Pastoral Centre at the time of the transition of responsibility early in 1999.

Introduction – Jury Backs Bishop's Deal

Bishop De Roo Vindicated

Washington State jury backs land deal cleric made in U.S. with church funds

By Robert Matas

Excerpted from the May 31, 2005 edition of *The Globe and Mail*

VANCOUVER — Months after Roman Catholic Bishop Remi De Roo retired in 1999, church officials shocked the country with accusations that the popular theologian had misspent millions of dollars from a nuns' trust fund buying land in the U.S. for a quick flip.

Six years after the explosive allegations were made, a jury in the Superior Court of Washington has vindicated the bishop.

Contrary to allegations by church officials, the jury decided the bishop, who was head of the Victoria diocese, had made a solid investment. During the 2 ½ week trial in Olympia, the state capital, the court heard that the land at the center of the controversy may have increased in value as much as fivefold since its purchase.

The church had no grounds for violating its contract with U.S. businessman Joseph Finley after Bishop De Roo retired, the jury found in a vote of 11 to 1.

The jury awarded $8.2-million (US) to Mr. Finley for damages caused by breach of contract and $4.2-million for breach of fiduciary duty. A date has not yet been scheduled for a judge to confirm the jury's verdict and set the payment that Mr. Finley will be entitled to receive.

"They have exonerated him. The decision validates [Bishop] De Roo's financial judgment," Patrick Jamieson, managing editor of the *Island Catholic News*, said yesterday in an interview. "This judgment proves he was not such a bad administrator."

Mr. Jamieson said the controversy arose from church politics. Bishop De Roo was well known for his liberal views on gays, married priests and women in the church. The Catholic Church has become more conservative in recent years, Mr. Jamieson said. "He was caught in a back tide."

Church officials who did not support the former bishop on church issues were too quick to accuse him of fiscal mismanagement, Mr.

1

Jamieson added. None of the church leaders in Canada spoke in Bishop De Roo's defense when allegations of fiscal mismanagement first surfaced. The land deal would have worked out if the church had honored its deal with the U.S. businessman and had not attacked the former bishop in public, he said.

Bishop De Roo, 81, was not available for comment yesterday. He apologized publicly in June of 2000 for his "errors." Recently, according to his website, he has been lecturing and holding retreats.

Victoria Bishop Richard Gagnon said yesterday the Catholic Diocese of Victoria plans to appeal the jury's decision.

"The diocese does not agree with the decision by the jury... The diocese believes an appeal will lead to a reversal of the verdict and dismissal of Mr. Finley's claims," he stated in a prepared statement sent to *The Globe and Mail* in response to a request for an interview.

Bishop Gagnon did not comment on the possible impact of the court award on the diocese.

However, Mr. Finley's lawyer, Randy Gordon, said Mr. Finley is not looking for the church to sell assets to pay out the court award.

The church's obligation could be met without interrupting its good works, Mr. Gordon said.

The sale of the property at the center of the controversy for its true value may be more than enough to take care of the court award, he said.

Mr. Finley would like to work with the church to reach a settlement, he said.

"Our goal is not to hurt the church, just to have [it] fulfill its legal obligations." However, if the church pursues its appeal in the court, "all bets are off," Mr. Gordon said.

The land at the center of the controversy is a 65-hectare industrial site in Lacey, Wash., a community of about 30,000, outside the state capital Olympia. The land was bought at a foreclosure sale for $5.3-million in 1997 by a partnership formed by the Victoria diocese and Mr. Finley.

Mr. Finley put the deal together; the diocese provided 100 per cent of the financing.

The partnership took out a mortgage on the property for $7.5-million in 1998 and anticipated reselling the property within 24 to 36 months for about $15-million.

But months after the bishop retired in 1999, his successor, Bishop Raymond Roussin, said the diocese did not have funds to make the mortgage payments. He tried to break up the partnership and accused Bishop De Roo of financial mismanagement.

After the diocese defaulted on payments, the mortgage holder imposed severe penalties, accelerating the debt. The diocese eventually raised $13-million (Canadian) from parishioners to pay off mortgage holders.

The Washington state jury received two appraisals of the land. Mr. Finley's lawyers called an appraiser, who said the land was worth $28-million (U.S.).

The diocese appraisers valued the land at $15.5-million to $20-million.

1.

As the above article from *The Globe and Mail* exposed, there was a solid case for the thorough vindication of Bishop Remi De Roo in the Lacey land scandal of 2000-2007. This book presents the evidence and circumstance of that case.

The argument started to play out in my mind as soon as the scandal was announced in March, 2000. There was too much evidence supporting the counterclaim and not enough credibility for the characters making the charges. Besides, I was in the middle of writing a book on the very subject, the political discrediting of Catholic leadership figures like Bishop De Roo, who stood out against the mainstream conventional wisdom on the basis of the ancient prophetic tradition of the Christian Church, a tradition that goes back thousands of years.

He was just the latest in a series of Canadian figures who were treated the same way in the last fifty years dating back to the former Archbishop of Montréal Joseph Charbonneau, who died in Victoria about 50 years prior to the outbreak of this latest scandal. That work anticipated the current development. In an intuitive way I knew that there was a story behind the headlines that would take some effort and digging to unearth.

2.

The opening chapter of this book was written nearly ten years ago. It was composed as a closing chapter for the aforementioned volume on the same subject. It was meant as a summary of the then current situation and I think it reads well enough as such a summary, but it was intuitively written.

I was finishing this biographical study of Bishop Remi De Roo when what I have come to call the 'Lacey Land Saga' flared up, in March of 2000, causing me to slow down the publication of *In the Avant Garde, The Prophet Catholicism of Remi De Roo* by nearly two years.

It was such a complex and antagonistic episode that it seemed very important to see what it was all about and how it could colour the reception and perception of Bishop De Roo for the future. At the same time I had a deadline to meet so could not then take the full amount of time to do all the necessary research for a definitive summary of the situation.

This was especially true because most of the developments could only be anticipated, including the jury trial in Washington in 2005, which resulted in his 'vindication'.

I have spent a good part of the last decade systematically reflecting on the facts of the case and this book is the result of what was written and concluded about it all, including the discrediting of Bishop De Roo. The tarnishing of his reputation at the time of the writing of my biographical study was a great shock to many as prior to that time it was virtually impeccable.

My own reaction to the news of the financial scandal, as it came to be called, was coloured by my research so I was very suspicious of the motivations at work. The subtitle of my book was the politics of the Catholic Church and I felt I could smell politics at work here.

By putting together my original version as portrayed in Chapter 1 of this book I was leaving myself vulnerable. The intuitive pattern was clear but would the actual facts bear it out? As it turned out, they did and this book is a testament to this fact.

The following summer after the publication of *In the Avant Garde, The Prophetic Catholicism of Remi De Roo and Politics within the Catholic Church,* I had the opportunity to make the acquaintance of Joseph C. Finley in a lawyer's office in Victoria.

This, I knew, was the moment of risk. What if he entirely or even partially contradicted all my so-called theories about the situation? Here was the actual business partner of Bishop De Roo and the Diocese of Victoria. If his version of the facts did not bear out what I had to speculate about, I would have to rethink the whole situation.

Up to this time, *Island Catholic News*, between February 2000 and the summer of 2002 had published virtually nothing about the story which had been played out fully in the pages of the *Times Colonist*, Victoria's daily newspaper. One exception was the statement by Bishop Raymond Roussin alluded to in the Preface.

3.

Three of us met with Joe Finley for a three-hour interview which was to prove momentous to the story. Finley was being depicted as a dark and mysterious if not outright unsavory character in the local press. He was the one, they said in so many words, who had lead the church down the garden path, bilked the bishop, etc. etc. What was he really like?

I found him a reflective, eloquent, enthusiastic, courtly 'southern gentleman', a lawyer and a business man, a former American military man (who had met two U.S. Presidents) and a Christian of the Southern Baptist persuasion. Moreover everything he told us that day confirmed my worst fears about the case. He confirmed my intuition that there was strange politics at play. It was the only explanation of certain glaring anomalies.

After two of us were de-briefed by a larger group, we decided it would be wise to invite Finley tell his side of things publicly. Let the parishioners decide for themselves. On November 26, 2002 we held an evening session at a public meeting room at the Central Library in Victoria and around sixty people attended. It was videotaped professionally and received media coverage. This started the process that was the foundation of this book.

A Special Edition of *Island Catholic News* dated January 2003 carried a full report on the library meeting which focused on Finley's version of the situation. In addition there was included in the special edition all the regular media reporting plus some letters about the impact of the meeting.

Included was Robert Matas' earlier article dated September 26, 2002 in *The Globe and Mail* which reported that court records were directly contradicting what the Diocese of Victoria was claiming about the case. If the contradiction was true the debenture bond issue of $13 million (CDN) was rendered unnecessary.

The opening paragraph of the article reads: "A special plea from the Diocese of Victoria for funds to stave off bankruptcy that followed a controversial land deal by Bishop Remi De Roo was unnecessary, according to records in a U.S. court case..."

This was the first serious contradiction to what the people of the Diocese on Vancouver Island had been told by their Catholic Church leaders and justified in itself the invitation by people of the Island to hear Joseph C. Finley's explanation of the fuller picture they obviously were not getting.

No mediation of a middle ground or hint of reconciliation was possible however. The legal process trumped the Christian values. The reaction was quick and vindictive. *Island Catholic News* was condemned publicly from the pulpit by Bishop Roussin who said in a CBC radio interview that no discussion was possible because the situation was in court. It was in court because he wanted it there. Finley was open to mediation outside the court process.

From that time forward *Island Catholic News* was not to be made available in the parishes of the Diocese. The cost to the little paper from loss of advertising and sales revenue would reach tens of thousands of dollars over the next seven years. None of this loss was necessary if an open and honest discussion of the subject had been encouraged by the powers that be. The church was returning to the mentality that error has no rights; and the church has all the right answers.

A Ten Year Process

When I think of the 'Lacey Land Saga' as I have come to call this story over the years, I can't blame people for losing track of the plot and losing interest in the details as the story has run at least since 2003.

It is so bizarre and incredible that it defies credulity. The implications are even more staggering. It is the evidence of a huge and tragic paradigm shift concerning how the Catholic Church is run.

But it is a story that I have come to love and this book is that labour of love.

I have come to believe that the 'Lacey Land Saga', far from being an oddity and a rarity is pretty much how the Catholic Church works now.

This book is entirely my own responsibility. The original articles might have been published elsewhere but I always had my own slant on the facts and subsequent developments have, in my mind, born them out; or at least reaffirmed my theories around it all.

On one hand, I know enough about abnormal psychology to recognize the possibility of a magnificent obsession or a delusion of grandeur. Deciding what is the truth of the situation will be the reader's assignment; and the ultimate purpose of the book. This is my argument with the authorities.

This opening chapter will recount what I have come to realize from my perspective from a very close study of the material over a decade. Of course, I bring an analysis to the subject matter. In application of my analysis I have come to a certain interpretation of the facts which I wish to share with the reader.

The reporting and close observation have already been printed elsewhere with one exception.

This 'exception' is what I have titled 'the lengthy confidential memo' which was necessarily written to explain to confidantes, supporters and advisors about some explosive developments which were emerging at a key moment in the case.

These were critical developments just at the time of the major trial in Washington between the Diocese of Victoria and their alienated business partner of the Lacey land property.

4.

A word about my journalistic background would seem appropriate.

I have been fully engaged within the Canadian Catholic Church since 1978 in the communication field.

I was the director of communications for the Catholic Health Association of Canada in Ottawa and the first lay editor of the Catholic newspaper, the *Prairie Messenger*, in Saskatchewan. I was the founding executive director of the Diocesan Health Care Council for the Diocese of Antigonish in Nova Scotia and established an independent Catholic newspaper for Vancouver Island in Victoria in 1986 which persists to this day.

Somehow circumstance has placed me in a strategic position to trace this story which seems to have implications for the universal Catholic church.

I have many writing interests other than this sort of journalism and this particular story but I have taken a professional interest in tracking it. In my study of the documents, certain conclusions have been unavoidable.

There are many aspects of this story which have gone unnoticed under cover of the greater sensation of the barrage of headlines. Thirty times in six months the story was on the front page or the lead page of an inside section of the local newspaper of record.

February 24, 1999

The key moment in the story is February 24, 1999. Bishop Remi De Roo turned 75 years of age that day.

According to the norms of The Second Vatican Council, Roman Catholic Bishops are to offer their resignation at this age. The

8

resignation may or may not be accepted by The Vatican but officially they must be tendered.

Bishop De Roo's was accepted. In fact his successor was appointed six months prior to that date and was located in the Diocese of Victoria for that period. This would become a key point in what was to follow: his presence and how much the new bishop was briefed on the finances of the diocese by staff prior to De Roo leaving office. It is significant to the subsequent decisions that effected the financial demise of the Diocese.

What became apparent at the time of De Roo's resignation was since everyone knew precisely when he was leaving office, there was a plan in the works by a group that quickly surrounded his successor and nothing was left to chance in taking control.

Due to her age, De Roo's financial officer also chose to resign at the same time his resignation took effect. This was both naive and unfortunate for the fortunes of the Diocese.

De Roo was appointed in the fall of 1962 in a surprise move by the pope at the time. He was only 38 years old and due to his gifts was seen as a rising star in the Canadian Church all during the period of the Second Vatican Council, 1962-65, and the following decade of reform.

It is no overestimation to say that he was an important figure in the progressive developments of the Canadian Church in the wake of the council. And the Canadian Catholic Church was one of the most progressive worldwide in terms of fully implementing the far reaching if not radical reforms of The Second Vatican Council. The backlash to this would form part of the 'Lacey Land Saga'.

It would seem odd that such a progressive individual would emerge out of a sleepy little backwater like Victoria but of course he was not formed in Victoria, but rather Winnipeg.

Manitoba had a strong self-confident Catholic culture as embodied in the fact three archdiocese are centered there – Winnipeg itself, The Ukrainian Eparchy and most significant to our story, the historic and French Saint Boniface, the seat of all western Canadian Catholic development after 1836. De Roo was a priest of the Diocese of St. Boniface.

It was Saint Boniface that formed Remi De Roo. He says that the three bishops of the church there were three giants who were instrumental in his formation, and it is said, subsequent appointment. He worked intimately with these men as an able young prelate coming out of the village of Swan Lake, Manitoba, south west of Winnipeg.

Obviously De Roo was not meant to remain in Victoria for very long, but the pope who appointed him died during the Council. Within five years' time he had crossed another even larger giant of the church, Cardinal McIntyre of Los Angeles, who I have written about elsewhere. As a result he was left to linger in this English-Irish enclave with a population who viewed him as 'other', as French, as a foreigner to their concept of village Catholicism. On the other hand, he also found willing disciples to his form of prophetic Catholicism.

However, over those nearly forty years a good deal of resentment built up locally, in reaction to the thoroughgoing way he implemented the council in the diocese. He kept certain would-be powerful figures at bay – clergy and laity alike. Some of these figures were exactly the ones who took control of the new situation and in effect the new bishop once he was appointed. This resulted in specific anomalies within the new bishop's situation, especially the financial arrangements.

De Roo's immediate successor was Raymond Roussin, another Manitoban, who had been the Bishop of Gravelbourg, Saskatchewan. He had been appointed bishop there in order to close and attach it to the Archdiocese of Regina.

In hindsight, it was not a good sign, yet De Roo publicly expressed his great pleasure at Roussin's appointment. And he meant it. He told me directly at the time of the announcement of the appointment how pleased he was and that he had not expected to get such an appropriate replacement. We were having coffee together on a break at an event held in the cathedral on View Street.

Marnie Butler, editor of *Island Catholic News*, 1993-2004, had predicted Roussin would be the one to replace De Roo. During an interview with Roussin at Queenswood Retreat Center, months prior to the news, she had told him it would happen. He had denied the possibility, saying he already had a diocese. When Butler ran her intuitive prediction past Bishop De Roo, he said: "You'll never be so lucky."

When one considers the sort of neo-conservative ordinaries that were being appointed by Rome, Roussin appeared almost a worthy successor to the progressive legacy in Victoria which had been developed between 1962 and 1999.

He was certainly not of the intellectual stature of De Roo and would be the first to admit this. In an interview with Butler when he first arrived, Roussin candidly stated that he did not even want to be a priest, never mind a bishop but had been forced by authorities and circumstances to accept the steps.

Pope John Paul II had seconded fresh religious orders like Roussin's, The Marianists, who had not distinguished themselves as producing any bishops over the years.

It was the Polish Pope's way of skirting historical politics with religious orders and getting firmer control of his appointments, who unfortunately, like Roussin, found themselves out of their depth. In his case he was to suffer a mental and emotional breakdown once appointed to serve as Archbishop in Vancouver after five years in Victoria. But the signs were there when he was still in Victoria.

Roussin had wanted to remain a simple brother in a minor religious order based in Switzerland and if lucky, be sent to a mission territory in Asia to help with street orphans. Instead, Roussin let loose forces in Victoria that virtually destroyed the Catholic church there, certainly entirely dismantled De Roo's progressive program, which was seen as a model of sorts for the universal church. After Roussin, the church was but a shell of its former self on Vancouver Island. De Roo's universal progressive model was scuttled.

Remi De Roo was not considered much of an administrator but the facts do not bear out this contention. Because he was considered such a prophetic speaker and teacher, De Roo's administrative abilities were always played down, especially by his critics but the truth was that being such a small diocese, he probably had more direct and difficult administrative responsibility when he was in Manitoba than Victoria required.

In 1962, when he arrived as a 38-year old *wunderkind*, the total budget for the diocese was less than $250,000 and the land value less than a million dollars. The previous bishop, Michael Hill, ran the whole place almost single handedly between 1946 and 1962.

At the time of Hill's death evidence was found of his style. He micro-managed the entire operation like a large parish. In his desk at the rectory of the cathedral on Blanshard Street, he left a hand written mass schedule drafted for the week, detailing all the clergy mass times. The diocese was of such a tiny stature that this was possible and seemed to many of the local priests as the only way to do things.

Seriously, this required modernizing and updating, which De Roo easily accomplished. The challenge of Victoria would never be that onerous to De Roo.

Even conservative estimates for 1999 when he left office were in the 90 million dollar range for the property value of the diocese. He had provided his critics who surrounded the new bishop with plenty of property to play with, which they quickly began to do. This was property he had always carefully stewarded. Victoria is a very desirable real estate location for the retirement of the rich and leisurely.

Its drawback from an investors' point of view is that it is on a peninsula and the property is limited. A stage of overdevelopment existed as the millennium drew to a close, the only land still available for rich and wealthy developers was the church reserves. This was the land they went after under the cover of the financial crisis which surrounded De Roo's orchestrated demise.

A good example was the allotment garden property next to Holy Cross parish in Gordon Head. A later chapter delineates this typical travesty of a created situation where the land was gobbled up by developers in conjunction with some of the decision makers through symptomatic cronyism.

One year after De Roo left office this new group started to make financial and administrative decisions that devastated the diocese. These decisions had nothing directly to do with any programs or processes De Roo had set in place. They took things entirely into their own hands, but in typical political fashion blamed it all on the previous administration.

5.

With foresight for the long term needs of the Diocese, De Roo had purchased the Allotment Garden lands shortly after becoming Bishop and 'land banked' them for the future. Over the years there had been innumerable requests from developers to buy the property. De Roo had always refused. Victoria was developing and the land might be needed in decades to come. Sale of those lands might be regretted as had the sale, in the 1930s, of the lands adjacent to St. Andrew's Cathedral by an earlier bishop.

Before leaving office as bishop, De Roo had banked the land for one hundred years. He had notified the group of gardeners, who had a thriving community garden on the land, to that effect. They were said to be delighted to know that the Diocese had land banked their community garden lands for a century at an affordable rent.

There is a sharp contrast between how De Roo dealt with land and how his successors did. When De Roo decided to sell some surplus land on Edgelow Street in Gordon Head, the matter was handled in-house. Kevin Doyle, the diocesan lawyer during the late 1980s and 90s, took charge of subdividing the Edgelow land, making the re-zoning applications, hiring the contractors to service the lots, advertising the lots for sale, selling off the parcels to successful bidders and keeping all the profits from the development entirely for the benefit of the diocese, not for outside interests.

As part of the Diocese of Victoria's efforts to recover losses on the Lacey Land, in October 2004 the diocese sued Kevin Doyle in the Supreme Court of British Columbia alleging that he had acted negligently throughout his dealings with De Roo, Finley and the

Lacey land. The Law Society of British Columbia reviewed Doyle's conduct over the years that he had acted as De Roo's and the Diocese of Victoria's legal counsel. They exonerated him and hired at their own expense, lawyers to defend Doyle. After four years of pursuing their claims, the diocese abandoned their claims against Doyle, but not before spending an estimated $150,000 in a futile effort to discredit him and his professional reputation.

6.

All of this would be bad enough if that was all that was going on.

Fifteen million dollars of diocesan property was sold at half value. The Lacey land itself was sold at half value losing fifteen million dollars (US). The court costs of fighting against the diocese's business partner is in the millions of dollars.

The travesty continued in terms of unnecessary costs, both monetary and moral. A thirteen million dollar debenture bond issue was raised to buy the mortgage of the Lacey property using the money of ordinary parishioners. Court records indicated there had been an offer to buy the Lacey property which would have made this unnecessary.

Land was sold for half price and used to make large profits for people who had nothing directly to do with the diocese, or its well-being, when the diocesan decision makers could have easily made the same profits to help the church itself. As mentioned, at an earlier time, under Bishop De Roo, land was developed by the diocese itself, then sold to raise needed funds and pay off debts.

This idea did not seem to occur to the new diocesan administrative and financial committee decision makers, despite the fact they all make their living doing precisely this sort of thing.

None of this was necessary. As early as November 26, 2002 Joseph C. Finley, the Diocese of Victoria business partner in *Corporate Business Park*, said publicly in Victoria he was ready to move into mediation to settle everything out of court. But Finley, for these agents seemed the devil incarnate. They never seemed to be able to fully account for their personal dislike of Finley.

Island Catholic News did a special edition at the time to help solve the problem. The little independent Catholic newspaper was treated to condemnation from the pulpit by the bishop of the day which cost it $150,000 in revenue over the next five years when its annual income dropped from $60,000 to $30,000 per annum due to cancelled ads by Catholic businesses and cancelled bulk subscriptions by parishes on Vancouver Island after fifteen years of successful enterprise at the much higher revenue level.

Three years later Finley won an $8.167 million dollar (US) judgment which was eventually reversed on a technicality. Finley proved by the facts of the case he was cheated -- breach of contract and breach of fiduciary responsibilities.

The deeper question is why did any of this have to happen? This book is an attempt to gain a clear-eyed look which only the passage of time and the lessening of the heat of the fray can allow.

Much of the answer lies in the changing of the guard in the universal Roman Catholic Church. In a paradigm shift in the leadership priorities of the Roman Catholic Church worldwide, there has been, since 1990, a political sea change in the Catholic church and Remi De Roo and his former diocese were its casualty.

7.

The Objective Facts of the Case

An objective statement of the legal facts of the case is in order at this point. To ensure objectivity, it is reprinted from a late court document, one which contained a decision favourable to the Diocese of Victoria in the last stages of the seven-year legal process.

Due to its dry and technical nature, the reader may wish to skip past it at this point, but know it is available for future reference at some point in the story if you feel a need for a clarification of fact.

On the other hand, it does provide the essence of the case and is a more than useful summary of the facts including the salient

15

one that it was under Bishop Raymond Roussin's administration that the crucial decision was made which cost the diocese its financial losses. It is the court record which confirms this fact which was the basis of Joseph Finley winning the trial jury judgment based strictly on the facts of the case.

As pointed out, this particular summary statement of facts is taken from the higher court decision which reversed that judgment, not on the basis of facts, but on a point of law about the nature of limited liability partnerships.

One criticism that can be expected of a book such as this is that since the Diocese to its own satisfaction 'won' the case against Bishop De Roo's business partner, how can he be considered 'vindicated' in any sense?

This book is not so much about the ins and outs of the legal battle (which most people in the Diocese quickly found tiresome) but rather is about what was revealed in the process. The real story is in the sub-text of the plot. Why did it have to happen in the first place? Why was it handled like this? How did corporate business values come to supplant Gospel values? What is the ultimate cost to the church of 'winning' in such a manner? Why did Bishop De Roo's reputation have to be sacrificed on such an altar, and why did he not defend himself?

Court of Appeals of the State of Washington Findings

Title of Case: Bishop of Victoria Corporation Sole, Appellant V. Joseph C. Finley, Respondent, Date Filed: June 17, 2005. Judge Signing: Honorable Paula K. Casey

The Bishop of Victoria Corporation appeals a jury verdict in favor of Joseph Finley for damages resulting from a breach of fiduciary and contractual duties, arguing that the court should have granted its motion for judgment as a matter of law. We must decide what duty the manager-members of a limited liability company owe to each other and whether the evidence in this case supports a jury finding that this duty was breached. We reverse.

Excerpts Regarding Facts

In the late 1980s, Joseph Finley formed Swiftsure Farms, an Arabian horse breeding business in Auburn, Washington. The Bishop of Victoria Corporation Sole (BV), the corporation that holds the real property assets of the Roman Catholic Diocese of Victoria, British Columbia, Canada, gave a substantial loan to Swiftsure Farms after the business suffered financial trouble. Finley was never able to fully repay the debt to BV.

Finley and BV Form a Limited Liability Company

In early 1997, Finley approached the leaders of BV with an idea for an investment opportunity. Finley was aware of a large parcel of land in Lacey, Washington (the Lacey Property) that was being sold from a foreclosure lender for one-third its appraised value. Finley proposed that he and BV purchase the Lacey Property with the intention of selling it at a substantial profit, enabling Finley to repay BV for his previous debt. They agreed, and BV and Finley formed a company called *Corporate Business Park*, LLC (CBP) that would purchase the Lacey Property. BV and Finley were the two sole members of CBP.

The Operating Agreement specified that CBP was a "limited liability company," LLC, engaged "solely in the business of investing in, developing [,] and marketing real property located in the State of Washington." Members of BV and Finley later testified that Finley agreed to contribute his labor and expertise to CBP and that BV agreed to contribute financially to CBP. Finley had expertise, experience, and knowledge of the Lacey Property, and BV had financial capabilities and financial resources. *There was no evidence presented that either party's obligation to contribute was quantified.*

Under the terms of the Agreement, Finley and BV were both managers of CBP. The Operating Agreement did not specify the time in which Finley was required to sell the Lacey Property, but BV's financial officer testified that she expected it to sell quickly.

CBP purchased the Lacey Property for approximately $5,000,000 United States dollars (USD) and obtained a mortgage for $5,250,000 in order to have excess proceeds to pay the debt service on the mortgage for one year. CBP first listed the property for sale for $18,000,000.

The Lacey Property did not immediately sell, CBP missed several payments, and CBP exhausted the excess proceeds from the mortgage.

17

BV and Finley then refinanced the first mortgage with AG Capital Funding Partners, L.P., (AG) for $7,500,000. On behalf of CBP, they executed a promissory note and deed in trust for the Lacey Property to AG as security for the refinance.

For a time, CBP was able to make the payments to AG from the excess proceeds from the refinance. Eventually, the reserve again ran out, and BV started making monthly payments to AG on behalf of CBP. *BV made monthly payments of $81,250 to AG.*

Leadership at The Victorian Diocese Changed

On February 24, 1999, there was a change in leadership at the Victorian Diocese when the old bishop retired and a new bishop replaced him and hired his own staff. As part of this change, the new bishop replaced BV's financial officer.

This change in leadership marked a shift in BV's approach to CBP. The new bishop did not approve of the Diocese's involvement in CBP. BV's new financial officer explained that BV was suffering financially from the mortgage payments to AG and that *the new leadership was concerned that the Lacey Property would never sell.* BV's priority became only that the Lacey Property be sold and the debts be satisfied. *During trial, the financial officer admitted that, under the new leadership, BV was willing to forfeit any potential profit to CBP in selling the Lacey Property, as long as CBP's debt was satisfied.*

Each party suspected the other's motives. The new leadership at BV took the perspective that "Finley has no personal interest in selling the Property unless he can sell it for a premium price that may never be available." Finley accused the new leadership of wanting "to sell the property for pennies on the dollar so that it can withdraw from what the new regime considers to be a bad investment."

In April 1999, the new bishop decided not to make CBP's April payment to AG. After this missed payment, the interest rate on the principle rose and AG sued CBP, Finley, and BV for foreclosure.

On May 5, 1999, Finley and BV then signed an Addendum to CBP's Operating Agreement. The Addendum specified that Finley owed BV $1,463,936.97 Canadian dollars (CAD) and that CBP owed BV $1,662,666.01 (CAD). *It stated that, before allocating any profits of CBP to the members, BV would first receive full payment of all outstanding debts to BV.* As security for repayment, Finley assigned his interest in CPB to BV. Lastly, the Addendum stated that BV "may, but has no obligation to, make further advances to

[CBP]." *Both parties later testified that before this Addendum, BV had agreed to finance CBP's debt service.*

AG obtained a judgment of $8,154,895.83 against CBP, Finley, and BV and a decree of foreclosure on the Lacey Property. The trial court issued an order to allow AG to apply the proceeds from a sheriff's sale of the Lacey Property toward payment of the judgment.

BV began exploring options to satisfy the foreclosure judgment. BV's financial officer informed Finley that he would contact other Dioceses in attempt to gain financial help with the foreclosure judgment. *At one point, BV offered AG $1,000,000 to release BV from liability under the foreclosure judgment, relieving BV's individual responsibility, but leaving CBP and Finley responsible. BV admitted that this arrangement would have been detrimental to CBP. At trial, BV's financial officer stated that BV should never have been involved in CBP* and that BV was interested in ceasing its dealings with AG, the foreclosure judgment, and CBP.

The Debentures

In 2000, BV raised $13,000,000 CAD dollars from the parishioners of the Victorian Diocese and issued debentures[1] in exchange for their money. In a deed of trust, BV *pledged all land BV owned in British Columbia as security* for repayment of the debentures. In a supplemental deed of trust, BV purportedly pledged the proceeds of the "Judgment, Mortgage and Loan Documents" as additional security for the debentures.

The Bishop issued an information statement disclosing that BV planned to use the debenture money to reduce its indebtedness. In the statement, he claimed BV planned to either: (1) reach a settlement with AG; or (2) take over AG's position, recover the Lacey Property, and offer it for sale.

The parishioners' funds were transferred to Fisgard Asset Management (Fisgard),[2] a trustee set up on behalf of the parishioners. BV and

---

[1] A debenture is a bond that is backed only by the general credit and financial reputation of the corporate issuer, not by a lien on corporate assets. Black's Law Dictionary 430 (8th ed. 2004).

[2] Fisgard was formerly called United Homes Victoria, Ltd. Throughout the trial court proceedings, and the first appellate review of BV and Finley's transaction, Fisgard was referred to as United Homes. But, the parties refer to the trustee as Fisgard, and we will continue to do so here.

Fisgard agreed that Fisgard would purchase the judgment from AG. The interest on the judgment had accrued and the amount due had grown to $8,701,832.07 USD. Figard negotiated with AG and bought the judgment at a discount for $8,296,056.00 USD. Thereafter, AG assigned the judgment and decree of foreclosure to Fisgard.

Relations between Finley and BV came to an impasse and, in September 2000, BV filed a petition seeking appointment of a receiver for CBP. The trial court appointed the receiver as custodian of the assets, operations, and business of CBP. The receiver had the power to manage and operate CBP's assets or to dispose of CBP's operations.

In an order dated May 25, 2001, the trial court ordered the receiver to enter into a partial settlement with Fisgard, in which Fisgard agreed to stay foreclosure actions over the Lacey Property for one year to allow the receiver to sell the property. If the receiver did not sell the Lacey Property by April 26, 2002, the court ordered the receiver to surrender a deed-in-lieu of foreclosure to the Lacey Property to Fisgard. The trial court, the receiver, Finley, and BV all signed the order agreeing to the deed-in-lieu.

The receiver was not able to sell the Lacey Property and, on June 25, 2002, he issued a quit claim deed for all of CBP's interest in the Lacey Property to Fisgard in satisfaction of the judgment and foreclosure actions. A foreclosure sale was not necessary because all title to the Lacey Property passed to Fisgard under the quit claim deed.

On April 5, 2002, Finley filed a motion in the trial court requesting the trial court to find that AG's foreclosure judgment has been satisfied, and requesting the trial court to direct CBP's receiver not to transfer title of the Lacey Property to Fisgard.

The trial court denied Finley's motion and Finley appealed. In an unpublished opinion, we held that (1) the judgment was not satisfied because Fisgard was clearly a separate entity from BV, and (2) Finley had no claims to the Lacey Property and the receiver had full right to issue the deed to Fisgard under the trial court's order. *We explained that we could not reach Finley's claims for damage arising from the relationship between Finley and BV because the trial court had not ruled on these issues.*

Finley Pursued His Remaining Claims

On remand, BV moved for summary judgment of Finley's claims on several grounds, but the trial court only granted summary judgment to BV on the issue that CBP's Operating Agreement was the controlling contract between the parties and CBP. It ruled that parole evidence could

20

not be used to alter the written terms in the Operating Agreement or Addendum.

After all evidence had been presented to the jury and before the jury deliberated, BV filed a motion for judgment as a matter of law. BV argued that, as a matter of law, the trial court should dismiss the claims against BV. Without ruling on BV's motion, the trial court allowed the jury to deliberate.

The jury issued a verdict in Finley's favor for approximately $8,169,000 on his breach of contract claim and approximately $4,200,000 on his breach of fiduciary duty claim. After the verdict, the trial court heard argument on BV's motion for judgment as a matter of law and denied BV's motion. BV now appeals.

The Canadian
$2.50
MAY 1990

Forum

Bishop Remi De Roo
Committed to social action

The state of theatre across Canada ■ Killing off the DCB ■ Gregory Baum on post-modernism ■ Poetry by Abbott Anderson ■ Plus a short story by Lorna Jackson

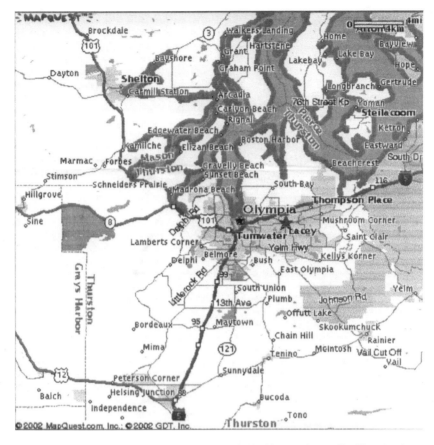

Lacey is situated near Olympia the capital of Washington State. Significantly, the Corporate Business Park property was located near the Interstate 5 freeway which is one of the main commercial thoroughfares running between Canada and Mexico.

Chapter 1 – Smashing The Icon

Chapter 18 from *In the Avant Garde: The Prophetic Catholicism of Remi De Roo* (published in 2002)

"And others are those sown among the thorns: these are the ones who hear the word, but the cares of the world, and the desire for other things come in and choke the word, and it yields nothing.

"And these are the ones sown on the good soil: they hear the word and accept it and bear fruit, thirty and sixty and a hundredfold."
–Mark 4:19-20.

ૐૐૐ

Questions Raised About Politics Behind Church Crisis

De Roo supporters wonder what role politics is playing in crisis rocking Catholic Church

By Mark Browne, Weekend Edition Staff
Friday, June 2, 2000–*Victoria News* 'Feature' Weekend Edition

As retired Roman Catholic Bishop Remi De Roo faces criticism over bad investments he made while bishop of the Vancouver Island Diocese, some local Catholics are convinced that forces within the Catholic church are out to get him.

"There seems to be a concerted effort to discredit him," says Patrick Jamieson, a board member and past editor of the *Island Catholic News*. Jamieson is currently writing a biography on De Roo who retired last year after thirty-seven years as bishop for the Vancouver Island Diocese.

Jamieson is also author of *Victoria Demers to De Roo, 150 Years of Catholic History on Vancouver Island*.

When news first surfaced that the diocese was $17 million in debt because of unsuccessful investments made by De Roo (involving Arabian horses and a subsequent risky land deal), Jamieson says the way the Roman Catholic Church handled the matter is suspicious.

He says he finds it strange that the National Post was inquiring if the local diocese was in trouble because of investments made by De Roo a few days before the church made an official statement on the matter earlier this year.

"The National Post called and they had wind of it which seemed curious to me because surely they weren't monitoring every Catholic diocese's financial problems," says Jamieson.

He notes that Conrad Black, the owner of the *National Post* who became a Catholic several years ago, and De Roo engaged in very heated debates with each other in 1983 when Canada's bishops addressed the economic and unemployment problems of that period.

Speaking on behalf of the country's bishops, De Roo expressed views that were very anti-capitalist in nature – something that Jamieson says didn't go off too well with Black.

"It got quite personal," he recalls.

Jamieson says it's important to note that the tides of political conservatism that swept across the Western world in the 1980s posed a threat for the left-leaning social justice policies that De Roo and the Catholic church in general had endorsed.

As the political power in the Vatican experienced a shift to the right in the 1980s, De Roo became quite unpopular with the right-leaning echelons of the Catholic church hierarchy who had assumed power, he says.

Jamieson argues that the discrediting of De Roo has its roots in that shift of power within the Catholic church.

On a local level, Jamieson contends that ill feelings towards De Roo from other priests have a lot to do with a position taken by such priests that wealthy people weren't donating much money to the local diocese because of their opposition to De Roo's left-wing social views.

"There are certain priests here that used to say to me "If we could just get Remi (De Roo) out of the way, the money would start to flow," recalls Jamieson. "So there was this circle in the diocese that was hyper-critical of Remi on precisely those grounds."

But while Jamieson feels that some of the local church hierarchy have been out to discredit De Roo, he stresses he is not convinced that Bishop Raymond Roussin, who took over from De Roo as the Bishop of the Vancouver Island Diocese, is part of that circle. The forces against De Roo have been in play for a long time, notes Jamieson.

24

However, Jamieson remains critical of how the new administration under Roussin was quick to release information to the media on the diocese's financial crisis and De Roo's involvement. He says the "tradition" would have been for the diocese to initially attempt to resolve the matter "in-house" out of respect for De Roo.

Jamieson says that within a few months of the new administration it had become apparent that the "right wingers" in the diocese had taken control. And that is particularly evident at the meetings the diocese has been holding in an attempt to address the current situation.

"I was kind of shocked and surprised by the level of negativity and antipathy towards Bishop De Roo that comes out at some of those meetings," says Jamieson.

De Roo isn't too popular with the right-wing of the Catholic church at Saint Boniface in Winnipeg either.

Jamieson notes that when De Roo went there to do some confirmations (a request that the late Archbishop Antoine Hacault made on his death bed) local right-leaning parishioners insisted that it wouldn't be appropriate for De Roo to handle confirmations of children since he was the subject of a canonical inquiry.

As for De Roo maintaining his silence on the issue, Marnie Butler, editor of *Island Catholic News,* says that she has been told by De Roo's lawyer, Chris Considine, that he will likely come forward and speak up on the matter after the canonical commission releases its findings on July 10.

Butler suggests that De Roo's reputation is unlikely to be tarnished given that several dioceses across the country are facing financial trouble. Butler says she feels that most people are intelligent enough to see beyond the negative statements being made against De Roo.

Jamieson says he doesn't think that De Roo's reputation will be ruined, while reiterating that there are those among the right wing of the church who simply want the former bishop's name to suffer.

Tom Loring, a longtime social activists in the local Catholic community, says he doesn't feel that De Roo's reputation will be damaged to any serious extent. Most people who find themselves in a position like De Roo is in these days would leave questions to their attorneys, says Loring, who also suspects that there are those in the church that are deliberately trying to discredit the former bishop.

Alan Bailey, a local Catholic and self-admitted big fan of De Roo, says he can only hope that people will forgive De Roo for errors he made in regard to investments made on behalf of the diocese.

While Bailey says it's possible that some right-leaning members of the church are out to discredit De Roo, most Catholics in the community realize that De Roo is human, and like other humans, has made some mistakes.

The Arabian Horse Saga

1. FIRST OFF AT THE POST

It was the last Wednesday of February, 2000 I first caught wind of the financial scandal which rocked the Diocese of Victoria during the first year of Bishop Raymond Roussin's episcopacy at Victoria. This next episode, a surprise development, raised many more questions than it answered.

Roussin had been installed gradually as successor to De Roo during the previous twelve months, during 1998. There was a process stretching the solemnization over a six-month period during 1999 as well. De Roo had retired officially on his seventy-fifth birthday, February 24, 1999. The *Island Catholic News* has a series of unpublished photos of the moment De Roo handed the crozier to Roussin. De Roo was in tears, almost as if he could see what was to come.

De Roo was very pleased that "someone as good as" Roussin was selected as his successor. He stated this to me in the cathedral rectory kitchen early in 1997 when I said Roussin's name was being bandied about as a successor. In fact he framed it in negative terms, that we would not be so lucky to get someone as good as Roussin.

Island Catholic News editor Marnie Butler had a strong hunch that Roussin, a member of the Marianist order and the former Bishop of Gravelbourg, Saskatchewan would get the nod. Gravelbourg had been suppressed and attached to Regina due to failing financial support in the traditionally Francophone prairie diocese.

Butler interviewed Roussin early in 1997 at Queenswood Retreat Center in Victoria for a cover story in ICN. Butler told me at the time she knew he would be the one. She had announced this generally. When she related her intuition, Roussin dismissed the idea, telling her he already had a diocese. She convinced him to sit for a 'cover shot' any way. The diminutive bishop had been on the Island for a Western Bishops' gathering hosted by De Roo in Nanaimo.

At that particular weekend, some of the leaders of the diocesan Catholic Women's League had gotten hold of choir robes resembling red cardinal costumes and served the supper to the bishops dressed as Roman cardinals. According to De Roo, the joke went over well. It is hard to imagine any other western diocese where the bishop would have felt as completely comfortable with this prank and its oblique commentary on the church's official attitude toward women.

❧❧❧

The financial scandal proper was initiated when a special statement was to 'only be read' from the pulpits of all the parishes in the diocese on the first Sunday of March, 2000. It was not to be released in a written form at that time; or earlier. The priests of the diocese had been so instructed at a special meeting earlier in the week.

I was seated at my computer in a studio in Chinatown working on this book when Marnie Butler came to the door. She announced how I could make an easy two hundred dollars for simply tape recording this message from the pulpit for Marina Jiminez of *The National Post*.

Despite the secrecy request – or perhaps because of it – someone had obviously called *The Post* and they wanted to make an offer we could not refuse.

Coincidentally, earlier that day I had been working on the section of the book that deals with the controversy in the late 1980s between Bishop De Roo and Toronto based press baron Conrad

Black. Black had taken serious umbrage with De Roo's leadership style on the 'Crisis in the Economy' reflections of 1983.[3] *The National Post* being Black's flagship newspaper, this was an interesting coincidence. As a consequence neither Marnie Butler nor I was disposed to co-operate with the request.

❧❧❧

When Jiminez called the *Island Catholic News*, she said she was sure it was a juicy disclosure, probably sexual in nature but Butler knew it wasn't the case. She had been hearing odd rumors about financial shortfalls at the diocese, something to do with horses but did not think much of it for a variety of reasons. For one thing ICN had never bothered with the financial side of things in the diocese during its thirteen-year history.

She also knew that Muriel Clemenger was a horsewoman, and as financial administrator for the diocese she was known to be creative and energetic in her thinking about investments. If Clemenger heard about a good deal in her horse circles, she would try it out. It was in her makeup. If she thought some funds were sitting idle, she could easily move to use them to help the diocese in that manner.

In fact a minor horse cartel was formed among a number of Clemenger's friends and associates, some of whom were close to De Roo, but the bishop himself had nothing directly to do with it.

The comment by Eileen Archer, De Roo's executive assistant for thirty years, bears a certain relevance here: "One characteristic that particularly stands out in my mind is Bishop De Roo's understanding of human nature and his acceptance of people as they are ... He has always trusted people. He assigns a task and expects it will be done. No reminders, no interference. And he encourages people. I for one, have been challenged to do things I didn't know I could."

---

[3] See pp. 117-119 of *Behind the Mitre* by Tony Clarke for details.

This quality was precisely why I was happy to try to start an independent Catholic newspaper on Vancouver Island in 1985. I knew that I would never have to be looking over my shoulder, worrying about what the bishop thought. I also knew from our initial conversation on the topic that there would be no money available directly from the diocese; and this suited us both.

More important than money, I knew we would have his trust. De Roo was not a fearful leader at any moment in my experience of him.

2. THE DIFFICULTIES OF THE CASE

Our main contact in the diocesan finance circles was Al Heron, a professional fundraiser hired as a development officer to get donations up in the early 1990s. Heron was very helpful to *Island Catholic News*, coming up with personally creative manners of fund-raising for the paper apart from his job at the diocese.

In casual conversation he mentioned he had seen a couple of budget line items that puzzled him, for which he could not get any answers. One of these turned out to be the loss on the Swiftsure Farms investment. Swiftsure was an Arabian horse breeding operation.

Heron's boss Muriel Clemenger was not only appreciated by Remi De Roo for her creative financial work. During Clemenger's last few years at Victoria she was appointed by the Western Catholic Bishops to develop an idea she dreamed up: to form an insurance co-operative to pool their payments. Until then each diocese had made its own insurance arrangement. She reported the savings were substantial.

She and Al Heron managed the co-op after De Roo left office. At that point the new administration brought in its own financial officer, an accountant. Clemenger, who was also aged seventy-five, previously announced she would only be staying until De Roo retired. Al Heron applied for her job but was not granted the courtesy of an interview. It seems there was another plan in the works.

Other regional conferences of Canadian Catholic bishops had more than a passing interest in the insurance pool concept. Clemenger informed me in a conversation during the middle 1990s. The Atlantic Bishops were definitely positive, and even the Ontario bishops were wanting to get involved she said, but the latter group had some technical angles to work out. It was all very bright and positive sounding, especially given what was to follow. It was typical of my experience of her creative inventiveness.

When the investment loss made the headlines, the Western Bishops dropped Clemenger unceremoniously. Shortly after, the Ukrainian Eparch of Winnipeg arrived in Nanaimo to lay off Al Heron. He acted "like a bully," Heron told me in his matter-of-fact collected manner. This was all in spite of the savings Clemenger had creatively instigated. Some definite distancing was going on beyond the simple loss of capital. Heron has since received a financial settlement for 'wrongful dismissal'.

Clemenger and De Roo decided not to contravene the new bishop in public and kept silence on the whole issue despite what was being said and implied about them. Clemenger told me that Roussin and his new administrator asked her at the time of transition not to speak in public in case it contradicted them, and she told me she would honor this agreement which seemed to be logical at the time.

De Roo hired a sharp local lawyer, Chris Considine, to represent him and he did issue a general apology. The public apology meant he would take the fall and not pass any of it on to Clemenger or anyone else at the next level of responsibility.[4] Kim Lunman of the *Globe and Mail* told me in a telephone conversation she did not find any documents in Lacey, Washington, to do with a land investment, that had De Roo's signature on them.

---

[4] In a CBC radio interview Chris Considine explained that De Roo's apology meant he accepted ultimate responsibility for the problem but it did not imply he was personally to blame.

It was the land investment aspect rather than the earlier million dollar loss on the Arabian horse farm that caused the real financial difficulties for the diocese.

The farm loss had taken place in the late 1980s. Investing in the land in the mid-1990s had been part of a recovery scheme that Clemenger devised through the same agent as the original investment, American lawyer Joseph Finley. If there were any other signatures on those documents besides Clemenger, De Roo was protecting these subordinates by his silence and public apology. In effect he accepted final responsibility, by virtue of his office.

࿏࿏࿏

Remi De Roo's character in both senses was the issue at stake here. His was not a nature to give finances, and such, the importance it carried in the secular business world, or the corporate media. In simple terms, he did not really care about money. It was not a pastoral priority in itself.

He also was not going to get into any public dog fights about what had happened, and the details of who had done what to whom. He was not into blaming. I knew this from personal experience. During the six years as editor of the diocesan newspaper, the only editorial suggestion I remember him making was that the paper not cover every "dogfight in the diocese."

As Marnie Butler repeated often enough: "Remi did not care about money for its own sake." This was the reason why she and many other left-leaning converts were drawn to join the Catholic church during his heyday. He did however tell Butler that he did not feel uncomfortable with financial transactions.

One thing she meant was that while some bishops are noted for their fiscal administrative capabilities, this was obviously not De Roo greatest interest or aptitude; and she admired this about him. To the people around *Island Catholic News*, it seemed like judging the competence of an Old Testament prophet by the tidiness of his cave. It was entirely irrelevant to who De Roo was.

31

Besides that it seemed awfully coincidental to them that no significant publicly-known problems had arisen until after De Roo left office. In fact the net worth of the diocese had risen astronomically during his four decades.[5] Admittedly this was largely due to the overall development of Vancouver Island, but it seemed he should be given some credit for having the money there to lose in the first place. In addition there was a serious question about under whose watch the real losses had taken place.

3. STOPPING PAYMENTS

Here we are relying on the *Globe and Mail* reporting as contrasted to the local *Times Colonist*. In her June 17, 2000 feature, Kim Lunman points out that the most serious loss was actually due to action taken by the new finance administration team, not by De Roo and Clemenger:

"But the land... never sold and the diocese was faced with $130,000 in monthly mortgage payments. *It stopped paying when Bishop Roussin took over a year later* [italics mine] and the lender, AG Capital Funding Partners of New York, took the church to court in May 1999.

"In March (2000) a judge ordered the land foreclosed and ordered the diocese, Mr. Finley and *Corporate Business Park* to pay $12-million to AG Capital. The interest alone is now accruing at $7000 per day."[6]

---

[5] De Roo's '*Ad Limina*' report to Rome in 1968 was published in the *Western Catholic Reporter*. Financially the diocese was worth $840,000, half of which was in real estate. Five years later the same report had the figure just over a million dollars. At the time of the scandal in 2000 the net worth was over a hundred million dollars. De Roo may have been 'caught out' by this radical escalation of property value during the 1980s.

[6] p. A 11, *The Globe and Mail*, Saturday, June 17, 2000 "The lawyer, the bishop and the money pit, It started with a $30,000 investment in horses. The next thing anyone knew, Vancouver Island Catholics were $17-million in the hole" by Kim Lunman in Lacey, Wash.

So, according to *The Globe and Mail*, due to a decision taken by the new administration the payments jumped from $130,000 per month to $210,000, escalating the crisis into a catastrophe. In addition, the land was now at risk. In the pages of the *Times Colonist*, which just happened to be owned by Conrad Black at the time, this little distinction was glossed over. The *Times Colonist* was in a feeding frenzy for all the good copy De Roo's purported 'fall from grace' was providing.

In the six month period between February and September 2000 the story made the front page headline of the T-C nineteen times (and the lead page of another section ten times).[7] The tip of the Richter scale may have been reached Saturday, May 27 with: "Ex-bishop gambled assets from convent, De Roo chased losses and had two sets of books, concludes Roman Catholic Church Commission."

Despite the fact that Roussin's last diocese, Gravelbourg, had to be closed and attached to Regina due to financial shortfalls; despite the fact that it was decisions taken subsequent to February 24, 1999 that caused the most serious crisis, De Roo was the only one 'investigated'. In fact he was not investigated at all. He was presumed guilty and it was a blame-affixing exercise that followed.

If there was a moment when De Roo could have started to present his side of the story – an objective moment not driven by media frenzy and pejorative headlines –then he could have been heard in a comprehensive manner, the formal canonical inquiry, requested by Bishop Raymond Roussin and established by the Canadian Conference of Catholic Bishops, would have been it.

After all he had served the CCCB in responsible positions for decades and he had displayed extraordinary gifts of articulation on complex and subtle issues. He would need an occasion like this to explain himself comprehensively, and it seemed simple justice if not courtesy that De Roo would at least be granted the opportunity.

But it was not to be. The changing of the guard was complete.

---

[7] See appendix 'Selected reporting on post-retirement year 2000 financial saga'.

p. 266

4. THE COMMISSION OF INQUIRY

The hearings were scheduled on the only days when De Roo had stated earlier he could not be available due to prior commitments elsewhere in North America. The report itself when it did come out reflected only one point of view on the whole matter. It did not indicate that any voices dissenting from the conventional wisdom espoused in the press had been heard at all.[8]

The report could have been written from Ottawa or Toronto, the locations of the principal members of the inquiry group. It entirely reflected the media reports and could have been written from such clippings, saving the price of the plane tickets of these busy and important men.

In interviews prior to the release of the report, Monsignor Peter Schonenbach, General Secretary of the CCCB and a member of the inquiry group, prejudiced and pre-empted his own report with pejorative comment. Canada's top Catholic church bureaucrat was quoted in the press comparing De Roo's behavior to that of a gambling addict. Peter Schonenbach was quoted making one-sided statements of fact that he must have known would be interpreted negatively in the un-nuanced reporting of the daily press.[9]

This was a full month before the report was released.[10]

---

[8] Muriel Clemenger, who spoke before the Commission, stated that she 'was not heard' at the hearing, saying she could have "saved the price of her gas."

[9] Paragraphs from the *Times Colonist* banner headline "Ex-Bishop gambled assets from convent" by Gerard Young read: "The former bishop of Victoria used money from a closed nun's convent to invest in Arabian horses, then later, like a gambler on a bad streak, chased his losses with a risky land deal....As well, the former bishop apparently was operating two sets of books for the diocese, (Monsignor Peter Schonenbach) said.

[10] The date of the "Report of Commission of Canonical Inquiry to Most Reverend Raymond Roussin, SM, Bishop of Victoria, BC" was dated June 26, 2000, Schonenbach was quoted in the *Times Colonist* on page one May 27, 2000.

The appropriate way for the CCCB General Secretary to con-duct himself on the issue would have been to see that a competent inquiry was appointed, presumably one that had at least one member from western Canada and someone who was knowl-edgeable about and sensitive to De Roo's pastoral style.

The General Secretary himself should not have served on the board but rather reviewed its findings objectively for the princi-ples of breadth of perspective, balance, objectivity and compre-hensiveness. He should not have allowed himself to be inter-viewed casually on so sensitive a subject, which only served to fuel the speculation that De Roo was being discredited for politi-cal reasons.

Schonenbach's actual behavior was very surprising because the CCCB had distinguished itself with stellar professionalism in its general secretary role, dating back to Rev. Everett MacNeil in the 1960s and 70s and Monsignor (later Archbishop of Winnipeg) James Weisgerber in the 1980s.

5. DIOCESAN FINANCES

In the *Times Colonist* reporting, there was never any indication that a workable payment structure was in place when De Roo left office, one that had been operating well enough. Obviously the loan arrangement was predicated on the premise that the property was valuable enough to cover its cost and would eventually be sold, probably recouping as well the original loss.

The real losses that drove the diocese into desperation mode were due to the subsequent court judgment, but even this was blamed on De Roo. With the *Times Colonist* and *The Post*, from the very start, the wheels had already been put in motion in one defi-nite direction.

As a student of media-church relations, the significant aspect to me was that the *Times Colonist* was privy to information about the diocese that is given to few if any newspapers about the Catholic church. It had a field day. This attitude toward the wind-mill-tilting crusader against corporate capitalism by its lapdog press was not something surprising at this point.

Coverage of De Roo in the pages of the *Times Colonist* during the 1980s and 1990s had soured radically compared with the glowing reports of the 1960s and 1970s when 'the boy bishop' could hardly set a foot wrong in the pages of either then-competing papers, the *Victoria Times* and the *Daily Colonist*.

6.   ADMINISTRATIVE GENIUS

Victoria was always a pretty small place, and did not require much administrative genius to keep it rolling. De Roo recognized this from his first days when he found the finances run on a rudimentary model, more suitable to an educational institution.[11]

Roussin had come to Victoria from the Saskatchewan Diocese of Gravelbourg, where he had been put in charge in order to close it down. The Franco-Catholic population was no longer sufficient to keep it financially viable so Gravelbourg was suppressed and attached to Regina.

As a result he would be expected to be a touch sensitive about finances, certainly more than De Roo, who after thirty-seven years in charge would be confident of the overall situation.

The most significant aspect of De Roo's financial administrative style was in how he kept certain types – power brokers, high priced lawyers, accountants, financial wizards and money men, et al – from taking over all the key positions in the financial administrative management of the diocese.

He and Clemenger made sure that farmers, ordinary workers and women maintained a balance on such key committees; and, of course, they were not popular in certain quarters for this.[12]

---

[11] The overall holdings of the entire diocese in 1968 was less than a million dollars, according to the *Ad Limina* Report to Rome by Bishop De Roo for the five-year period 1964-1968.

[12] For example, on page 6 of the inaugural edition of the *Diocesan Report* (An Organizational and Financial Report of the Diocese of Victoria, Vancouver

Most other dioceses had capitulated in these areas to 'the experts'. De Roo was always wary of such experts as his battle over the economy with corporate Canada in the early 1980s showed. While this allowed a different model of church to emerge, it also made him a nemesis in those circles; certain 'successful' types who quickly moved in to fill the vacuum.

All these types of people came to make up Roussin's financial-administrative inner circles during this controversy. The shift was functional on two fronts: Control was obtained of the key money matters in the diocese by a select group of experts who never did have that much time for Remi De Roo and his prairie populism priorities; and De Roo was made to wear the blame and thus publicly discredited.

As in the Charbonneau case, De Roo's good nature was used against him. He said he did not want to contradict his successor in public and thereby jeopardize the subsequent bond issue being raised.

Speculation started early that Roussin would not stay in the diocese for many years. Right from the start his health was suffering from the stress of the situation. He also had a serious auto accident that eventful summer of 2000, which added to his nervous stress and physical ailments.

ॐॐॐ

When De Roo had taken over after the death of Bishop James Michael Hill in 1962, the diocese was literally run on a shoestring. It was bankrolled on one annual 'Pentecost' collection. Hill had kept a small college going in rural New Brunswick during The Depression and so knew how to stretch a dollar.

Once De Roo arrived, the financial footing of the diocese was put on a whole other basis and there was nothing of any irregular note for thirty-seven years. On the contrary, he was considered a fiscal

---

Island), of November 2001, not one woman is named as a member of the seven key finance and administrative committees. Two women are named on the publication committee.

conservative, never a lavish spender. Living very simply despite being a 'prince of the church', he was far from being a gambler of any sort.

De Roo's travel money was taken from his fees as a speaker. He took only the same salary as the youngest priest. Things were not flush but they continually improved over three and half decades. Then a full year after he leaves office, skeletons were supposedly found in the closets by a new administration, one steeped in the practice of forensic accounting.

Not only were these bones discovered but they made a great deal of noise in their rattling. The bad news was released immediately to the regular press. This was the first objective sign that something strange was afoot; apart from the allegations of fiscal irregularities.

7. CHURCH-MEDIA RELATIONS

The Catholic church is still one of the most secretive organizations in the history of the western world. It does not trust the media. It does not, repeat does not, give away information to the regular media except for a specific purpose. The Catholic press itself is notoriously dull because it is generally the official organ for managing information, which is still a one-way street.

The normal procedure for a crisis of these purported proportions would be to hush it up and protect the former bishop, if only because it reflects badly on the church as a whole. Use of the local Catholic press would be solely to get the story quietly to the effected population – the people in all the parishes and organizations of the diocese which could be relied upon to recoup the loss and keep the affair as quiet as possible.

There would be rumors, of course, but nothing would be confirmed. The loss would be dealt with internally. The Catholic church does not air its dirty laundry in public. A decision to the contrary was taken and there had to be 'a good reason' for it.

In other words, the gain had to outweigh the loss of the bad publicity. The greatest gain would be that the shock would result in the loosening of private purse strings. The loss would be the discrediting of a bishop, a retired bishop, but one who in the view of the majority of principal decision makers was easily expendable for any number of reasons.

In the collective view De Roo was a liability that could be cut. In their view he had brought it on himself. He was to blame. That would be affixed indelibly in the public consciousness, the better to open some of those larger and too-long-closed purse strings. In the interviews for this book De Roo himself admitted that certain well-heeled members of his congregation were withholding in reaction to his social stands.

And it worked. Not only did the money pour in but a *carte blanche* arrangement for any further financial decisions would be granted. Retreat centers could be closed with a minimum of questioning. It was all necessary for the good of the diocese. The fact that Bethlehem Retreat Center conducted 'progressive' spiritual development courses, now out of favor by Rome, was simply an added bonus.

8.   OUT OF THE LOOP

For some reason *Island Catholic News* was entirely kept out of the loop. It was never approached to help with the situation. Further, ICN Editor Marnie Butler asked the diocesan finance people most privy to information to clarify the financial facts "for the record." While they assured complete openness within the Catholic community these "facts" were never forthcoming. Instead the regular media, which in the usual view of the church is seen as unequivocally antagonistic, was fed information and was trusted to fuel and steer the controversy.

In my twenty-five years of experience as a church journalist who was fascinated by this problem of media relations, I have never seen this done before. Normally the Catholic church assiduously avoids even responding to media inquiries on anything so potential damaging as financial irregularities.

At best the media is viewed with suspicion by church personnel because it is seen as unmanageable and asks difficult questions that are based on secular (i.e. non-Christian) values.

Ironically this is one of the areas where De Roo made some positive contribution during his earlier career. As a writer and editor who worked within the Canadian Catholic Church from 1978, this attitude on the part of the church always seemed counterproductive.

De Roo's reputation for exercising a candid style with media interviews was one of the reasons *Island Catholic News* was set up on Vancouver Island. I felt the paper could succeed in Victoria on an autonomous basis, and it had.

As a journalist I knew that De Roo would wait until there was an objective moment, when he could do what he did best, communicate from a position of personal authority. It was only then that he would feel confident in presenting his side of the truth of the situation; of it being actually heard. As the local media hysteria mounted and the blistering pejorative headlines continued unabated, I sensed this moment was slipping away and would never come.

Local antagonism had built up over the years. The very fact he was blamed in public was definitive testimony. Rome and The Vatican were opposed to his style and his program of implementing Vatican II in its intent.

His hope of a balanced objective moment could only come, if it was going to arrive at all, when the Canadian Conference of Catholic Bishops were brought in to do a competent review of the situation.

Nothing would be further from the truth. This report was the hardest blow yet. The top bureaucrat in the Catholic Canadian Church would pre-empt his own report in an entirely prejudicial manner. It was a scandal in its own right but would pass unnoticed in the general mud-slinging frenzy and confusion which kept getting worse and worse for six months and beyond.

9. FACTS OF THE CASE

In the late 1980s a short term loan, lent by the diocese to Swiftsure Farms in Washington, was not repaid. Swiftsure was brokered by a Seattle Lawyer, Joseph Finley and Muriel Clemenger knew him through her horse circles. Clemenger and her brother, a California horseman, both raised Arabians, which are show horses, contrary to the implication of the *National Post* when it broke the story.

The Post reported that the investment was in race horses, and that a later land deal to try to pay off the 1.1 million dollar loss had something to do with a race track. It gave *The Post* its typical spin, that extra salacious twist.

Neither Clemenger nor De Roo ever broke silence to speak on the issue, but Clemenger told me in a telephone briefing that there never was any question of "investing in horses, or buying horses," which at that time in early March, 2000, was the general tenor of the local reporting. I was going to be interviewed on the radio about the financial scandal and wanted to make sure that some of my impressions were accurate, so Muriel Clemenger and I had a conversation.

She said that the arrangement was a short-term loan at a very good fee, "irresistible, in fact." She said the problem was created when the American tax structure around show horses changed at just that time: "You could not believe how fast things changed."

She said that they should have gotten out earlier and maybe only lost half the amount but "Remi felt sorry for the farmer and we stayed in too long. Remi did not want to make things worse for the man."

It was then Muriel Clemenger told me there was never any question of the diocese investing in horses or owning horses: if there was they certainly had their chance when they were owed all that money.

According to Muriel Clemenger it was his compassion that got De Roo in trouble. This was in the late 1980s, and the money used had been from a defunct trust fund set up to look after some elderly nuns who had been left stranded when Mother Cecilia quit the Catholic church in the 1960s.

Cecilia, an animal protectionist, had a lot of press about her extreme compassion for animals in the local Victoria papers in the 1950s and '60s. Her extremism got her into hot water with the local bishop as well as Rome and she was ordered by Rome in March, 1965 to cease and desist.[13]

De Roo inherited this problem when he took over the diocese and the trust fund was a solution to a difficult situation. Land had been sold that belonged to Mother Cecilia's order and the funds were used to pay pensions for the members of her order.

Perhaps it was a residue of the Protestant Ethic in Muriel Clemenger that did not like to see funds sitting idle; as the few remaining nuns were comfortably supported. Whether it was her Evangelical background that reasserted itself or not, she tried to do something about it. It was these funds that were used for the ill-fated loan. Technically it did not require the usual checks and balances of diocesan funds because it was outside those regular parameters.

This debt was still outstanding in the middle 1990s when the land deal came along as a solution to paying it off. The idea was that the land would eventually sell covering the old debt and making more money to boot. It might have worked out if De Roo was not required to retire at age seventy-five. At that time it still had not paid off.

Al Heron suggested that the monthly payments were of such a size that a larger supporting body may have had to guarantee the loan. It was suggested the Archdiocese of Vancouver guaranteed the loan that required hundred and thirty thousand dollar payments each month.

In the end the Diocese of Victoria was probably large enough to float its own loan and the diocese was able to get a line of credit to make the monthly payments.

---

[13] A biography of Mother Cecilia Mary, OSB *A Nun Goes to The Dogs* by E.D. Ward-Harris was published in 1969.

This was the arrangement when the new administration in Victoria took over under Raymond Roussin in February 1999. For whatever reasons, the new finance-administration committee were antagonistic to this arrangement and they pulled the plug making the situation that much worse.

On the face of it, there is really not anything very sensational in all this unless you want to dress it up. So why was it all made into a public scandal?

10. THE BETTER REPORTING

The better reporting on the story was done by the *Globe and Mail*. The local daily, the Victoria *Times Colonist*, seemed to get much too close to the story to do an objective job on it.

It was the difference between a story intelligently told with journalistic objectivity; with a beginning, a middle and an end; and some designated purpose to its telling versus one thrown together constantly in a feeding frenzy because the story had proven a juicy one for the local market. *The Globe and Mail* looked at the court documents.

The *Times Colonist* virtually accepted everything the Diocese issued at face value. Their conclusion to the fact that neither Clemenger nor De Roo would give their sides was simply not to provide any counterbalance in their own reporting. It's typical of lazy journalism, encouraged by a publisher's presumed prejudice.

The story hardly got off the front page for months and this seemed to satisfy the *Times Colonist*. In the fifteen years I have been reading it as the local paper of record, The T-C has never distinguished itself with investigative journalism.

De Roo's reputation was dismembered in every day's trouble. I sent three or four lengthy op-ed pieces to challenge the conventional wisdom, but none were published. My letters that were published were short ones on specific points of accuracy. It was all very dismaying. Eventually, after all the damage was done, Don Vipond, a former editorial writer with the T-C, talked them into running an appreciation piece on De Roo, which by its nature did not attempt to address any of the prevailing issues.[14]

Kim Lunman's piece in *The Globe and Mail* had greater balance and integrity.

Her story was datelined Lacey, Washington where the questionable investment property is situated. She told me that while there she found no court records or documents with De Roo's signature on them, perhaps contributing to the sympathy she said she had for him as a figure in the whole debacle.

"The promissory note for the mortgage was signed by the diocese's financial administrator, Muriel Clemenger, who retired at the same time as Bishop De Roo," her piece read.

"Ms Clemenger, a former missionary who now lives in Nanaimo, recently defended the investment to the newspaper *Christianweek*. 'I remain convinced that we'll come out of it all right because it is a good investment,' she said. 'I'm very much at peace and at rest in my own heart.'"[15]

Clemenger said the same thing to me at the time of my earlier telephone briefing: "They say God is in reality, so God is in this somewhere, we'll just wait and see how."

11. WHAT IT'S ALL ABOUT

Such a coincidence that after thirty-seven and half years as bishop, within the twelve months after he left office, so much after all is found to be wrong with De Roo's administrative manner.

---

[14] "The Crucifixion of Bishop De Roo – Great deeds of a good man are forgotten" by Don Vipond, Sunday August 20, 2000, p. A7, *Times Colonist*.

[15] *The Globe and Mail*, June 17, 2000. On August 28, 2001 on page B1, the *Times Colonist* carried the headline "Church deal falls through" reporting that an offer of $9.6 million US had not been successful. The approximately $15 million CDN was still the estimated market value of the land at this date even after all the confidence-threatening turmoil, validating Clemenger's confidence in the property as a 'good investment'.

Was Rome asleep at the switch for four decades or are we to assume that perhaps, just perhaps, there are some other dynamics at work here? Certainly things lined up well against De Roo.

At the bottom level, locally, nearly forty years of a certain sort of antipathy was finally given its full play. Within the church, there was that block of clergy that chafed under De Roo's leadership style, who badly wanted him gone so that one of their own could have his day.

Add to this traditionalists who resisted Vatican II tooth and nail. In addition, there were recently converted or returned social conservatives who were embarrassed that a left-wing radical was in charge of their church, especially that he received so much adulation and media coverage for views that drove them crazy.

Of course, Rome's disposition was well known. The new top down authoritarianism was in direct opposition to De Roo's advance. Even the normally unflappable De Roo had been expressing concern at just how bad it was getting in Rome, what he had experienced during his *ad limina* visits.[16] Rome was not a debatable point.

The top level within the church and the local level were all settled in their indigestion. The local situation had shifted further that way with him out of office. But the big surprise was in the middle where he could have expected to be cut a bit of slack.

If there was going to be a neutral forum where he could have his say, it should have been provided by a balanced intervention from the Canadian Conference of Catholic Bishops where De Roo had made such a critical contribution over many decades.

---

[16] After his mid-1990s visit De Roo who met often with small groups and in small group settings where an extraordinary candor was shared about the state of the church, De Roo was saying openly among friends that he felt he had seen the face of evil on his latest trip to The Vatican. He told some confreres that he feared that the next pope would be extremely right wing.

I knew from the start that De Roo would not respond to the media frenzy, that he would not allow the media to set the agenda where he was expected to speak about his side of the affair.

Catholic bishops are a small and exclusive club. They are in the habit of controlling the venue where they have their say. When the Canadian Bishops Conference agreed to do a canonical inquiry, this could be the opportunity when he felt that a neutral opening was available.

But he would never be granted this moment. The report and the reporting process and the inquiry itself was not conceived in those terms. He was too powerful a speaker to be allowed to have his complete say. After all that was what had made him so unpopular with the other side in the first place. He could marshal facts and ideas and insight of analysis in so masterful a manner it made his enemies see red; and his disciples gasp with inspiration. This was precisely his area of leadership within the church and within Canadian society.

To be able to move such an institution as the Catholic church in the way he had demonstrably done for fifty years, this required a special set of skills – political skills that got things changed and also made fiercely irate enemies.

❦❦❦

The Editor
The Globe and Mail
June 30, 2000

I appreciated Kim Lunman's piece on the Diocese of Victoria's financial woes (G&M 17-6, p. A11). She did a good job of tracking the financial line of the story. Of course there are those who feel that this is really a political story – church politics.

It's interesting, in this vein, that she was only able to find tenuous direct connections between Remi De Roo, Victoria's bishop from 1962 to 1999, with the line of the story. She acknowledges that the earlier financial strategy was entirely the creation of Muriel Clemenger, the former administrator; and it was her job to do such creating.

De Roo had the reputation for 'not caring about money' and for delegating in a manner that included a lot of trust and little if any second guessing. It is interesting as well that the verdict is still out as to whether the property in question will sell; recovering the entire 'loss' as Muriel Clemenger was still convinced it would even after the original story broke in late February. Clemenger and I had a candid conversation about the topic then when I needed to be briefed prior to a radio interview on this issue.

The fact the story was broken by the National Post bears some close scrutiny. Their reporter called the *Island Catholic News* with what was supposed to be an irresistible offer of two hundred dollars to tape the message that was only to be read from the pulpit the following Sunday. It is amazingly diligent of *The Post* to be closely monitoring the financial troubles of every Catholic Diocese in the country – some seventy in all. As the one who was supposed to be doing the taping, the request made the hairs stand up on the back on my neck in a sudden alertness that something funny was afoot.

I well knew that the owner of *The Post* (and a few dozen other newspapers, including the local Victoria *Times Colonist* at the time), one Conrad Black, was reported in your pages ferociously attacking De Roo in the 1980s over his role in the Canadian Bishops' critique of the crisis in the Canadian economy. It got all rather heavy and personal.

The Post angle about race horses became the hallmark headline of the story despite the fact Arabians are show horses. The gambling edge had to get in there. Muriel Clemenger stated to me there never was any question of buying or investing directly in horses. She said it was a "simple bridge financing arrangement with a healthy fee" that went afoul leading to the losses and then to the recovery strategy of flipping the property at Lacey, Washington, which Kim Lunman tracked. Clemenger told me that it was De Roo's compassion for the horse farmer at Swiftsure Farms that would not let her pull the plug earlier.

Back home here on Vancouver Island, the new diocesan administration was very quick to publicly affix blame to the previous administration and yet I see that Ms Lunman correctly indicated that it was the decisions taken by the new group that resulted in the escalation of the financial problems, caused by the foreclosure and the court ordered jacked-up interest rates. The new administration refused to continue payments thus resulting in the crisis becoming a catastrophe which was all blamed on De Roo despite his being out of office when these subsequent decisions were taken.

Clemenger obviously had a workable payment strategy in place with the Lacey property but it was promptly abandoned, exacerbating the difficulties. Clemenger was requested by the new administration not to speak in public, a promise she keeps to this day.

Even the way the information was released was very curious at best. The clergy were forbidden from distributing the statement, which was only to be read from the pulpit. This reverting to ancient secrecy methodology caused the maximum media curiosity; and subsequent furor, anger and confusion among the general Catholic population.

On the other hand, it worked and Bishop De Roo in the collective view was entitled to wear all the blame. The new financial administrator, by the way, was hired out of the circles in the diocese that had always been hypercritical of De Roo's administrative style. Clemenger was not popular among the traditionalist clergy, either because she was a woman or as a scapegoat for their feelings about the boss; feelings which could not be directly expressed.

Meanwhile back in Rome, as Garry Wills argues in his new book, "Papal Sin" (reviewed by Michael Valpy in your same edition) very little will be tolerated in the way of church reform or progressive theology. Unfortunately De Roo made the mistake in February '99 of announcing such would form a distinct part of his retirement program. Shortly after that he was silenced for the first time in his career when scheduled to speak in Atlanta at a married Catholic clergy conference. Then as now he has suffered in complete silence, knowing this is hardly the time for speaking out, or his program, yet knowing as well how things can shift in the Catholic church.

Less than twenty years ago he peaked a twenty year run of social and theologically progressive leadership with the 'Reflections on the Crisis in the Canadian Economy' on New Year's Day, 1983. This event made him a household name – fifteen minutes of fame that was extended for fifteen years.

Rome's disposition and the changing of the guard in Victoria are no big surprise nor was the retrograde reaction of Conrad Black who became a Catholic through the back door about the same time De Roo was championing the rights of the unemployed in the early 1980s. De Roo would not be the individual running the church of his choice.

According to Ron Graham's 1990 book "God's Dominion," Black was welcomed into the church at a champagne breakfast by Cardinal Emmett Carter of Toronto without the privilege of the usual one-to-two year discernment process the Catholic church requires of its entrants. Perhaps Black's theological acumen was the basis for the exemption, with his strong suit the church's social teachings.

The surprise area of attack was the Canadian Bishops Conference which was called in by the new Victoria Bishop, Raymond Roussin, to do a formal canonical inquiry. While their report has yet to be released, its chairperson Rev. Peter Schonenbach, General Secretary of the CCCB, was headlined in the *Times Colonist* comparing De Roo's situation to that of a gambling addict. The general secretary thus pre-empted his own report in a prejudicial manner; hardly professional behavior from the Canadian Catholic church's top bureaucrat.

Roussin, by the way, seems a complete innocent in these political matters, as evidenced by the breakdown of his health under the pressure of the financial quandary and the discrediting that De Roo, his friend and colleague, has suffered.

Coming out of Vatican II, the Canadian Conference of Catholic Bishops could be said to have lead the universal church in its celebration and manifestation of collegiality, a central principle emerging out of Vatican II. An apt example was the infamous birth control controversy in 1968. At the time De Roo led the conference in its all but dissenting pastoral application of the papal encyclical 'Humanae Vitae.'

The general Catholic outcry against the teaching by Pope Paul VI created a crisis of confidence in the church's central teaching authority from which the Catholic church is still reeling. Collegiality was the coming of age of global Catholicism, where the local national church would decide how best to apply the papal teachings; but it has all but been abandoned.

In the 1990s Cardinal Ratzinger of the Curia has made it expressly clear that under the present papal regime the national colleges of bishops have no canonical status or authority. So it is not surprising to see the CCCB fold entirely under Roman pressure, although it must be sorely disappointing for De Roo who was a leading figure in the development of the collegial principle both at the Council (1962-65) and in Canada after as a Council Father.

Remi De Roo, a national icon, has suffered from an orchestrated effort to discredit his legacy, to distract him from adding to it. With his linguistic capacity and actual theological acumen, he was once among the very few Canadian Bishops with legitimate papabilia potential. That was all cancelled from 1968 when he crossed the American king maker Cardinal Francis MacIntyre of Los Angeles and had his advancement card indelibly soiled in Rome.

It must be very painful for him to be protested against in Saint Boniface, Manitoba recently when parents complained about having children confirmed by a bishop under threat of canonical censure. De Roo, a priest of that diocese, was anointed for succession at Saint Boniface by Archbishop Baudoux, his mentor, but it was never to be, due to the above difficulties. The mitre was passed to his classmate and cousin by marriage Archbishop Antoine Hacault who died of cancer in April and asked De Roo from his deathbed to make his confirmation rounds.

My own intuition about the financial dimension of this story is that there will be, lo and behold, *a deus ex machina* manifestation and the financial situation of the diocese will be fully restored by the selling of that much-cursed and joked about property. But the permanent impact will be the discrediting of the reputation of Remi De Roo, the actual purpose of the entire saga.

Not for the first time have such cruel, clever politics been so manipulated in the Canadian Catholic Church (or the Diocese of Victoria). Remember Archbishop Joseph Charbonneau, the social justice advocate of Montréal. He 'retired' for ten years to Victoria prior to his death in 1959, and he too refused to speak out about his shafting because he did not want to add to 'the scandal about the church'. I am afraid the scandal of the church is all too apparent to those who have the eyes to see and the ears to hear.

Patrick Jamieson
Victoria, BC
[unpublished]

'People of God' Pull Together to Reach Goal

Diocesan Debt Repayment Plan reaches target

By Marnie Butler

Island Catholic News, Volume 14, No. 8, September 2000

VICTORIA (ICN)—After over three months and many hundreds of volunteer hours of work by a dedicated and experienced group of Vancouver Island parishioners, the inaugural stage of the Diocese of Victoria's Debt Repayment Program is closing.

As of August 31st the diocese will have raised over $13 million through the issuance and sale of bonds and the generous donations of organizations, parishioners and other individuals, principally on Vancouver Island. Everyone deserves a rest this Labour Day.

Bishop Raymond Roussin will celebrate a Mass of Thanksgiving here September 14th, 7:00 pm at St. Andrew's Cathedral. It will resonate with the many prayers offered up by the faithful over the past months.

At its inception in mid-May, Ellis Achtem, who, together with Monsignor Michael O'Connell, co-chairs the fundraising effort said: "We are undertaking this unfortunate, but necessary campaign to honour commitments made in the name of the Diocese." Members of the Roman Catholic Church here obviously took this commitment to heart and rallied to the cause.

The diocese was struggling under 18 per cent interest payments on a defaulted mortgage of a property in Washington State. The campaign explained to parishioners throughout the Island that over $12 million needed to be raised to remove this burden from the diocese.

Retired attorney, Ellis Achtem, Monsignor O'Connell (Rector of St. Andrew's Cathedral), Diocesan Financial Administrator Vern McLeish, and Bishop Raymond Roussin, together and individually, travelled to every region in the diocese, holding meetings with parishioners and explaining the new financial plan.

The bond issue is part of a business plan that will effectively see the Diocese "become its own banker over the next three years," Achtem explained to the sometimes irate parishioners at these meetings. Anger abated, the urge to blame set aside, Catholics on the Island rallied and supported the Diocesan plan.

Through the issuance of bonds, the Diocese has borrowed money from parishioners and others at a minimal interest rate. This allows the Diocese to undertake an orderly sale of some of its real estate assets. The proceeds from the sale of assets will be used to clear the debt and repay the bondholders. The bonds are secured by a mortgage to be held by a trustee charging all of the land and buildings of the Diocese.

The 13 properties available for sale have an estimated value of $9,745,000. No church or school buildings are presently being offered for sale.

Some surprise investors came forward to assist the Diocese. Naz and Yasmine Rayani, local Muslims called Ellis Achtem to offer their financial support.

"This is not an issue of faith", said Naz Rayani, "the Catholic church is much more than a place to worship. I look at what the Catholic church does in the community – at the social programs, hospitals and schools that it supports – and I realize how important the activities of the Victoria Diocese are to all of us, regardless of our denomination. When I think of the religious turmoil that exists in the world, I cannot help but think how much better things would be if all religions could recognize each other's good works in times of trouble."

A Sacred Heart parishioner tells of the enthusiasm of a Jewish friend in Toronto to invest in the bonds: "It's just for three years and the interest rate is decent [six percent], why not?" said the investor from afar.

There have been some surprises in the parishes on Vancouver Island. Each parish determined, in consultation with the Debt Repayment Committee, an appropriate goal for bond sales. Several were kept low because of the severe unemployment in resource based communities, where revenue from logging, fishing and mining has declined in the past years. Most of these parishes topped, even doubled, their goals.

Bishop Ray Roussin, who has served as the chief shepherd of the Diocese for only 18 months, has been joyfully overwhelmed by the response to the campaign:

"A simple 'thank you' does not seem enough to convey to all of my gratitude for your prayers, efforts and contributions to address-ing our financial dilemma," said the bishop in a July 26th letter dis-tributed in many parishes and addressed to 'Dear Brothers & Sis-ters in Christ'.

Bishop Raymond continues: "The Debt Repayment Committee and its uncounted number of volunteers... have earned the thanks of all throughout the Diocese and they are grateful in return for the enthusiastic participation of not only our own parishioners but sympathetic people from other faiths."

And what of the property in Washington State? Its value has been estimated by various sources as between $5,000,000 to $12 million (US). A special task force has been established to manage the Seattle land investment as well as the diocesan debt. It consists of Ian H. Stewart, Q.C.; Norman Isherwood, International residen-tial and commercial real estate management and development; and David Osmond, President, Victoria Properties former manag-er, HSBC (formerly Hong Kong Bank of Canada).

Their responsibility surely must feel less onerous, given the impressive support of the "People of God on Vancouver Island."

island catholic news

Additional Distribution Sites page 12

$2.00 PER COPY

Volume 16 Nº 12   January 2003   Independent Voice of 'Prophetic Catholicism' for Vancouver Island & the Gulf Islands

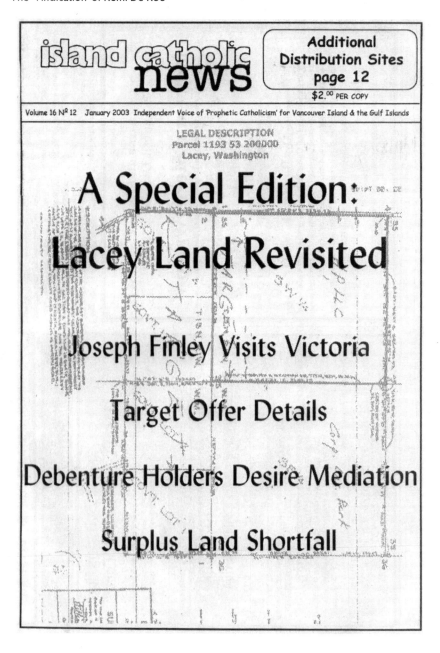

LEGAL DESCRIPTION
Parcel 1193 53 200000
Lacey, Washington

A Special Edition:

Lacey Land Revisited

Joseph Finley Visits Victoria

Target Offer Details

Debenture Holders Desire Mediation

Surplus Land Shortfall

Chapter 2 – Lacey Land Revisited

Debenture Holders Desire Mediation in Diocesan Dispute

Island Catholic News Volume 16, No. 12, January 2003

VICTORIA—Joe Finley was in town in late November and the impact of his information is still being felt throughout the Diocese.

At a public meeting November 26, 2002 in the city library on Broughton Street, Joseph Finley of Bellevue, Washington took two and a half hours to explain his experience of fifteen years of financial dealings with his business partner, the Diocese of Victoria. Some sixty people attended, including some significant diocesan debenture bond holders, such as the Oblates of Mary Immaculate, represented by Rev. Terry McNamara of Vancouver.

After a half-hour opening statement, Finley fielded questions for another two hours. At the meeting's close, according to CBC Radio reporting on November 27, 57 of the 60 who attended voted by show of hand to say they were in favor of mediation as a means of solving the messy business problems between the two parties.

Joseph Finley and the Diocese are partners since 1997 in *Corporate Business Park*, a hundred and sixty acre piece of industrial property on the Interstate 5 corridor, ten miles from the state capital of Olympia, Washington. However selling the increasingly valuable piece of real estate as partners has proven to be consistently difficult, especially since the departure of the former Bishop of Victoria, Remi De Roo, in February 1999.

De Roo was Bishop of Victoria from 1962 to 1999, and in the late 1980s Finley, and De Roo's financial administrator, Muriel Clemenger came to know each other through their common interest in raising Arabian horses, in which they invested together.

Arabians are show horses, not to be confused with race horses, as they regularly were in some of the early media reporting on the financial revelations that emerged exactly one year after De Roo left office. *Corporate Business Park* was an effort at eliminating an earlier loss by the Diocese through a loan to an Arabian horse farm owned by Joseph Finley in the 1980s.

From March, 2000, however, it was extensively reported how the current administration at the Victoria Diocese took a very dim view of the *Corporate Business Park* arrangement; how it decided it was too rich for its blood despite its contractual obligations. Unfortunately, it has not proved so simple to escape contractual business arrangements, not without a great deal of expense in the process. Various kinds of expenses.

By this time the Diocese was being administered in a different style under its new bishop, Raymond Roussin, who had been appointed by Rome to replace De Roo from the day of his seventy-fifth birthday, February 24, 1999. The fifty-nine-year-old Roussin came to Victoria from Gravelbourg, Saskatchewan some six months prior to that date. He worked with De Roo until the time of his official retirement.

Roussin put in place an entirely different administrative team and just more than a year after taking office, in late February, 2000, a huge financial crisis was loudly announced by the Diocese. They claimed, it was widely reported, the crisis was due to investments made by the former bishop. These were typified as 'bad investments' or 'questionable investments' at best.

New Revelations

Now information is emerging through Joseph Finley that contradicts that conventional wisdom. Finley claims it was a wise investment that matured when expected and could have paid big dividends on time if the new administration had not scuttled an offer of twenty-three million dollars Canadian from a large American retail firm in the summer of 2000.

He also claims that the Diocese did not inform him or *Corporate Business Park* about the Target Corporation proposal but instead tried to eliminate him as their business partner.

56

As he expressed it over the phone on Boxing Day of 2002: "There was a Target deal; there were negotiations all through the summer of 2000 to hold the Target deal until the Diocese could grab the Washington land; their lawyers advised them badly and their plot failed."

"We still could have sold the property to Target had they co-operated in February 2001; the actions of the Diocese on this raise securities issues under B.C. law, they are in violation of their fiduciary duties to the bondholders and to the *Corporate Business Park* and me."

"The surplus lands appear to have been squandered under very unusual conditions. How much does it take to get a groundswell to call the Diocese on the carpet? Hopefully, not waiting until August 2003 when the Diocese will be begging the bondholders for more time because they will not have the money unless this mess gets resolved."

Three Years Ago

In February, 2000 the 'financial crisis' information was directly released to the secular media. As a result the whole issue was blown entirely out of proportion. For six months the reporting was sensationally persistent, resulting in a hotly charged atmosphere of blame, anger and threatened recriminations. De Roo's role was examined by a Canonical Inquiry out of Ottawa, an extraordinary measure requested by his successor.

As a direct consequence two things resulted. The Diocese launched a debenture bond sale which resulted in some thirteen million dollars being lent to the Diocese to help it out of its announced crisis. This money came from a combination of ordinary parishioners, religious orders who wanted to help out, non-Catholic churches such as the local Anglican diocese, as well as sympathetic people who had heard about it through the media reporting.

The other major effect was that Bishop De Roo's reputation was severely tarnished. De Roo, something of a legend in the Canadian Christian Churches after Vatican II (1962-65), had methodically established a unique role as the social conscience of the country during the 1960s, 70s and 80s, when he served as chairperson of the Canadian Bishops social affairs commission.

By consistently applying the Catholic church's social teaching in the context of emerging social problems, De Roo is said to have transformed Canadian Catholic social teaching in the direction of 'prophetic Catholicism.' The Catholic church, under De Roo's leadership, adopted the model of liberation theology to the Canadian context and the result was politically controversial.

By charging the church's social teaching with a fresh voltage, the bishops animated direct action by Catholics and other ordinary Canadians on a multitude of issues. The effect was to challenge the governing power elite. In the process De Roo, as the principal spokesperson, was widely admired on the left, but deeply despised on the right, both within the church and Canadian society. As a result he gained an international reputation for human rights work.

So, while the Diocese of Victoria was said to be suffering from financial losses as a result of these unlikely revelations, the blow to De Roo's reputation held a wider and deeper symbolic effect in Canadian social and political culture. This was at a point when Canadian culture was reeling from twenty years of social neoconservatism that was effectively rolling back fifty years of previous gains under the aegis of fiscal restraint.

Within the church, the quality of length of service by Bishop De Roo seemed to be lost to view as did the perspective and balance afforded by the gospels as the controversy raged on. For many it all left a foul taste in the mouth from the acrimonious politics possible within the Catholic church.

Public Library

On Tuesday, November 26, 2002, Joseph Finley told the library audience that from his experience of the past five years, something notably irrational seems to be at work in the financial affairs of the Diocese of Victoria; a mysterious element that has made the situation much worse than it needed to be, he said; a strange attitude that still has him scratching his head.

Joseph Finley is a lawyer and a businessman based in Washington State. As an American businessman, operating in a fiscally conscious culture, he is not used to business partners turning their nose up at twenty-three million dollar offers for land that cost them less than half that amount, especially when that same partner has announced huge debt problems which the sale would completely eradicate.

But that is the problem Finley offered to explain at the professionally videotaped meeting November 26. He said he came to Victoria at the request of a group of parishioners who wanted a fuller explanation of the situation as he saw it. He confessed that he finds the non-co-operative attitude baffling at best. He cannot, in rational terms, understand the antagonism toward his involvement. If the Diocese finds him so difficult as a business partner, one would think that working together to complete a sale would be the quickest way to be rid of him; not prolonging the agony.

The Target Offer

In a sworn declaration dated August 26, 2002 in the Superior Court of Washington for Thurston County, Finley states that he has evidence that Target Corporation, an American retail chain, approached the Diocese of Victoria in the spring of 2000 with a proposed purchase agreement for the *Corporate Business Park* property at a price of $13.9 million (US). He says that was at the same time the Diocese was raising $13 million (CAN) from its parishioners to refinance the property.

Finley says that Target was described by Donald Moody, the realtor who brought the deal to the diocese, as "in the Fortune Five Hundred." He also questions the legality of concealment of the offer by the Diocese.

Moody testified under oath in the United States Bankruptcy Court, Western District of Washington at Seattle, on March 6, 2001, that he came to the Diocese of Victoria with a purchase offer. Vernon McLeish is the financial administrator of the Diocese of Victoria.

Segments of that deposition upon oral examination read: *Q. "Did you have a purchaser at that time that was interested? A. We had a purchaser that was interested… Q. How did you decide that the church was the person that you needed to talk to? A. That was the name that was given to me…. Q. And the $13 million price, is that one you set or is that the one the Church told you? A. That's one I set…. Q. Did you contact the Bishop of Victoria Corporate Sole…? do you recall exactly who? A. I called up and asked who would be involved in the piece of real estate. I'm not sure who I talked to that first time. I have a list of phone calls… it would probably have been Dave Osmond. Q. Do you ever recall speaking with Vern McLeish? A. Yes…I talked to Vern – I took the purchase and sale agreement to Victoria… These are calls that were logged in to me, not calls that I made out. What I'm saying is that I probably returned a phone call on each of these… I talked to Vern McLeish one other time… they came down to Seattle – three or four of them – and I talked to Vern a second time at that time. Q. Do you recall when that was? A. …it probably would have been around June of 2000. Q. And do you recall who was present? A. Well, I'm sure that McLeish was present, probably Dave Osmond… Q. At that meeting in June of 2000, what were you told about the property? A. I was told that they were very anxious to sell and that I was supposed to leave my listing with them… They were very positive about selling the piece of property. Q. Did they tell you anything about clearing title? … Did they discuss how long it would take to clear title? … Were there ever any discussions as to how long it would take to clear title? A. It probably would have come from my side. They were always very positive that they were going to be able to meet any deadlines.*

Finley Statement

In his August 26, 2002 sworn statement Finley says: "In August 2000, I entered into a listing agreement with Trammell Crow Company in my capacity as co-manager of *Corporate Business Park* property... The value derived by Trammell Crow for the *Corporate Business Park* property for the 160 acres (was) $18,469,440 (US) ... After the fact, I learned that in May/June 2000 CB Richard Ellis (agent Donald Moody) had approached the Bishop of Victoria corporation with a proposed purchase and sale agreement and a listing for the *Corporate Business Park* at a price of $13,939,200 [US]. The Bishop of Victoria concealed this opportunity from me until I discovered it in February 2001... From early 2001 through July of that year, I had direct involvement with the Target Corporation's purchase of 142 acres of land adjoining the *Corporate Business Park* property (and knowledge of the price paid by Target Corporation), a purchase Target made only after the Bishop of Victoria had refused to cooperate with me to make the *Corporate Business Park* property available to Target... I believe the current value of the *Corporate Business Park* property is not less than $18 million (US) and could be higher than $21 million. I believe that the failure to sell the property to Target Corporation or to other users is directly and solely due to the actions of Bishop of Victoria Corporation Sole, its officers and agents, and to the actions of United Homes Victoria (now Fisgard Asset Management Corporation) its officers and agents."

United Homes Victoria, which became Fisgard Asset Management Corporation, is the purchaser of the mortgage of CBP as provided by the $13 million (CDN) received from the Catholic parishioners and other debenture bondholders.

Concealment

Finley alleges that in the United States concealment of this purchase offer from both the debenture bond purchasers and himself, as business partner, is a breach of fiduciary duties and a breach of contract.

Court documents, including a hundred page deposition by the diocese's financial administrator Vernon McLeish, dated May 7, 2002, have been obtained by the media. In his statement McLeish admits that there has been a shortfall on the monies earned from the sale of surplus lands which the Diocese used to guarantee the return for debenture bond sales; a return due in less than eight months, in August, 2003.

As a result the story has been picked up by reporters Robert Matas of *The Globe and Mail* (September 26, 2002), Candis McLean of *The Report Magazine* (October 21, 2002) and Mark Browne in *The Victoria News Weekend Edition* (October 18 & December 13, 2002). [*These stories are reprinted*]

The deal was turned down, Finley claims, because the Diocese told Target the land was tied up in litigation, but that litigation was, in fact, the Diocese' efforts to get rid of Finley as a business partner; something he contends was strictly their doing not his. His legal actions, he said on November 26, were not commenced until spring of 2001 and "were purely defensive measures" in re- sponse to aggressive moves" to have him removed from the con- tract equation.

The summer of 2000 was the summer when the diocese was raising its $13 million dollars through debenture bond loans and also starting its program of selling off 'surplus lands' in order to recover that money and pay back the parishioners and other loan- ers in August 2003; and those eight months are ticking away. Quoted in *The Report* magazine article, Ian Stewart, Chairperson of the Diocese Finance Committee, "We're in terribly, terribly bad shape; people have no idea of the problems going on. Where the $13-and-a-half million we need next August is going to come from, I don't know."

Two disturbing and opposing sets of questions arise at this point. If Finley is manipulating the situation for his own ends, how exactly does making up a Target Corporation offer help his cause?

What was Donald Moody talking about if there was no serious interest in an offer? On the other hand, if the Diocese did this seemingly 'irrational' act of turning away a potentially solid offer, what could be the reasons? To answer these questions we need to revisit the history of the *Corporate Business Park* investment.

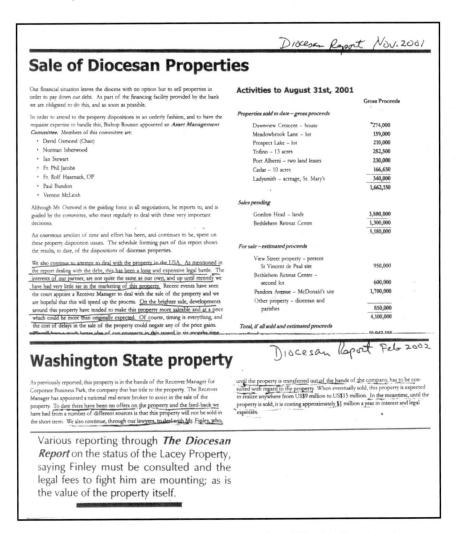

Diocesan Report Nov. 2001

Sale of Diocesan Properties

Our financial situation leaves the diocese with no option but to sell properties in order to pay down our debt. As part of the financing facility provided by the bank we are obligated to do this, and as soon as possible.

In order to attend to the property dispositions in an orderly fashion, and to have the requisite expertise to handle this, Bishop Roussin appointed an *Asset Management Committee*. Members of this committee are:

- David Osmond (Chair)
- Norman Isherwood
- Ian Stewart
- Fr. Phil Jacobs
- Fr. Rolf Hasenack, OP
- Paul Bundon
- Vernon McLeish

Although Mr. Osmond is the guiding force in all negotiations, he reports to, and is guided by the committee, who meet regularly to deal with these very important decisions.

An enormous amount of time and effort has been, and continues to be, spent on these property disposition issues. The schedule forming part of this report shows the results, to date, of the dispositions of diocesan properties.

We also continue to attempt to deal with the property in the USA. As mentioned in the report dealing with the debt, this has been a long and expensive legal battle. The interests of our partner, are not quite the same as our own, and up until recently we have had very little say in the marketing of this property. Recent events have seen the court appoint a Receiver Manager to deal with the sale of the property and we are hopeful that this will speed up the process. On the brighter side, developments around this property have tended to make this property more saleable and at a price which could be more than originally expected. Of course, timing is everything, and the cost of delays in the sale of the property could negate any of the price gains.

Activities to August 31st, 2001

	Gross Proceeds
Properties sold to date – gross proceeds	
Dawnview Crescent – house	274,000
Meadowbrook Lane – lot	159,000
Prospect Lake – lot	210,000
Tofino – 13 acres	282,500
Port Alberni – two land leases	230,000
Cedar – 10 acres	166,650
Ladysmith – acreage, St. Mary's	340,000
	1,662,150
Sales pending	
Gordon Head – lands	3,880,000
Bethlehem Retreat Centre	1,300,000
	5,180,000
For sale – estimated proceeds	
View Street property – present St Vincent de Paul site	950,000
Bethlehem Retreat Centre – second lot	600,000
Pandora Avenue – McDonald's site	1,700,000
Other property – diocesan and parishes	850,000
	4,100,000
Total, if all sold and estimated proceeds	10,942,150

Diocesan Report Feb 2002

Washington State property

As previously reported, this property is in the hands of the Receiver Manager for Corporate Business Park, the company that has title to the property. The Receiver Manager has appointed a national real estate broker to assist in the sale of the property. To date there have been no offers on the property and the feed-back we have had from a number of different sources is that this property will not be sold in the short term. We also continue, through our lawyers, to deal with Mr. Finley, who,

until the property is transferred out of the hands of the company, has to be consulted with regard to the property. When eventually sold, this property is expected to realize anywhere from US$9 million to US$15 million. In the meantime, until the property is sold, it is costing approximately $1 million a year in interest and legal expenses.

Various reporting through *The Diocesan Report* on the status of the Lacey Property, saying Finley must be consulted and the legal fees to fight him are mounting; as is the value of the property itself.

In February 2002 the people of the diocese were being told "to date there have been no offers on the property" despite two Target approaches, the second coordinated by Finley who is blamed for "$1 million a year in interest and legal expenses" in the above text.

Three Bishops and a Businessman

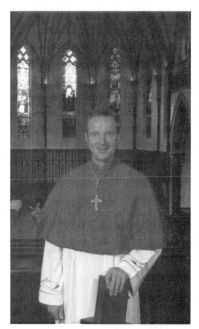

Remi De Roo (1962 – 1999)

Joseph C. Finley

Raymond Roussin (1999 – 2004)

Richard Gagnon (2004 -)

Chapter 3 – A Debt Left On The Books

Island Catholic News, Volume 16, No. 12, January 2003

At the public library meeting, Joseph Finley typified his dealings with Muriel Clemenger and Bishop De Roo as very pleasant. He said that they were always open, cordial and, even when dealing with difficult issues, very positive. There was a feeling of good will and good faith with each other. Those were the good days, he stated.

As he tells it, through Ms Clemenger there were a number of individual people who were parishioners on Vancouver Island who had invested in Arabian show horses. The Diocese entered directly into the equation only at the point when an effort was needed to save Swiftsure Farms, a horse breeding operation which would benefit all concerned.

The Diocese's loan was initially guaranteed by a reputable Toronto investment house, he said. The tax structure around Arabians subsequently changed for the worse and the value of horses for investment purposes dropped to five per cent of their original value. As a result that money was lost, approximately a million dollars by the diocese.

Two options were possible at that time Finley said. He was advised by legal counsel to walk away from the situation which he could have done under the law. Instead he chose the second option, telling the Diocese to keep the debt on the books and that he would find a way to pay them back over time. The Diocese agreed. This loss took place in the late 1980s.

A number of years later, in 1997, Finley says he kept his word and brought the Lacey land deal to the Diocese. (He said he never forgot the debt nor the honorable way he was treated throughout the difficult episode.) This was a hundred and sixty acre parcel of industrial land that was being sold for what was still owed on it, $5.5 million American.

The appraisal on the land was $14 million (US) but the appraiser said it would take around thirty months to sell. The final cost after remortgaging was $7.5 million and the Diocese signed as a backer on the debt. Finley put none of his own money into the deal. His role was broker, agent and partner based on expertise and input of time and effort. The purpose of the deal was primarily to pay off the debt – after that was taken care of, to split the profits after the Diocese received its original investment of $7.5 million (US). The alleged Target offer in 2000, some thirty months later, was for $14 million (US), approximately $23 million (CAN).

After De Roo had left office, Vernon McLeish told Finley there would be no more payments "until they figured out what was going on." On May 15, 1999 they signed an Addendum to the *Corporate Business Park* Agreement, which was to allow the resumption of payments but they did not recommence. McLeish then told Finley this was because the Diocese was going to refinance to get a lower mortgage rate but in September, 1999 the refinancing fell through.

By then the lender, AG Capital, had commenced their lawsuit which continued although the Diocese brought all payments current through the end of 1999. In January, 2000 Allen Vanderkerkhove made an offer to buy CBP for $7.5 million (US) which failed and after that the Diocese made no more payments and AG Capital took a judgment against CBP. At this point the Diocese cooperated with AG Capital to try to collect from Finley, which also failed. It was this series of decisions taken by the Diocese which precipitated the huge 'financial crisis' according to *The Globe and Mail* reporting at the time.

Then in the summer of 2000, the Diocese sold the debenture bonds and bought the AG Capital judgment.

Looked at over the longer view, especially in light of an actual offer, the value and schedule of the land bought by De Roo were accurate and *Corporate Business Park* was actually a good investment. This was certainly Joseph Finley's contention on November

26, and he seemed to convince some 95 per cent of those in attendance at the public library.

Profit Arrangement

One of the things he explained was his own profit arrangement through the original *Corporate Business Park* contract with the Diocese in 1997. Since the overall purpose of the deal was to pay back his debt, he could only receive financial benefit after: 1) the original debt was repaid; 2) the repayment of monies invested by the Diocese to purchase and develop the property for resale and 3) the diocesan share of the profits. Only after all that, he said, he would get his share which depends on the final selling price.

He admitted freely that he did not put up any of his own money. His earnings are based upon his investment of time, legal and business expertise, management role and, in effect, a finder's fee. There is no doubt that Joseph Finley wants his share of the profit once CBP is sold, but as he stated, that is what he agreed to when he signed the contract. The key question seems to be what is the truth of this Target offer allegation, or why was Target concealed from the bondholders and Finley; not why should Finley be getting anything out of the sale?

The Other Question

If what Finley has sworn to be true in his court deposition, and if the sworn testimony by Don Moody, the Washington realtor – that he brought the deal to the Diocese only to be eventually turned away – is true; why would the Diocese be acting the way it has? If Finley's recorded explanation at the public library is factual, who could be gaining from such a strategy?

Has anyone within the administrative team ever confirmed that there was an actual offer from Target that was turned away for whatever reason? The mentioned newspaper accounts all have diocesan officials saying there was no formal offer from Target;

but as Candis McLean and Mark Browne point out in their pieces, the operative term seems to be 'formal offer'.

No one is denying that some negotiations with Target took place in the summer of 2000. The Moody statement on that is strong and clear. Finley also talks about further negotiations in February, 2001. What were the nature of these negotiations? Before we get into that, how should the Diocese be relating to its business partner, no matter how reluctant the arrangement?

One of Finley's main complaints against the Diocese is that when this approach – and we can at least call it that – was made, he as their business partner should have been informed, so that he could get directly involved and bring it to fruition. He says he only found out in early 2001 from Seattle area realtors which was confirmed by the sworn deposition of Don Moody, the realtor, on March 6, 2001.

Finley claims that the contract he signed with the Diocese, after De Roo left office, when the new administration was starting to try to get him off the deal, imposed 'a fiduciary duty' for the partners to inform the other if there was serious interest in the property. This claim forms a central part of the court struggle between Finley and the Diocese at present.

The Target interest in land in that area would have to be categorized in the 'serious' category. This is clear because they bought a smaller parcel of land immediately adjacent to the CBP site, a site that did not suit their needs as well because it was too small at 120 acres and required that they purchase an additional adjacent 22 acres, which the owner was reluctant to sell.

A lot of the February, 2001 negotiations between the Diocese and Finley (**see Chapter 4**) had to do with his expediting an easement to the CBP lands so that CBP would be that much more attractive to Target due to this other size difficulty.

This proved ironic given the fact a diocese spokesperson, a member of the Lacey property committee, Norm Isherwood told me on the phone December 11th, after the adverse media publicity, that Target did not want the CBP property precisely because the fit was not right. (*The Diocese of Victoria was invited through Norm Isherwood, to provide an explanation of its version of these same events on a page of this issue of ICN*).

In light of the facts, this sounds like a rationalizing excuse for what appears otherwise to be an irrational decision. Earlier, in September, 2002, Norm Isherwood explained on the phone to a third party that there had been an offer from Target but that it had to be turned down because the land was tied up in litigation.

Since the only litigation surrounding the land when these events occurred was the Diocese' efforts to get rid of Finley as a business partner, this would appear to be only a lame excuse. Finley said at the library meeting that he would have agreed to an offer like the Target offer "at the speed of light." The litigation story sounds like a pretext to make the refusal sound rational.

An Expensive Antipathy

It is obvious the current administration at the Diocese does not like Mr. Finley, or at least the arrangement with Mr. Finley. They do not accept, apparently, his version of the nature of it.

But is that all it is, an antipathy toward an individual or his dealings? If so, it is an expensive antipathy, one the Diocese should be the first to admit it cannot really afford, especially at this time. Why would they declare a 'financial crisis' and then embark on an estimated $2 million legal campaign rather than simply working to cooperate with their partner? Why not just deal with him as quickly as possible, and have done with it, if it is simply a matter of distaste?

According to church teachings, such antipathy is not really supposed to be the primary basis for such dealings even if heartily felt. According to the Gospel mandate – and the 2000 years of church teaching – love, peace, forgiveness and reconciliation are to be the primary values aimed at ameliorating even business tensions.

Behind The Scenes

What are the other, more rational possibilities behind this 'irrational' attitude? Could it be serving someone's interest? Could anyone be gaining behind the scenes from this strange log jam? Who is ultimately gaining from the fact that diocesan surplus lands are put up for sale, and why those specific lands?

These are certainly the questions that started to arise from the give and take, questions and answers at the library session; and follow-up kitchen meetings around the issue.

After explaining the history of the deal, Finley responded to questions and queries, statements and postures at the meeting by media reporters, debenture holders, parishioners from most of the major parishes in Greater Victoria, defenders of the Diocese, as well as members of the general public. Some were certainly antagonistic, at least at the start, but at the close one fellow got up to say he expected Finley to have horns when he arrived, but had grown to quite like him.

Speculation did arise. For example, focus has fallen on the land in Gordon Head next to Holy Cross parish, the former Allotment Garden lands. A number of parishioners were far from pleased when this land was lost as surplus land. (*See Chapter 8 for a close examination of one such sale as 'surplus lands', the Gordon Head Allotment Gardens.*)

According to diocesan released figures, that parcel sold for $3.8 million. Compared to a smaller piece of property in that area sold by the diocese in the late 1980s, it has been suggested that much more could have been made from that land if subdivided by the diocese itself as the earlier property was by the earlier administration.

During the late 1980s and 90s, a piece of property on Edgelow Street in Gordon Head was subdivided and sold. Most of the profit is made in the subdividing such as they did then, not in the simple off-loading of property.

Why the relative giveaway? This is an especially pertinent question when the monies raised on the surplus lands are in short-fall. This has been admitted by the present diocesan administrator in a sworn statement in the Superior Court of Washington for Thurston County.

The McLeish Deposition

Compared to the fifteen million dollars' worth of property listed at the time of the debenture loan issue, only some 7-8 million will be gained, admits Vernon McLeish in pages 64 to 78 of his deposition; and very little of that has been set aside to pay back the debenture holders according to McLeish. The sale of the Lacey land is stated by the Diocese as the other source of funds for this purpose. But the Lacey land without mediation will be tied up in court for at least 18-24 months. (*It finally came to trial in the spring of 2005 with a May 28th decision.*)

In the February 2002 *Diocesan Report* tabloid newsletter, the vehicle the Diocese has used to get out information to people in the parishes, a one-paragraph statement under the heading 'Washington State property' reads in part: "To date there have been no offers on the property and feed-back we have had from a number of different sources is that this property will not be sold in the short term... In the meantime, until the property is sold, it is costing approximately $1 million a year in interest and legal expenses."

In a sworn deposition before the Superior Court of Washington for Thurston County on May 7, 2002 (in hearings that were part of Finley's measure to stop the diocese from having him removed as their business partner on the *Corporate Business Park*) McLeish admitted that paying back the debenture holders from the sale of surplus lands was impossible.

Question: The Bishop Corporation pledged as collateral a great deal of lands as part of this debenture offering, correct? Answer: Correct. Q: I want to ask about the surplus lands that were pledged as part of this debenture offering... So the $13 million figure that's used as an approximation of the *value of the surplus lands, that was Canadian funds, correct? A. Correct... Q. Has the bishop sold any of the surplus lands? A. Yes. Q. How much money has the bishop derived from those sales? A. To date. Its $6.6 million Canadian. Q. Was that $6.6 million Canadian paid back to the trustee on behalf of the debenture holders? A. No – $4.6 has gone to the bank for monies we owed for bonds... there were other debts other than the judgment dealing with Corporate Business Park's debts. So that 6.6 is gone. 4.6 to that and the other 2 million is held by the diocese right now and is being used for reconstruction of a church on the north island. (Comox Valley) So probably down to $300,000 left... Q. Do you know which properties were sold? ... A. Gordonhead (sic), there referred to as the Gordonhead lands. The Bethlehem retreat center. There was some land in Ladysmith parish. There was two or three residential lots. The majority of the money that we've raised has just come from two or three properties, Gordonhead, Bethlehem and Ladysmith... That accounted for 5 million of the 6.6. Q. How much was the Gordonhead lands worth? A. That was 3.8 million... Q. Is the church currently attempting to sell additional surplus lands? A. There are still a few under negotiation...Q. Any sales pending on any of those lands? A. Not at the moment... Q. Of the lands that have not already sold, are the remaining surplus lands currently being marketed and being attempted to be sold? A. Yes, but no sales pending and best estimate of what we'd get for that is 1.7. Q. For the remaining properties? A. Yes. Q. That would only be 8.3 million; is that right? A. That's right. Q. How is that – why is that different than the $14,867,000 in the offering statement? A. Well, the 14.8 was a property assessed value and it soon became apparent once you try to sell properties, that you don't come anywhere close to what you would like to get... that's about all we're going to get. Q. You don't expect to recover enough proceeds from the sale of the surplus lands to be able to pay off the debenture offering, is that right? A. Absolutely.*

The Distinct Feeling

One could get the distinct feeling that the surplus land sales stopped suddenly once someone got their hands on the 'Gordon-head' properties, as they are called. Further questioning of McLeish revealed that he believes that once the thirteen million plus interest ($15,622,000 according to *The Diocesan Messenger*, October 2002) was paid back to the debenture holders, Fisgard Asset Management Corporation (the successor to United Homes Victoria as the trustee of Bishop of Victoria Series A Debenture Holders) would get whatever extra there is. Furthermore this idea that it would not come back to the Diocese is also held by the Diocesan lawyers, according to the deposition transcript.

Since the shortfall from the surplus lands sales must be made up by the sale of the Lacey lands and the Lacey property is gaining in value every day and could bring in over $21 million (US) (according to Finley's sworn statement), that would be quite a windfall.

On page 13 of the October 2002 *Diocesan Messenger* (the new name of the *Diocesan Report* newsletter) under "Debenture debt," the shortfall is expected to be $12,405,000 with "Balance due, which will have to be repaid from the sale of the property in Lacey and other diocesan properties."

There would appear to be an advantage to the Diocese if the shortfall is higher and is to be repaid from the sale of the Lacey property since according to Vern McLeish and the Diocese's Washington lawyers, anything over the $15,622,000 owed to the debenture holders can be claimed by Fisgard Asset Management as trustees for the bond sales.

Beginning on page 82 of Vernon McLeish's deposition under oral examination, it reads:

Question: What is your understanding of what will happen if the property sells in an amount in addition to the amount owed for the debenture offering? A. Depends on how that comes about, but my understanding was that if it's an excess, then United Homes, I guess, has the surplus funds, and what they do with them, I guess it's up to them... as I say, I've thought about the debenture issue myself and thought what – who legally owns – say if the property went to the trustee and he sold it for more than the judgment, in my mind, I think that money probably belongs to the trustee... Q. Is there any agreement between the Bishop Corporation and United Homes Victoria or its successor company about where the money would go if there is a surplus following the sale of the property? A. No agreement whatsoever. Q. Mr. McLeish, are you aware that your counsel has taken the position in this litigation that United Homes Victoria would receive all the excess funds in that situation? A. I didn't know that... Q. My question was: Do you know that to be the position of the Bishop of Victoria Corporation now? A. Only because you told me. If you are telling me the truth then I have to accept that."

A Second Look

All these things need to be looked at more closely by an informed group of parishioners and debenture-holding public. Who was it that got their hands on the 'Gordonhead' and other properties, whose money did they use to acquire and develop it? Where did they get the funding? Who is making the real money off that side of the deal?

Is there any connection between the various parties who are legitimately gaining from the delay in sale of the CBP property? These include the Washington law firm that is fighting Finley on behalf of the diocese? An estimated two million dollars has gone their way. How were they selected, whose recommendation?

United Homes Victoria, now Fisgard Asset Management seem to stand to gain inordinately if the Lacey land sells for some of the more optimistic values.

Third, the people who were able to get their hands on the surplus land and develop it for resale, most particularly the Gordon Head property next to Holy Cross parish. Who ultimately benefits?

All important and legitimate questions, the answers to which go a long way in explaining this 'irrational' refusal by the Diocese to work in the right way with the right people to sell *Corporate Business Park* in the summer of 2000; or the spring of 2001 when Finley first discovered the concealment and then worked to realize the Target option.

Surplus Lands Revisited

The only other pieces of property sold, according to McLeish's answers to questioning during deposition, were the Bethlehem Retreat Center bought by the Benedictine Sisters in Nanaimo and "two or three residential lots." Bethlehem went for 1.1 million and Gordon Head for 3.8, McLeish stated that day. The maximum to be gained he claimed would be 8.3 million to cover the 13 million plus interest, to be paid back in August.

According to the information on page 13 of the October 2002, *Diocesan Messenger* newspaper, there is more than $12.4 million (CDN) to be collected for repayment, and this will have to come primarily from the sale of the Lacey land.

McLeish also says that the money for the Washington lawyers came out of that $6.6 million as did $2 million to fix up the ten-year-old Comox Valley parish church. The pastor of that parish eventually was given charge of St. Andrew's Cathedral as rector despite costing the Diocese so much by previous poor planning and administration. Another large amount was going for bank debt. All from the money that was to be designated to pay back the debenture bond purchasers in eight months' time. A July 24, 2002 confidential memorandum in print, obtained by ICN from Joseph Finley states:

1. *"Summer 2000. BV (Bishop of Victoria) received an offer from Target Corp. broker to purchase the CBP (Corporate Business Park) land for $14 M (14 million dollars American). BV did not tell CBP or Finley. BV did not tell the debenture purchasers that it had received this offer – it would have made the debenture offering irrelevant. BV hid this offer until debentures were sold. When BV could not get rid of Finley in fall*

2000, Target was told to look elsewhere – Target purchased 142 acres of adjoining land for $14 M; closing occurred in July, 2001."

2. "BV misled debenture purchasers by concealing Target offer."

These two cryptic paragraphs spell out the entire difficulty if true, (and according to the jury trial results of May 2005, they turned out to be). There would appear to be misappropriation of funds under the terms of the debenture offering. The Diocese has told the media that it is not true but statements to the press do not have the weight of sworn statements in court, so the Diocese has further explaining to do.

As Finley said on November 26, 2002 in Victoria, if mediation does not take place so that everyone, the Diocese, CBP and debenture purchasers are all winners, it will take two more years in court and they could all go over the cliff together. He stated that he feels he has a very strong case.

The irony is that Joseph Finley could be Bishop Roussin's best friend if what he is saying is true and yet he still wants to settle out of court. In court cases both sides always feel they are going to win but two more years of lawyers' fees and other related expenses might not leave that much at the end of the day for the Diocese and the bondholders – they all might go over the cliff together.

A Leadership Question

As Father Terry McNamara, OMI, was quoted on the CBC Radio on the morning after the November 26 public library meeting, we are not really getting good leadership on this issue. His point was not to criticize Bishop Roussin, or Bishop De Roo, but to underline how dysfunctional the situation has become and state that only honest mediation will clarify and resolve it all.

Joseph Finley was interviewed on the morning of November 26 prior to the meeting, and Bishop Roussin was interviewed November 27 when he ruled out any possibility of mediation because, he said, the question is working its way through the courts. It may have been a mistake for the bishop to engage himself at this level of the process. It might have been much better to have sent one of his advisors to deal with the technical questioning which he did not go near himself.

The final authority card should be saved, because if it does not entirely satisfy then there is nowhere else to go. The bishop should be seen to be above the fray in these sorts of matters. It is a mistake to get too closely associated with one side or the other because his role is the final resolution of it all, apart from the courts.

In the end it is the Bishop as Corporation Sole who wears it; not his advisors no matter how prestigious, honest, honorable or otherwise. The lesson of Bishop De Roo is surely not lost on Bishop Roussin; how listening to your advisors no matter how well intentioned and able can get you into serious trouble.

A certain amount of independence of mind is required. When conflicting information starts to emerge such as it has now, it is no good to bury yourself more deeply on one side of the dispute. It is the responsibility of the leader to take a wider view, to weigh and consider it all in an entirely (if not radically) independent manner so that the truth is followed; and, secondarily, so that one does not get into further legal and financial trouble.

The back cover of the Special Edition on the Lacey Land issue of *Island Catholic News*, January 2003.

Chapter 4 – Doubts Cast

Records Cast Doubt On Victoria Diocese Cash Plea

By Robert Matas, Vancouver
Excerpted from the September 26, 2002 edition
of *The Globe and Mail*

A special plea from the Diocese of Victoria for funds to stave off bankruptcy that followed a controversial land deal by Bishop Remi De Roo was unnecessary, according to records in a U.S. court case.

The diocese had been approached with a proposed sale agreement for the property at a price of $13.9-million (US) about the same time the diocese was raising $13-million (Canadian) from parishioners to refinance the property, investor Joseph Finley states in a sworn deposition.

Diocese officials say they never received an offer on the land. "If we had an offer, we'd jump all over it," the diocese's financial administrator Vernon McLeish said in an interview yesterday.

The conflict is part of a legal dispute between Mr. Finley and the diocese over control of the land.

Earlier this month, Mr. Finley filed notice of an appeal of several earlier court orders relating to the land deal in the Superior Court of Washington for Thurston County. The appeal is expected to be heard sometime next year.

A 65-hectare industrial site in Lacey, Wash., a community of 30,000 outside the state capital, Olympia, is at the centre of the controversy.

The land was bought for $5.5 (US) in June, 1997, by a partnership formed by the Victoria diocese and Mr. Finley.

It was refinanced in 1998 for $7.5-million.

Months after Bishop Remi De Roo retired as head of the Victoria diocese in 1999, his successor, Bishop Raymond Roussin, said the diocese did not have funds to meet financing payments for the land. Bishop De Roo, one of Canada's most controversial religious leaders, was criticized for incurring extraordinary debt by acquiring the land with church funds.

In response to an emergency appeal, parishioners gave $13-million (Canadian) to the church, buying so-called church bonds which were to be repaid with 6-per-cent interest in August, 2003.

Documents in the court case show the diocese has not stuck to commitments made to parishioners when soliciting the funds.

As collateral, the diocese pledged the U.S. property and 28 other properties that were considered surplus to the church's needs. An information circular to debt holders, dated June 1, 2000, stated that the surplus properties were worth $14,867.00.

In a sworn deposition taken this summer for the court case, Mr. McLeish stated the surplus lands were now considered to be worth only $8.3-million, about 44 percent less than the value stated when they were soliciting funds.

"The 14.8 was a property assessment, and it soon became apparent once you try to sell properties, that you don't come anywhere close to what you would like to get, so as much as we would love to sell for 14, … [$8.3-million] is about all we're going to get," Mr. McLeish said.

He said in an interview the properties were sold for the best price the church could get. "There's nothing magical about it," he said.

In his statement, Mr. McLeish said $6.6-million has been raised from the sale of some of the properties and the estimated sale value of the rest is $1.7-million.

His statement also says that $2-million from the sale of properties was used to fix up a church building. In the interview, he defended the use of a portion of the funds to renovate a church building. "We were entitled to use $1-million on renovations of buildings."

He did not say why $2-million from the proceeds was spent on renovations. Details about diocese finances will be sent out to parishioners next week, he said.

Mr. McLeish's sworn statement, which has been circulating quietly in the diocese, has upset parishioners who lent money to the church, said journalist Patrick Jamieson, the founding editor of the *Island Catholic News*, who has been an outspoken critic of the current diocese leadership.

"People I speak to are startled and dismayed at the shortfall in the sale of the properties and at how the funds are being used," Mr. Jamieson said in an interview.

The diocese may not have needed to borrow any money from its parishioners, he added. "There's anger out there in the community," he said. "There needs to be a full accounting."

Mr. Finley declined to comment on the court proceedings.

Mr. Finley went to court in March, 2001, to contest Bishop Roussin's scheme to pay off the debt, alleging that the scheme was illegal under Washington state law.

A Real Hornets' Nest

The Diocese of Victoria is Accused of Refusing to Co-operate in Bailing Itself Out of Financial Difficulty

By Candis McLean
(*The Report*, October 21, 2002 pp. 50-51)

When the Roman Catholic diocese of Victoria went cap-in-hand to its parishioners in the spring of 2000, it said it needed their help in raising millions of dollars to cover part of the cost of skyrocketing financing charges connected to an ill-advised U.S. real estate transaction that had been initiated by the diocese's recently retired bishop, Remi De Roo. The crisis is still far from resolved, and now church officials stand accused, by the American at the middle of the deal, of ignoring an offer to buy the property.

Moreover, the lawyer and real estate developer Joseph Finley says he has a solution that would resolve the Diocese of Victoria's financial problems. "If you believe that, I could sell you shares in an empty, salted gold mine," responds Ian Stewart, a member of the diocese special task force on the diocesan debt. These are the latest jabs in a two-year, knock-'-em-down, drag-'em-out match as two hostile parties attempt – and, so far, fail – to do business together.

The mismatched team of lawyer-turned-land developer and the Roman Catholic Diocese of Victoria are yoked together through complicated financial deals that go back to 1988, when people on Vancouver Island became involved in the glamorous world of Arab show horses. A good number had invested in Swiftsure breeding farm, which Mr. Finley and partners owned in Washington state, when suddenly the market took a tumble. In an effort to survive, Mr. Finley needed a

$500,000 bridging loan. The diocese's financial officer, Muriel Clemenger, a horsewoman and pharmacist who had spent 15 years as a medical missionary in India, suggested to Bishop De Roo that the bridging loan would be a good investment opportunity for the Priory fund – the trust account for aging sisters which he personally controlled. "We saw it as an opportunity to get a finder's fee, help someone and get a return fairly quickly," explains Miss Clemenger, now 78. "We were supposed to get the money back in six months." But the timing could not have been worse: within months the value of the exotic steeds plunged from $100,000 to $5,000, their investment banking group defaulted on underwriting the farm and the bishop lent him another $500,000. "Swiftsure Farm and I were obligated to the bishop," states Mr. Finley. "I have never attempted to deny that." Meeting with Bishop De Roo and Miss Clemenger, he says he promised to repay the debt, and the bishop agreed to cooperate by not pressing for repayment." In the 1990s I pursued other things, mindful that I had to take care of this obligation."

In 1997, the developer learned of 160 acres of rolling land one mile from Interstate 5 and 10 miles from the state capital of Olympia; someone had lost it to the lenders. An appraiser valued it at US$15 million, warning it would take up to 30 months to sell. "Since our purchase price was $5.5 million, the bishop, the financial officer and I saw it as an opportunity to repay the debt. The diocese's advisors approved it, so it's unfair to put the decision on the back of the bishop," Mr. Finley says. The bishop invested $150,000 from the Priory fund, his partner arranged virtually 100 percent financing and the diocese guaranteed the mortgage. Mr. Finley produces the deal they signed, which stipulates that when the property sold, any surplus proceeds would go first to the old debt plus accrued interest; second, to all diocese funds advanced in connection with the land investment plus interest, before any surplus would go to Mr. Finley.

- In 1997 *Corporate Business Park* purchased the property.
- For the first year, an interest reserve covered payments; when that ran out, they refinanced for a higher amount at the same interest cost.

Safeway considered the property, then balked; the interest reserve expired, and the diocese took over interest payments of $81,250 per month.

Bishop De Roo retired in March 1999; under Bishop Roussin, the diocese stopped making payments.

An amended agreement was written up; Mr. Finley claims that representatives of the diocese assured him that if he signed the agreement, they would once again pay interest payments, but did not.

On May 15 they signed the agreement, the lender started legal proceedings over arrears and interest started to accrue at a default interest rate of 18 percent – an additional $40,000 per month.

Eight months into arrears, loss of the property was imminent when at Christmas 1999 the diocese paid $500,000 to bring the payments current.

"Then a curious event occurred," Mr. Finley says. "December 31, 1999, diocese lawyer Paul Bundon and new financial officer Vernon McLeish came to Seattle, met with me and the lawyer for *Corporate Business Park* and announced, 'We're out of money, we can't make any more payments and we're not going to.' I was shocked; they had just brought it current. They said, 'We have an offer from a parishioner, Allan Vanderkerkhove, who will buy the property for the amount of the debt, US$7,500,000. If you will agree to this, we will wipe out any claims against you or *Corporate Business Park.*' But it was less than half what it was worth. The *Corporate Business Park* lawyer said 'If you're willing to make that agreement with Vandekerkhove, why not make that agreement with Finley?' They reluctantly agreed to consider it, but when I tried to get refinancing, no one wanted to touch it because of the legal action taken against the property." By now the lender had a decree for foreclosure and a money judgment against the bishop and Mr. Finley, but was not acting on it.

In spring 2000 the diocese launched an emergency appeal, selling debentures to pay off the debt; parishioners purchased $13 million worth. Last month, in a sworn deposition filed in the Superior Court of Washington for Thurston County, Mr. Finley claimed the debenture issue had not been necessary because the diocese had already received an offer to buy the property for US$13.9 million. He points to a deposition of real estate broker Don Moody which was taken in March 2001, in which Mr. Moody talks about meeting with Dave Osmond and Vern McLeish in May 200 in Victoria: "I took the purchase and sale agreement to Victoria, and I think that I talked to Vern at that time," Mr. Moody stated under oath.

In an interview with this magazine, however, Mr. Moody explains, "I talked to them, but I never offered to buy the property. I've had buyers in the past shown the property and turned it down for one reason or another. But it's about ready to come into its own now because the Target building [which was recently built on the adjoining land] has helped bring in infrastructure." Mr. Moody adds, "I have never known either the church or Finley not to try to sell."

Mr. McLeish concurs: "The diocese has never received a formal offer. We've been dying to get rid of the property, but how? We can't sell when Finley keeps going to court with legal obstacles. He should back off. He lost his opportunity for a surplus long ago. But if he has an offer, put it in writing and our people will look at it."

Mr. Finley responds, "Interestingly, McLeish's wording of 'formal offer' leaves the door open to other 'offers' having been made, while Mr. Moody's statement contradicts his testimony given under oath." In fact a source connected to the diocese, who wished to remain anonymous, told this magazine that there was indeed an offer. And, according to documents produced by Mr. Moody during his deposition, there clearly were faxes, phone calls and documents exchanged in the summer of 2000 between the diocese and the broker consistent with a property sale in progress.

In a carefully worded comment, Mr. Finley states: "There is a viable solution that would accomplish repayment of the debentures in full and pay out all sums properly owing to the diocese under its agreement with *Corporate Business Park* and me, but that solution would require the co-operation of both parties, and the diocese would have to abandon its campaign to take the *Corporate Business Park* property."

Responds Mr. Stewart, "We're faced with having to close either a parish or a school because we're running out of surplus property to sell while Mr. Finley has fantasies about what he can do and a rather less than clear commitment to the church. I'm not going to do business with the enemy."

"I have devoted years and sacrificed other opportunities for this project, but what have they done?" retorts Mr. Finley, 56. "They've refused to sell the property when opportunities have arisen for reasons that are unfathomable except that perhaps those sales would have vindicated Bishop De Roo's investment."

With one last jab, Mr. Stewart demands, "Ask Mr. Finley about his offshore company."

"I don't have an offshore company, and I don't have an onshore company," responds Mr. Finley. "I've been financially decimated because of the actions taken by the diocese since Bishop De Roo's departure. All Mr. Stewart knows of me is what he's heard. But now I may have a solution, and I am told that he is a sophisticated and responsible person; I challenge him to meet with me, person-to-person, to try to solve the problem instead of hurling accusations at me that are unfounded."

An observer cannot help but wonder if it will be a fight to bankruptcy.

'Like The Enron Scandal'

Attempts by the Diocese of Victoria to sell off 28 surplus properties as collateral for their debenture may realize only $8.3 million, not the $15 million at which they were assessed. "Our situation right now looks bloody awful," declares retired-lawyer-turned-car-dealer Ian Stewart. "We're in terribly, terribly bad shape; people have no idea of the problems going on. Where the $13-and-a-half million we need next August is going to come from, I don't know. It's like the Enron scandal. But we're not going to waste time with the bellyachers; we're assembling our own war cabinet with a number of us who are pushing 70, using all the expertise we've got: financial, legal, developmental. And we're going to get our money back, or my name's not Ian Stewart."

Mediation No Solution to Diocese Woes

Reprinted from November 30, 2002 edition of the *Times Colonist*

Last Tuesday, at a little-advertised public meeting, Lawyer Joe Findlay [sic] described his version of the events that led up to the financial crisis in the Roman Catholic Diocese of Victoria.

As the *Times Colonist* has reported, these views do not agree with those stated by the diocese. The majority of the 50 people present were persuaded that the situation was somewhat like the difficulties experienced by married couples and could be resolved by mediation. This is patently untrue.

In effect there are three parties involved, not two. The first party, the former bishop, Remi De Roo, and others associated with him, were persuaded by the second party, Findlay [sic] into making two unwise investments.

The first involved taking advantage of a tax loophole relating to the breeding of Arabian horses, which failed when the loophole was closed. The second involved the purchase of land in Washington with the object of re-selling it with sufficient profit to recover the earlier losses.

Findlay [sic] put no money into either of these ventures, however he persuaded Bishop De Roo that all the liabilities associated with these ventures could safely be borne by the diocese.

For reasons that have been well aired, the re-sale did not take place, massive interest payments were required and the diocese came to the brink of bankruptcy.

All of this was entirely hidden from members of the diocese, until the arrival of the third party, namely Bishop Raymond Roussin. He, with his advisors, gradually uncovered the enormity of the situation. He resolved to bring everything out into the open and to ask for parishioners' financial help to start the painful process of restoring stability.

To return to the marriage analogy, the abusive relationship was only between the first two parties who behaved like addicts and the codependents, who compounded the problems by their enabling actions.

The present administration is not part of that sad story. It is determined to put the diocese firmly on the road to recovery. The openness and dedication, which it continuously displays, will prevail, but the duplicity of the past actions can be no part of the solution. We are talking about recovery, not mediation.

Rory Kirby,
Victoria

Facts About The Lacey Land

Alleged Purchase Offer by Target Corporation

*Handout issued by the Diocese of Victoria, at the
November 26, 2002 meeting held at the Victoria public library*

The Diocese never received an offer from the Target Corporation to purchase the Lacey land.

The only offer ever made for the Lacey land was an offer by Barclays Bank North, Inc., in April 2001 to purchase the land for (US) $9.6 million dollars. Both Bishop of Victoria and Joseph Finley consented to sell the Lacey land at this price. In the absence of a better offer, the Barclays Bank North offer was eventually accepted. Unfortunately, Barclays Bank North cancelled the deal before the scheduled closing.

In June of 2000, the Diocese was approached by a real estate broker named Don Moody. Mr. Moody would not disclose the name of his client, however he indicated that he was aware of a "Fortune 500" company that was interested in several properties in the Seattle area and the Lacey land was one of those properties. Representatives of the Diocese told Mr. Moody that the Diocese was very interested in selling and hoped that Mr. Moody could obtain an offer from his client. Mr. Moody's client never made an offer for the property.

Mr. Moody has confirmed that the Bishop's eagerness to sell the property. In a sworn deposition, Mr. Moody testified that the Diocese was "very anxious to sell" and was "very positive about selling the piece of property." Mr. Moody also testified that his client investigated the Lacey land, but decided that another property was better suited to its needs.

Joseph Finley was not present during the June 2000 meeting with Mr. Moody. Mr. Finley's claims about an alleged "offer" from Target Corporation and the alleged response by the Diocese are not accurate. As a legal tactic, Mr. Finley often refers to an unsigned broker's "listing agreement" as an "offer" to purchase the Lacey land. Mr. Moody presented the draft listing agreement to the Diocese before he realized that the Lacey land **was already listed for sale** by the national brokerage firm called Trammell Crow. The Diocese made it clear to Mr. Moody that while it could not sign his broker's listing agreement, the

Diocese was still eager to sell the Lacey land to his client or to any other buyer.

From the time the Lacey land was acquired in June 1997, until the court appointed a Receiver in April 2001, Joseph Finley was the person responsible for finding a buyer for the Lacey land, so that Mr. Finley's debt to the Diocese could be repaid. Mr. Finley never found a buyer. After the new administration came in, the Diocese asked Mr. Finley to give up control over the marketing of the land. Mr. Finley refused, and the Diocese eventually filed a court action to free up the Lacey land for sale.

Lawyer Files Suit Against Diocese

By Mark Browne

Reprinted from December 13, 2002 issue of *Weekend Edition*

A lawyer from Washington state has launched a civil suit against the Victoria Catholic diocese.

The suit was launched in Washington state by Bellevue, Washington lawyer Joseph Finley. Finley's lawsuit is centered around a 142-acre piece of property in Lacey, Washington, which was bought for $5.5 million in June, 1997 by a partnership between the Victoria Diocese and Finley, according to court documents from Washington. The investment was part of a strategy to recoup losses from an earlier loan made to Finley in the 1980s.

The property was refinanced in 1998 for $7.5 million.

As the property was assessed at $14.8 million, the idea was to sell the property within two years and make a profit.

According to a sworn statement by Finley, the diocese had been approached with an offer in the summer of 2000 from Target Corporation, a large U.S.-based retail chain, to buy the property for $13 million (US).

Vernon McLeish, the diocese' financial administrator, earlier maintained that there was not an offer from Target Corporation.

Finley's lawsuit essentially centers around his allegation that he was pushed out of the partnership with the diocese. As well, Finley notes that his contention that there was an offer from Target Corporation to buy the property is central to his lawsuit against the diocese.

The diocese raised $13 million from parishioners, who purchased what are known as church bonds, to refinance the property in Washington state. The arrangement called for the parishioners to be paid back with six per cent interest by August, 2003.

Many parishioners gathered at a meeting in Victoria last month with Finley who maintains that he would prefer to have the issue dealt with through mediation.

Patrick Jamieson, the past editor of *Island Catholic News* and strong supporter of De Roo, notes that 57 out of 60 parishioners expressed their support to have the matter go to mediation.

"The real purpose of the meeting, in my view, was to create a third force of debenture holders who would pressure the diocese, who would be aware if a new offer came in so that it wouldn't be able to be concealed," he said.

Finley concedes he wasn't sure what to expect when he showed up at the meeting with parishioners.

"I was kind of amazed at the end of the meeting because I figured I was going to walk in there and deal with some hostile people and some people who were prepared to not be receptive," he says about his surprise that so many of the parishioners expressed support for an out-of-court resolution to the matter.

While mediation isn't binding, Finley says it's a process that will essentially provide a forum where the matter can be dealt with to everyone's satisfaction.

Roussin did not return the *Weekend Edition's* calls before our Thursday morning deadline.

February 2001 – A Chronology:
Cooperating Toward Target

Island Catholic News, Volume 16 , No. 12, January 2003

On February 6, 2001 Joseph Finley telephoned Vernon McLeish and Paul Bundon, a lawyer for the Diocese, when he learned that Target Corporation was trying to buy the land adjacent to the

Corporate Business Park location. He says he learned this from a representative of one of the owners of the adjacent land. Finley says they refused to meet with him, instead Norman Isherwood and Dave Osmond, who serve on the Lacey land committee for the Diocese, were coming to Seattle the following day and Paul Bundon arranged for him to meet with them.

The next morning at 8 a.m., he met with Isherwood and Osmond in a coffee shop at the airport at Boeing Field in Seattle where Finley met their flight "to discuss the purpose of their trip and to discuss Target."

Finley has written up his version of the period between February 6 (after he learned of the Target possibility) and February 14, 2001 (when he received a dismissive letter from Vernon McLeish on behalf of the Diocese):

"Norm Isherwood told me that they had been dealing with Don Moody (Target broker) for many months and that Moody had refused to disclose the identity of his buyer to them but assured them it was a major 'Fortune 500' type company. They had told Moody they wanted to sell but had 'title issues' to clear... But Moody and people from the Diocese had continued to meet over the summer of 2000."

"Norm Isherwood also informed me that he and Dave Osmond previously urged the Committee to 'quit worrying' about whether I would receive money from a sale and just sell the property to cut off the interest expense and legal fees." (boldface added)

"We talked about the history of the property deal. It was not at all clear that they had been informed that I had a written contract with the Diocese. Norm Isherwood told me that after I had filed the Chapter 11 bankruptcy proceedings in November, 2000, he and Dave Osmond were instructed to tell Moody that he and his buyer would have to look elsewhere, again because of 'title problems.' There was no contact with me at the time, and I was unaware of the buyer and Moody until early February, 2001."

"I explained to Norm Isherwood and Dave Osmond that the neighbour who had been approached by Moody to sell 22 acres was more interested in clearing up an easement problem than selling to Target and would co-operate with us. **This would have stopped the other deal because Target needed a minimum of 140+ acres for their building and parking and open space requirements, etc. Without the 22 acres, the other site had only 120. This was why Moody approached the Church in May 2000 – our site worked for Target.** Isherwood and Osmond were excited about getting the Target deal back on track."

"I met again with Norm Isherwood. and Dave Osmond for dinner in Seattle on the evening of February 7 and we agreed to meet again the following day at the offices of Trammell Crow (the broker I had hired) and to have Moody come to that meeting. **They seemed to believe that the best solution for all concerned was to get Target back on track.**"

"On February 8, 2001, I met Norm Isherwood and Dave Osmond at the offices of Trammell Crow in Kent, Washington. Present also were Nick Casino and Mike Hubbard, both Trammell Crow brokers. Casino and Hubbard explained the listing agreement I had with them and their efforts to sell the CBP property. The listing covered CBP and other acreage that I had an interest in or was trying to get under option for the purpose of avoiding the very competition among property owners that had developed. There was no conflict of interest as McLeish later alleged. The purpose was to make sure that CBP sold first."

"**We discussed the Easement relocation that would effectively block Target from the adjoining site.** Casino and Hubbard also defended the listing price at the time of $2.75 per foot ($19,166,400 US) for CBP. Their internal analysts had done a residual land value analysis to arrive at that number."

"We were then joined by Donald Moody. When he learned that Trammell Crow had the listing, he became visibly angry and had difficulty maintaining his composure. He obviously had visions of a full 5% commission on the sale going to him ($700,000

US at 14 Million). He now realized that if Target bought our property he would have to share 50/50 with Trammell Crow."

"Norm Isherwood, Dave Osmond and I told Moody there were no title issues and that *Corporate Business Park* **was ready to sell to Target.** Moody said he would inform his client, but from his comments and demeanor it was clear he was not going to push our deal. His commission had just been cut in half, and by then he had two and a half months invested in the other deal. As to price, we told Moody that we were not inflexible."

"February 9, 2001, I drafted the easement Relocation Agreement and presented it to Agnes Kwan, the manager of the company (HP, LLC) Target and Moody were trying to buy 22 acres from. (*See attached sketch of properties on page 90*) **I discussed it with Mrs. Kwan. She agreed to the terms, but being a Catholic, she was not willing to sign until the Diocese approved and signed the deal.**"

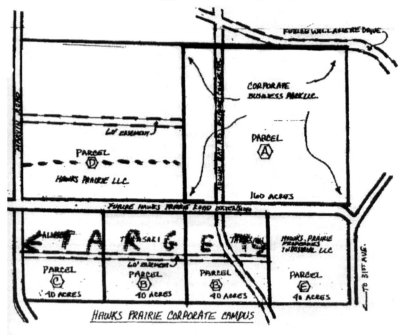

Target eventually bought a smaller tract of land immediately adjacent to the diocese property, a piece of land which did not suit their purposes as well as Corporate Business Park, necessitating the purchase of another piece of property which the owner was not keen to sell. According to court documents in 2001, Finley worked with this owner to bring the deal back to CBP but the diocese would not cooperate.

"February 10, 2001. Per prior agreement, **I took the float plane to Victoria to meet with Norm Isherwood, Dave Osmond, Paul Bundon and Vernon McLeish.** Isherwood met me at the inner harbour, we then went to the Chancery office. We spent half an hour going over the numbers that CBP and I owed the Diocese, and McLeish admitted that he could reduce those numbers somewhat because they included attorney's fees that are not my obligation under the agreement with the Diocese, and there were credits missing for prior payments."

"**All five of us met for approximately three hours. We hashed over how to approach Target.** They wanted me to give them carte blanche to negotiate the price and terms with Target. I could not agree because they could lower the price just to protect the Diocese and cut me out."

"**We discussed the easement deal and they had copies of the agreement I proposed with Kwan. They were shown exactly how the agreement would work. I emphasized that it would cost no money or other hindrance but would guarantee Target coming back to us, and I emphasized that Ms. Kwan was ready to sign.**

"**At the end of the meeting Norm Isherwood proposed that I accept $100,000 to settle and walk away, leaving Target and the property solely to the Diocese. Since even at $14 Million, I was entitled to some $2.5+ million after the Bonds and Diocese were paid in full, I declined the offer.**"

"They informed me that, their committee would meet the following Tuesday and get back to me, and I left to return to Seattle to prepare a proposal to deal with the entire situation."

"February 12. I sent letters to Dave Osmond summarizing the situation so the committee would have them for their meeting on the 13th. **In telephone conversation with Dave Osmond I learned that Moody had come back contending that the CBP site 'would not work' even though it had been fine for the previous six months while Target and Moody were waiting for the 'title problem' (i.e. me) to be cleared.** I also learned that Moody advised against pushing the Target deal. He said he had another buyer, and the next deal would go for a much higher price.

"I received McLeish's letter which speaks for itself. (see letter dated February 14, 2001) **Someone on the committee (or someone influencing the committee) killed trying to put the Target deal back on track,** and without their co-operation on the easement deal, Target would not be blocked on the other site. After 2/14/01, communications with Norm Isherwood and Dave Osmond stopped.

June, 2001. The *Corporate Business Park* property is placed under contract to a company called Barclays North for $9.6 Million (US). Target is trying to get its site plan approved next door, but an easement through the site was a problem for them, so **Target has its Seattle attorney approach Barclays with a $14 Million offer,** *which is strange* for a property that did not work for its requirements! This offer was never consummated but only because Target's engineers found a way to work around the easement."

"But, the point is that the 'site won't work' excuse is just bunk and the Diocese knows it."

Finley Open Letter on Mediation with Diocese

Island Catholic News, Volume 16, No. 12 , January 2003

January 13, 2002
The Editor
Times Colonist

I attach the following Open Letter which I ask that you publish as it relates to a meeting on November 26, 2002 that was the subject of a published article in your newspaper the following day and the subject of a letter to the editor that was published on November 30, 2002. Apparently the author of that letter appointed himself as the head of a committee of three (being the only three persons out of 60 at that meeting to not favor mediation as a process for solving the litigation pending between the Diocese of Victoria and me).

With all due respect, the author of the letter published on November 30 (*see earlier Rory Kirby letter*) does not understand the facts or the dynamics between the parties, and certainly did not represent the overwhelming sentiment expressed at that meeting.

OPEN LETTER

To: Bishop of Victoria,
 Roman Catholic Diocese of Victoria
 All Purchasers of Bonds issued
 by the Diocese in August 2000
 All Parishioners of the Diocese

Dear Bishop Roussin, Debenture Holders and Parishioners:

I am writing this letter to fulfill a commitment I made at a meeting of Debenture Holders and Parishioners in Victoria on Tuesday evening, November 26, 2002. I attended the meeting at the specific request of some Parishioners who did not believe they had received enough information regarding the prior investment by the Diocese in land located in Washington State and the litigation that is currently pending. I believe the meeting was productive and mutually beneficial.

It never has been my preference to be involved in litigation, and I have attempted at different times and in different ways to come to a mutually acceptable solution. Thus far the lawyers and administrative staff of the Diocese have refused to consider any alternatives other than the litigation that so far has cost the Diocese not less than $2 million in accrued interest on the bonds and attorneys' fees since September of 2000. In my estimation, all of these costs were totally avoidable. This letter should not be taken as any indication that I am not prepared to continue with legal proceedings to obtain a just result. Just the contrary, if the court battle continues, I look forward to the truth coming out, and I am prepared to proceed to a final decision on the merits but with a profound sense of regret that this could not have been handled in a better way.

I will not attempt to restate the discussion that took place at the meeting on November 26. I believe that interested parties can obtain access to view a videotape recording of that meeting in its entirety. Suffice it to say that at the conclusion of the meeting, there was overwhelming sentiment to submit this matter to mediation. Out of approximately 60 people who voted, all but about three favored mediation as a means to cut off the costs and attorneys' fees and delay involved in the court proceedings. This vote has been reported in the media. Near the conclusion of the meeting, I was asked by one of those in attendance whether I would communicate a settlement offer to the Diocese. I indicated that I would even though prior attempts have been rejected in favour of continued litigation.

For example, I communicated an offer in writing to the Diocese in February 12, 2001. Had that offer been accepted, the Lacey property would have been sold by now or I would have transferred my interest to the Diocese. Regrettably for both parties, that offer was rejected out of hand by a letter from Mr. Vernon McLeish, Finance Officer for the Diocese on February 14, 2001. (**See appendix**) Since that time there have been no settlement discussions even though my lawyers and I have left the door open to that possibility. And as recently as October of 2002, the lawyers for the Diocese and the debenture trustee adamantly refused to enter into even a partial settlement discussion although the Judge in the case admonished all parties to make such an attempt.

The facts and legal issues involved are sufficiently complex that a monetary settlement offer might only open up the possibility of criticism that would be unwarranted if all facts were known. Any other offer that attempted to formulate an alternate solution could face a similar fate. Consequently, I believe the best approach to making a settlement offer is to accept the collective wisdom expressed at the meeting on November 26. I hereby formally state that I am prepared to enter into mediation in an attempt to reach a settlement that would fairly deal with all parties and create a mechanism for repayment of the Debentures on or before their maturity date of August 17, 2003.

The mediation process should proceed without delay, and it would not preclude or delay the court proceedings from going forward concurrently. I believe a formulation of settlement possibilities that could come from mediation will be far more effective than anything I might propose now. Mediation is non-binding but often very effective to create a dialogue when, as here, communication has broken down, and an effective forum to reconcile parties' differences. I understand that Bishop Roussin has rejected mediation, but I respectfully ask that he reconsider his position in the best interests of the Debenture Holders and the Diocese.

Need Mediation More Than Ever

Island Catholic News **Editorial,** Volume 17, No. 1, February 2003

I was a parishioner who attended the November 26 meeting at the public Library at which Mr. Joseph Finley had been invited to speak to an interested group concerning his perspective on the contentious situation regarding the Diocese' investment in land in Washington State. Consequently, I was somewhat surprised by the tenor and the content of a letter written by Mr. Rory Kirby that was published in the Special Edition on the Lacey land situation.

During the meeting Mr. Kirby interrupted Mr. Finley and others on more than one occasion with his stated concern that the parties should not focus on the past, but on the future with the paramount goal being to put an end to the "crisis" facing the Diocese. And yet, Mr. Kirby devoted most of his letter to restating the Diocese' position on past events and a small portion to applauding the present administration of the Diocese for its intention to "put the Diocese firmly on the road to recovery."

Mr. Kirby devoted no attention in his letter to any constructive solutions, and he ignored the overwhelming support that was expressed for mediation. Only three out of approximately 60 parishioners and bondholders did not adopt the resolution favoring mediation.

Mr. Kirby demeans the intelligence and good intentions of those who spoke in favor of mediation. We are capable of deciding who is telling us facts and not conclusions. We are capable of deciding whether a business dispute (and not just a marital problem) could benefit from mediation, and we spoke loudly and clearly. Mr. Kirby seems not to have been listening. If the reported information is accurate, the lawyers for the Diocese have received well in excess of $750,000 out of their representation of the Diocese. It is time to stop trying to find scapegoats and to focus on who is preventing a solution and what their motivation might be. It is time to find a solution, not a continuation of an ineffective and very costly strategy.

Bishop De Roo had a long and distinguished tenure as Bishop and undertook many projects that financially benefitted the Diocese in great measure. Are we now to believe he somehow became a person lacking both good judgment and good intentions? The present administration has spent millions in interest and lawyer's fees, and we have no solution. The presentation administration has presided over highly questionable sales of Diocesan properties that may have been totally unnecessary. With all due respect Mr. Kirby, pat someone on the back after they have accomplished something positive. What we have seen from this administration in its very brief tenure is a failure to solve what they call "the major crisis" affecting the Diocese. So, Mr. Kirby, who is really the lead player in the "sad story" you described?

We need a better solution than paying large legal bills to Seattle lawyers. We need to be just in our dealings with others. We need to solve this problem and heal divisions within the Diocese. If the administration refuses mediation, they should have a better solution than delay and more legal bills. They asked for money to buy bonds. Now it appears that might not have been necessary.

They already are hinting that they might not be able to repay in August of this year. That is not acceptable. They have a duty of stewardship to parishioners and bondholders and to the Diocese; refusal to mediate is evidence of insensitivity to the parishioners who supported them by buying bonds. They asked for our money (and our understanding), now we ask them to think of our best interests and our clearly stated wishes for mediation.

Joseph C. Finley

Attorney at Law

227 Bellevue Way N.E., No. 265
Bellevue, Washington 98004

Telephone: 425-221-6531
Facsimile: 425-454-2398

email: jcfcrg@aol.com

TIMES COLONIST · SUNDAY MARCH 5 2000 · X7

News Focus

MEN *of the* CLOTH

De Roo true to goals of Vatican II

Times Colonist staff

An ecclesiastical flower child, a product of the '60s revolution in the Roman Catholic church, Remi De Roo was a champion of social justice issues for all of his 37 years as bishop of the Diocese of Victoria.

Remi Joseph De Roo, former Roman Catholic Bishop of Victoria, said it is too soon to judge the impact of the changes in the church stemming from Vatican II.

Roussin hopes to bring a sense of spirituality

Times Colonist staff

Raymond Roussin, a Marian priest who came to Victoria as bishop from Gravelbourg, Sask., knew he would have a tough act to follow in Bishop Remi De Roo.

Vancouver Island Roman Catholic diocese Bishop Raymond Roussin sees a greater need for an awareness of the divine.

Bishops must often act like CEOs

By Kim Westad
Times Colonist staff

Horses a high-risk gamble, say investment experts

By King Lee
Times Colonist staff

Edwina MacDonald, owner of JEM Arabians, with her stallion Black Panther at her ranch near Sooke Lake. Arabians were part of the Catholic church's investments.

Loans: Diocese will have to sell some holdings

FROM PAGE A6

It's a big loss. It's not going to bring us down, but we will have to sell properties that have been earmarked for the future.

Part of a 2-page spread in the Sunday *Times Colonist* March 5, 2000

Chapter 5 – Bishop Regrets

Bishop Regrets ICN Special Edition on Lacey Land

Regrets ICN's Alternative Coverage but Commits to Providing More Information

Island Catholic News, Volume 17, No. 1, February 2003

January 26, 2003
Re: Statements made by the *Island Catholic News*

Dear Parishioners:

It is with sadness and regret that despite all of the information that has been shared by the Diocese with its members and the public, the *Island Catholic News* is still reporting as facts, or as legitimate questions, information which has been examined, refuted and rejected time and again by the Courts in the State of Washington. If anyone has doubts as to the events as put forward by the Diocese, they need only go to the official court record where they will see the history of Mr. Finley's claims and allegations and how the Court has dealt with them. Mr. Finley has been unsuccessful so far with all of his claims and allegations. The U.S. courts have affirmed the legal position advanced by the Bishop of Victoria and the Trustee for the bondholders in all substantive matters decided to date. Neither *Island Catholic News*, nor Mr. Jamieson, has made any effort to meet with myself and my advisors to review the record of the legal actions taken to date, instead they have relied solely on Mr. Finley's version of events.

Notwithstanding his lack of success, Mr. Finley continues with legal actions that are completely without merit or factual base. The Trustee for the Debenture Holders has recently filed a motion against Mr. Finley's appeal. This motion requests that his appeal be dismissed on various grounds, including the fact that it is frivolous.

It is hoped that the Washington Court of Appeal will rule on this matter within 60 days.

I wish to reiterate and confirm the following information:

In May, 1999, Joseph Finley promised to repay the Diocese the monies advanced from various Diocesan trust funds in the amount of approximately $1,500,000 with interest thereon at 8 percent from May, 1999. Mr. Finley has made no payment on account of this obligation.

The property owned by *Corporate Business Park*, LLC ("Lacey Land") was purchased for approximately $5.3 million US in June, 1997. Mr. Finley promised to resell the property promptly, at a profit, in order to pay his debts to the Bishop. From June, 1997, until the present day, only one offer has been made to purchase the land. In April, 2001, Barclays Bank North, Inc. [sic] made an offer of $9.6 million US. Both the Bishop of Victoria and Mr. Finley consented to sell the Lacey land at this price. Unfortunately, Barclays Bank North, Inc. cancelled the transaction before closing and forfeited their deposit of $100,000 (US).

The Bishop of Victoria has never received an offer either written or verbal, formal or informal from Target Corporation to purchase the Lacey land.

From the time the Lacey land was acquired in June, 1997, until the Court appointed a Receiver in April, 2001, Mr. Finley had the sole responsibility for finding a buyer. In almost four years, he failed to find a buyer for the Lacey land.

While the Diocese has expended in excess of $5 million on account of the Lacey land, Mr. Finley has never advanced any monies to pay any expenses.

Although Mr. Finley continues to speculate that the Lacey land has a value of not less than $18 million (US), and that could be as high as $21 million (US), an independent appraisal obtained in January, 2003 by Canadian Western Bank (bankers for the Diocese) put the value at $11.5 million (US).

A sale at $11.5 million US today would be insufficient to cover all of the costs to date on the Lacey land. We must remember, there is still no offer to purchase the Lacey land and, meanwhile, the Diocese bears the risk of continuing costs for interest and taxes of approximately $1 million per year. Mr. Finley claims to have no resources. He bears no risk if the property is not sold in a timely manner.

I am grateful for your support in the past and as your Bishop, I ask that you continue to support me, my advisors and the many volunteers who have assisted to date in trying to extricate the Diocese from its financial difficulties.

As matters unfold, I am committed to providing continuing reports to all members of the Diocese. And, to the extent that it is appropriate for the Diocese to do so, I will provide further requested information to all members of the Diocese and to the media. Please address any such enquiries to the Diocesan Chancery Office, 4044 Nelthorpe Street, Victoria, BC V8X 2A1, for my attention or that of Mr. McLeish.

+ Raymond Roussin, SM
Bishop of Victoria

Response to Bishop's Statements of January 26, 2003

Joseph Finley counters assertion, remains open to mediation

Dear Bishop Roussin:

I have read your statement to parishioners dated January 26. It is difficult to respond to unsupported sweeping statements, and I am loath to suggest your statements were intended to be disingenuous, but there are portions of your message to parishioners on January 26 that compel a response.

Your statement appears more likely to have been crafted in a back room in a law office rather than at your desk in the Chancery. Otherwise, it is surprising that you have such an encompassing grasp of all of the pleadings and all of the records and all of the decisions in the various Washington cases, which now fill, literally, several file boxes. But if this is your understanding, however acquired, it is woefully inaccurate.

There is no information that has "been examined, refuted and rejected time and time again by the Courts of the State of Washington." In point of fact, nothing of substance has been decided in the case against the Diocese and the Debenture trustee other than a holding on a motion to dismiss the Debenture trustee, not on the merits of the case, but on the interpretation of a so-called "partial settlement agreement" that was authorized by the Court but never implemented by the parties. That decision is on appeal, and its outcome will be determined by the Court of Appeals not your lawyers. There are miles and miles left to go in the litigation, and even if the Debenture trustee is dismissed, it does not affect the claims asserted directly against the Diocese.

Several points you raised require direct rebuttal:

1. Contrary to your assertion I have not defaulted on my payment obligations to the Diocese. It was agreed and understood when we signed the amendment to our written agreement in May of 1999 that any sums owing from me or from *Corporate Business Park* would be realized from a sale of the property. The relevant provisions are contained in paragraph 1 of the Addendum to Operating Agreement of *Corporate Business Park*, LLC dated May 15, 1999. This Addendum was signed on your behalf and is, therefore, equally binding on both of us. Before payments could have been made from a sale of the property, your administration at the Diocese acted to prevent a sale of the property that fully would have discharged my obligations.

2. When the Lacey land was purchased, all parties, including the Diocese, relied on an appraisal conducted by Mundy & Associates, an appraisal firm based in Seattle, Washington. Mundy's appraisal specifically stated that a minimum marketing time of 24-30 months would be required. The assertion that I promised an immediate sale is a fiction. If I signed such an agreement, please produce it.

3. The statement you made regarding a Target offer is refuted directly in sworn testimony by the Target broker. It also has been refuted by a member of one of your committees advising on financial matters. Other proof can and will be offered at trial.

4. The responsibility for selling the property at all times was vested in the Managers of *Corporate Business Park*, LLC. From and after May 15, 1999, Vern McLeish was a Manager. From that time until April of 2001, *his* only efforts to sell the property were the attempted clandestine sale to Target that was concealed from me.

5. I was never expected to provide funds to the Lacey property; the Diocese assumed that responsibility for the venture. It is curious that I am criticized for not doing something that was not my responsibility. This is an ongoing attempt by your administration at the Diocese and its lawyers to change, illegally and by force of economic pressure, an agreement that they have decided to breach notwithstanding that you, acting through your Financial Officer, affirmed it in writing on May 15, 1999.

6. I cannot respond to the allegation of a current appraisal at $11.5 Million. The administration at the Diocese has not provided a copy to me or to my lawyers. It is herewith requested.

7. Before you complain too loudly about the $1 million in interest and legal fees and costs that are accruing, you and others at the Diocese (and your lawyers) should remember that I made a settlement offer to the Diocese on February 12, 2001 (a copy of which was published by *Island Catholic News*) (**see appendix**) that would have resolved this matter completely without that expense and at no detriment to the Diocese. My offer was flatly rejected by the Diocese in a letter from your Financial Officer dated February 14, 2001 (a copy of which also was published by *Island Catholic News*) (**see appendix**). You also should remember that you are the one adamantly demanding that the court battle continue, even though a good number of parishioners/bondholders have requested you to consider mediation. It is your decision, and yours alone, to continue draining the resources of the Diocese.

It is not my place to offer advice to you, and in any event, you have numerous administrative officers, committee members and lawyers to do that. But I am and will remain open to a fair, just and rational settlement if you should decide that you really wish to extricate the Diocese from this limited part of its financial difficulties.

I realize what a burden it must be for you to wrestle with the Diocese' financial problems, and I know that you pray for guidance and divine inspiration. You should understand that I do the same.

Mediation Right Way

Island Catholic News, Volume 17, No. 1, February 2003

The Editor:

Thank you for making available the special edition (Special Edition of ICN-January 2003). I realize you will face criticism for making available some documents around the Lacey Property. These documents offer me interpretations that the diocese did not provide.

I believe everything is infused with the Spirit and it is each person's job to tap into the Spirit. The divine in my experience is never absent from the human and for me the capacity and urge to relate are at the heart of the gospel. All is interconnected and we all can, if we want, forge links and connections. In light of the diocesan bishop's refusals to go for mediation, this latest edition of the ICN is a gift – a starting point.

I believe we have much to change in our church structures. For example, in the Province of Québec the local bishop is not the Corporation Sole. This old canonical formula is not allowed by the legislature. Each parish in Québec is governed by an elected board of lay trustees. Needless to say Rome and the bishops tried in vain to resist this change.

We must find 'new eyes and ears'. We must dialogue and listen to the world. Mediation (refused by the bishop, in spite of recommendation of the People of God gathered that evening) might have allowed for the other truths to come forward for conversation and study.

Today we must find new ways in a totally new religious territory. I believe mediation has the right of way over lawyers, bishops and chancery folk. The People of God gathered were the ones that called for mediation to help us see with new ears and new eyes. Are we interested in seeing with a prism or are we choosing to remain locked in a prison preventing ourselves from seeing another world.

The Reign of God (which is often beyond the reach of lawyers) is so much larger and more important than the Roman Catholic church. The RC Church is supposed to be at the service of God's Reign – (*Redemptoris Missio* #1 18, 20) – even the regretted narrow ecclesiocentric perspectives of that document say that.

"Seek first the Reign of God and its justice and everything else will take care of itself." Matt. 6:33. Thank you Patrick for making available that documentation.

Jack Sproule, Pastor
Saanich Peninsula Parish
Diocese of Victoria

2.

Diocese Asks for Three Year Extension on Debentures

Extension Resolution requires 75 per cent vote of 50 per cent Quorum of Principals

Island Catholic News, Volume 17, No 2, March 2003

Lacey Land Blamed

With three letters dated February 26, 2003, the Diocese of Victoria asked some 2,000 debenture bondholders for a three-year extension on the debenture bond loans which come due August 31, 2003. The three-year bonds were to pay six per cent interest over the three years since some thirteen million dollars' worth were issued in the year 2000, but the diocese does not have the $15.6 million to redeem them at this time.

The letters were from Bishop Raymond Roussin, ordinary of the Diocese of Victoria; Ian Stewart, Chairperson of the Diocesan Administration and Finance Board; and Ellis Achtem, co-chairperson of the Diocesan Debenture Committee. Bishop Roussin said in part: "We all regret we have been unable to sell the land in the United States. It has not been due to our lack of effort in that domain... I come then to ask you simply and humbly to extend your debenture if you can."

Ian Stewart said in his letter: "Our financial problems exist because of the U.S. land. We have sold sufficient Island properties to pay down bank debt of approximately 4.6 million dollars relating to the U.S. land... However as the U.S. land has not sold, we do not have the necessary funds to redeem the debentures. As our interest, taxes and legal costs associated with this land continue, we are facing costs of operation which cannot be met from the day to day contributions made to the Diocese."

Ellis Achtem asked for more money particularly in the form of converting the loan into a gift: "We give all parishioners and the debenture holders an opportunity to help the Bishop with a charitable donation either by gift or by converting all or part of the principal or interest due on their loan into a gift."

The central theme of the letters is to blame the problems with the sale of the land in Lacey, Washington for the shortfall in pay-back funds. This is a recent development, as originally it was announced that the sale of surplus lands in the diocese would cover the pay-back. A close scrutiny of the debenture offering information packet details, however, also lists the Lacey land as security for the loans as well as "the sale of school and Church properties, if necessary" although these were originally underlined as untouchable.

Little mention was made of problems with sales of surplus land; or acceptance of any responsibility for the inability to sell the land to Target Corporation which was interested in the property but was discouraged by the Diocese from realizing any final purchase in the summer of 2000 and again in the early Spring of 2001.

The so-called surplus lands, which required 50 to 75 years of conscientious generosity by parishioners to build up, now are being spent at a rapid rate and represent a permanent loss of legacy as the lands must be considered fundamentally irrecoverable.

Extension Resolution

None of the letters mention the legal requirement for such an extension as outlined in sections 1, 4 and 8 of article ten of the Deed of Trusts and Mortgage that governs the covenants, premises and conditions of the administration of the debenture bonds.

Unless bondholders grant individual release of consent to extend debentures, a meeting is required representing debenture holders that includes a quorum of at least fifty percent of the principal amount of the outstanding debentures. Not less than seventy-five percent of the principal amount of debentures represented at the meeting is required to pass the extension resolution.

The letter sent under the signature of Ellis Achtem says that the support of the debenture holders for another three year period is to be completed in the month of March. The key to the strategy is to get bond holders to do individual releases.

In this vein Achtem faxed to parish debenture committees a sheet of suggestions and requirements which says "the 'CONSENT TO EXTEND DEBENTURE' [sic] form will allow anyone to extend the debenture for the three year period ending August 31/2006. This is *absolutely required* [italic boldface added] to allow time for the resolution of the legal claims against the U.S. land and the subsequent sale of the property."

Low Evaluations

On Friday February 28, this writer visited the offices of the Canadian Western Bank at Fort and View Streets in Victoria to look at the bank's independent appraisal of the value of the Lacey property. The Diocese has been insisting that the property is of much less value than their business partner Joseph Finley has claimed in sworn statements.

Whereas Mr. Finley states that *Corporate Business Park* property is worth between $18 and 21 million (US) at full, fair market value, Bishop Roussin in his January 26, 2003 said their appraisal figure is only $11.5 million (US), and that this will not cover all the costs associated with the land problem. This contradicts what is said in the February 26 letters which claim the sale of the U.S. land will settle the problem of paying back the debenture bonds in three years' time.

I was curious about the nature of this huge discrepancy in value – some 36 to 44 per cent difference. In his January letter Bishop Roussin also said that the media was welcome to view re-quested information, so I wrote and received permission to view the lower appraisal.

It turned out there were two stages to the appraisal that the bank had required over three years in order to loan money on the property. The original and thicker document was from December, 1999 and it appraised the property at $6.5 million (US). Three years later in January, 2003, the value had risen to $11.5 (US), nearly double in value. This was due, Gerald Laliberte of the bank explained, to the Target development of the adjacent property, which improved the infrastructure as the appraisal was estab-lished on the basis of comparative land value.

'Comparative land value' is an alternative method of measur-ing the value of the land as compared to the more rigorous 'Re-sidual Land Value Analysis' which Joseph Finley swears he had his realtors, Trammell Crow Company, do in August 2000.

Finley's method resulted in a value of $2.65 (US) per square foot while the Canadian Western Bank value was between $2 and 2.15 dollars (US) per square foot. Ironically it was because the Diocese reneged on developing a sale with Target when it twice had the opportunity, that the Lacey land, according to its measurement, radically increased in value as a result of the adjacent sale and construction by Target.

Their most recent appraisal per square foot value lies between 2 and 2.15 dollars (US) per square foot, while Finley's figure, from August 2000, is 2.65. This difference does not account for the huge discrepancy however. The Diocese's figure is so much lower because its appraisal was only on 126.5 acres (in 1999) and 130 acres (in 2003) instead of the full 160 acres which comprises the CBP property.

The assessor for the bank was Richard J. Briscoe of Terra Property Analytics of Union Street in Seattle, Washington and he assessed only on what he called the 'net usable land.' There are tree buffers on the property covering some thirty acres that can be removed if a lawsuit already pending is pursued.

Vanderkerkhove Offer

The Diocese has been consistent in its attitude of undervaluing the property. In the Debenture Offering information (June, 2000) the property was assessed at $7.2 Million (US) even though shortly before that time according to court documents, Allen Vanderkerkhove had offered $7.5 million (US) in a thwarted effort to purchase the land in the winter of 2000 at a distressed price.

7.5 million (US) is the renegotiated mortgage figure that the land actually cost in 1998. Another part of the debenture offering information reads: "The appraisal indicates a range in the value of the Washington Lands from $4,777,500.00 to $9,555,000.00 depending on the time taken to market the property."

Since 9.6 is double 4.8, the variation here seems remarkable. In terms of the Canadian Western Bank appraisal, 160 acres worked out at the $2.15 per square foot comes out over $14 million (US) which is exactly what records show Target offered; and exactly what Target paid for 142 adjacent acres.

It is obviously in someone's interest to leave the figure low and loose. Why not determine a realistic fair-market value price based on a more comprehensive measuring methodology such as

Mr. Finley had Trammell Crow do, and then there would be a firm and definite figure?

What is the actual value of the property? Without knowing that how can debenture bond holders have confidence that even in three years they will get their money back?

Three Years Back Taxes

Even the Thurston County Assessor believes the property is worth $1.46 million (US) more than the Diocese' appraiser. In the Thurston County Washington 2002 tax assessment on the property the assessment figure utilized is $12.96 million (US). Usually property tax assessment figures are lower than actual values.

More significantly perhaps, the Diocese was at risk of losing the property for unpaid back taxes allowed to accrue over three calendar years. Taxes were not paid during the years 2000, 2001, and 2002. On February 25, 2003 more than $473,000 (US) was finally paid as were other special assessments on the property, according to my conversation with the Thurston County tax assessment office.

The total due on October 31, 2002, billed to the trustee Fisgard Asset Management, had been $351,400.05 from the years 2000, 2001 and 2002.

These were taxes owed on 2002 land values of $12,960,00 (US). Apparently the Diocese does not mind paying taxes on this assessed value for a property worth only $11.5 million (US) according to its bank's appraisals. It is costly though, as is the tax delinquency. As of last August, 2002 the delinquent interest and penalty for the unpaid taxes was $64,010.88 (US), which is more than a hundred thousand in Canadian dollars.

Dubious Tactics

Regarding another related matter, the Diocese of Victoria may eventually have the dubious privilege of suing its current lawyers in the *Corporate Business Park* legal conflict, if things do not go as planned.

According to court documents, in 1999 Bogle and Gates [now Dorsey and Whitney], the Diocese's lawyers, were successfully sued by their clients Carl A. Anderson and wife for legal malpractice and breach of fiduciary duties in The Superior Court of the State of Washington for King County.

The Andersons were awarded a substantial settlement because their own lawyers were judged to have used questionable tactics in a legal case that bears more than passing similarity to the current one between the Diocese and Joseph Finley, its estranged business partner.

In September of 1999, the law firm now representing the Diocese settled with the Andersons after U.S. Bankruptcy Court Judge Thomas Glover severely chastised the law firm of Bogle and Gates [now Dorsey and Whitney] for engaging in questionable tactics. The same lawyers appealed the case to U.S. District Court and the U.S. Court of Appeals where Judge Glover's decision was upheld each time.

The Andersons sued their lawyers for faulty advice in a commercial property case which included a sale of a run-down service station to a party named Kim. After paying on the land for years, Kim wanted to renovate the service station and had been offered the money to do so by Chevron. But Anderson's (and the Diocese') lawyers refused to allow the renovation even though Anderson could not reasonably refuse to consent.

Ostensibly the goal was to push Kim into default so that Anderson could take the land back and make the deal with Chevron himself. Anderson did succeed in forcing Kim into bankruptcy and in taking the property back but the bankruptcy court held in favor of Kim who got money and damages and attorney's fees against Anderson and his lawyers.

Throughout this process Anderson and his lawyers adamantly refused to negotiate with Kim (in a similar way that the Diocese has refused to negotiate with Mr. Finley). Anderson lost the Chevron deal and had to pay damages and attorney's fees to Kim. As well the lawyers for Anderson were hit with severe penalties. The total was approximately a million dollars. The judge's opinion placed the blame squarely on Bogle and Gates for its tactics.

The Anderson's sued Bogle and Gates and settled out of court for a sum said to be in the hundreds of thousands of dollars.

3.

Not Due to Our Lack of Effort

February 26, 2003

Dear Debenture Holders,

Some two and a half years ago I wrote to you to thank you for your generosity in supporting the Diocese by your debenture purchase. I come today to reiterate my gratitude to one and all for this gesture. You all responded in the spirit of Christ to the crisis we faced at that time.

We all regret that we have been unable to sell the land in the United States. It has not been due to our lack of efforts in that domain. Nonetheless, such is what we face at this time.

I come then to also ask you simply and humbly to extend your debenture if you can. Details concerning this step are given in the attached letters.

Once again I thank you for whatever support you are able to offer the Diocese at this time. I also ask that, with me, you pray with God's guidance we will be successful in this endeavor.

Sincerely in Christ
+ Raymond Roussin, SM
Bishop of Victoria

Manage to the Highest Standards

February 26, 2003

Dear Debenture Holder

I am writing to you on behalf of the Finance and Administration Board of the Diocese to advise you of our financial status and to seek your continuing support.

The Board is striving to insure that the finances of the Diocese are managed to the highest standards of the civil law. Changes have been implemented so that the financial errors of the past will not be repeated. We have a Financial and Administration Board with various committees meeting on a regular basis. In addition, we have an annual audit of the financial records of the Diocese done by an independent accounting firm.

Our day to day costs for operating schools and Churches have improved so that they are near the break-even point. Our financial problems exist because of the U.S. land.

We have sold sufficient Island properties to pay down bank debt of approximately $4.6 million dollars relating to the U.S. land, and have sufficient funds on hand to pay debenture interest due Aug. 31, of this year. However as the U.S. land hasn't sold, we do not have the necessary funds to redeem the debentures. As our interest, taxes and legal costs associated with this land continue, we are facing costs of operation which cannot be met from the day to day contributions made to the Diocese.

Accordingly, we are asking you to extend the date of redemption of your debenture to August 31, 2006, to give us additional time to sell the U.S. land. We also ask for donations, from those able, of the interest and/or principal due under the debenture to help us meet the extraordinary expenses incurred by the Diocese in connection with the U.S. land. Your security for repayment continues to be the U.S. and Diocesan Lands, under the original Deed of Trust and Mortgage.

We will continue our efforts to liquidate remaining properties, work with the Bishop on the reorganization of parishes, and assist the schools in making meaningful contributions to the overall improvement of our finances.

Your loyalty and support has sustained all of us and we are thankful. Once again, we ask you to respond positively to the canvassers who will soon call on you. We ask you to consider the options presented to you, keeping in mind our most difficult present position and the fact that, even as we emerge from this dark episode, we will still have a debt – a debt that until repaid will overhang our abilities to fully pursue our Mission.

Yours truly,
Ian H. Stewart, Q.C., Chair,
Diocesan Administration and Finance Board

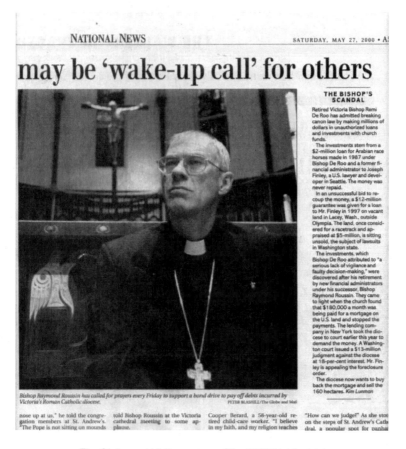

The Globe and Mail coverage of the 2000 'debt crisis'

Chapter 6 – Rejected Offers and Other Disturbing Factors

Diocese' Lawyers Fined for "Unprofessional" Practices in a Separate but Similar Case

Past Summer Sees Two More Rejected Offers

Island Catholic News, Volume 17, No 11, December 2003

The Facts

In a twenty page memorandum opinion, Judge Suzanne Barnett of the Superior Court of the State of Washington for King County fined two lawyers at Dorsey & Whitney, LLP $400,000 (US) in a decision rendered on October 16, 2003.

The two lawyers, Todd Fairchild and Richard Clinton were sanctioned and fined along with their firm Dorsey & Whitney for "making claims that were without sufficient basis in law or fact." She also fined their client $100,000 (US) for allowing the lawyers to harass the opponents in a civil case.

Dorsey & Whitney and Messrs. Fairchild and Clinton are the same ones fighting the case for the Diocese of Victoria against business partner Joseph Finley in the Corporation Business Park land case currently before the courts in Washington State.

Judge Barnett wrote in her Memorandum Opinion: "The court further finds that certain other claims, while marginally supportable under the facts and applicable law were nonetheless added to the complaint in this matter for the improper purpose of harassing the individual defendants."

In an interview, Joseph Finley declined comment on this recent turn of events. However, Mr. Finley did report that the Diocese and the debenture trustee recently asked the trial court to impose a requirement for an appeal bond or cash deposit on him for an additional $1.85 Million (US) even though the court previously had

117

ruled that his bond requirements to preserve the status quo on appeal was limited to quarterly bonds of $150,000 each. The request of the Diocese and the debenture trustee was rejected by the Court, which left the accruing bond amount virtually unchanged from a year ago.

Mr. Finley believes the bond to be a technicality because the debenture trustee can have no damage from the appeal, and he has asked his lawyers to consider filing a motion in the Court of Appeals to have the bond eliminated entirely.

This would mean that all of the accruing costs of the litigation and holding the Lacey land will fall on the Diocese with no hope to recoup any of those costs from the bonds, which in any event fall far short of covering the ongoing costs.

According to Finley, it appears that the skirmish over the amount of the appeals bonds (in light of the fact that the court already had determined the amount of the bond) is akin to the harassing tactics used by Clinton, Fairchild and Dorsey & Whitney in the other case. This could spell trouble for the Diocese if it allows the lawyers to pursue tactics designed for harassment rather than getting to the merits of the case.

Details From The Judge's Ruling

On page 19 of her Memorandum Opinion Judge Barnett writes: "It is not sufficient to search for a way to do the bidding of an influential client. It is unprofessional to accept at face value the emotional claims of one who, as in this case, is powerful, unaccustomed to being questioned, who feels he has been wronged … attorneys who are in the business to do their client's bidding are in the wrong business …"

"The testimony of the Dorsey & Whitney attorneys highlights the need for careful training and exquisite oversight of any major litigation in which the representation is undertaken by a team of attorneys. No matter what the resources of the client, no attorney can or should accept a document as handed over without critical inquiry into the bases for the averments and allegations it contains."

Judge Barnett's final paragraph reads: "Rather than advice and counsel, Dorsey & Whitney provided accommodation. For that failure of professionalism, the firm must pay a disproportionate share of the sanction."

"The court's analysis of these claims is based not on hindsight but upon review of thousands of pages of discovery, pleadings, notes and the testimony of plaintiffs' counsel themselves. The court determines that, in whole or in part, each of the eight claims upon which it conducted inquiry were either unsupported by reasonable inquiry into fact or law, or were asserted for improper purpose."

In a prior article, ICN reported that these attorneys were involved in a somewhat similar situation that resulted in a malpractice claim against the attorneys and also resulted in a devastating loss for their client who later sued them.

The Connection To The Lacey Land Litigation

How does any of this relate to the Lacey land case? Each involved a financially strong client (in each case the client of Dorsey & Whitney) against a much weaker one. Each involved allegations that were later proven to be false or not founded on the facts and applicable law.

What if it is proven that there was a Target offer in 2000 as Mr. Finley claims? That offer would have been known to the Diocese and its lawyers. Or, the lawyers at least had a duty under the ruling of Judge Barnett to get to the truth.

What if it is proven that Target was not opposed to buying the Lacey land, and that the Diocese' refusal to cooperate with Mr. Finley in February of 2001 was done with that knowledge?

What if it is established that the action of the Diocese in surreptitiously buying the judgment against the Lacey land was in fact "constructive fraud" as Mr. Finley has alleged? The whole premise of the Diocese' defense and its allegations as drafted by Dorsey & Whitney could fall like a house of cards and the financial stability of the Diocese along with it.

Related Matters – The Offers

Two separate offers of roughly $9 Million (US) each were turned down by the Diocese in July and September 2003. The Diocese wanted $11 Million (US) but the Lacey land is costing the Diocese roughly $1 Million (US) to carry, and the Diocese' lawyers have conceded (in fact represented to the court) that the litigation will continue for at least another two years unless some resolution can be found.

An August 28, 2003 Purchase and Sale Agreement for a sale at $11 Million (US) was presented to Madison Project One, LLC as a counter-offer to Madison's prior offer of roughly $9 Million (US) to the debenture trustee and to the Diocese. ICN has obtained a copy of the proposed Purchase and Sale Agreement and the prior offer. As part of each offer, Joseph Finley, the Diocese and the debenture trustee would have to release all claims of each one against the other and end the Lacey land litigation.

Under the terms of a document entitled "Settlement Agreement and Mutual Release" Finley and the Diocese and the debenture trustee were to waive "any and all lawsuits, appeals and other legal proceedings involving Joseph Finley or any other party to the settlement agreement, including without limitation: civil actions number 99-2-01006 and 00-2-01783-6 in the Superior Court of Washington for Thurston County and case number 29321-8-II in the Court of Appeals of Washington, Division II."

It appears that the offer by Madison Project One, LLC would have solved two major woes of the Diocese, namely: the ongoing cost of the Lacey land and litigation of over $1 Million (US) per year; and repayment of the debentures which still total roughly $12.4 Million (CDN).

If the debentures cannot be paid from the Lacey land, the Diocese is on record that debenture holders may have to forgive the debt or church properties and other properties essential to the operations of the Diocese may have to be sold as the so-called "surplus land" in the debenture offering has essentially been sold already.

Why the Diocese would not seriously attempt to negotiate a resolution of the situation that has been referred to by the Diocese' Administration as a "major financial crisis," and the "most serious problem facing the Diocese" seems inexplicable.

The expensive litigation continues; the cost to carry the Lacey land continues; the fees to the lawyers who were sanctioned by Judge Barnett continue at an apparent pace of $200,000 per year.

The possible solutions afforded by either of the two offers have not been reported by the Diocese, which continues to blame Mr. Finley for its woes even though he apparently was willing to settle all matters. There is a factual disconnect between what has been happening in Washington and what is being reported to the parishioners and debenture holders.

Reflection: Factual Analysis

In summary then, the situation is as follows: the Diocese is spurning offers even though those offers are consistent with what the appraisers for the Diocese say the Lacey land is now worth; the cost to carry the land and continue the legal battle goes on to the tune of $1 Million (US) per year; the exchange rates between the US and Canadian dollar are diminishing the Diocese' ability to recoup even enough to pay off the debentures if it does not act quickly.

Joseph Finley appears to be prepared to press the litigation if necessary – he posted the most recent bond required by the court on December; the lawyers for the Diocese have been severely punished in another case that raises serious questions about their objectivity and ability to represent the Diocese in a professional manner.

The debenture holders are being prepared by the Diocese for the possibility that they may not be repaid on the debentures in three years or ever without selling churches and schools at the same time that two offers were rejected that would in fact have repaid the debentures and relieved the Diocese of its ongoing cost of $1 Million (US) on the Lacey land that is wreaking havoc on the Diocese' financial viability; and instead of keeping the parishioners and debenture holders informed, the Diocese and the debenture trustee appear to be actively concealing what is happening from them. The last is a serious breach of trust with the debenture holders especially, as it is after all their money.

In Summary

1.

What has become increasingly disturbing is a lack of information coming from the Diocese about the matter, and the information that is forthcoming seems to be at odds with what is actually happening in Washington State.

For example, in the July 2003 *Diocesan Messenger*, the parishioners were told that the *"Trustee for the Debenture Holders continues to pursue avenues to effect an early settlement of the litigation surrounding this property so that it can be sold and the proceeds used to repay the Debenture Holders."*

And in the December 2003 *Diocesan Messenger*, Diocesan Administrator, Vern McLeish stated: *"Rest assured, the Diocese, together with Fisgard* [the debenture trustee] *are doing everything in their power to bring this issue to an early conclusion."* But in an interview with ICN in connection with this article, Mr. Finley reported that neither he nor his lawyers have ever been contacted by the Diocese or the debenture trustee or their lawyers about a possible settlement since the litigation commenced in the spring of 2001. Mr. Finley has a track record of wanting to resolve the dispute. The Diocese and the debenture trustee do not.

It will be remembered that Mr. Finley came to Victoria late last year and publicly stated (in an interview on public radio and at a meeting of debenture holders) that he wanted to resolve the Lacey matter. Mr. Finley and a fair number of debenture holders called upon Bishop Roussin to enter into mediation in an effort to do that. It also will be remembered that Bishop Roussin, also in an interview on public radio, dismissed those requests and was resolutely determined to proceed with litigation. Whether that was the appropriate decision remains to be seen, but in economic terms it has become worse than a nightmare for the Diocese.

In the December 2003 *Diocesan Messenger*, Vern McLeish also stated that *"We are no further along in the sale of the Lacey land."* However ICN has learned that the Diocese received two offers to purchase the land over the last 5 months, and that both were rebuffed with little or no interest in concluding a sale except at a price of $11 Million (US). It appears that both were credible buyers and at a price of roughly $9 Million (US) each.

Perhaps more significantly, each of the buyers claimed that they could obtain the agreement of Mr. Finley to cooperate with the sale and that all litigation pending between the Diocese, the debenture trustee and Mr. Finley could be ended. ICN in fact has obtained copies of the most recent offer and the counter offer made by the Diocese, and indeed, there are settlement and release documents attached to each, suggesting that the sale would in fact resolve the litigation.

2.

And while McLeish claims that there is no way to sell the Lacey land, it should be reported that it appears from pleadings filed in the Washington action that the debenture trustee has in fact "sold" part of the Washington land for supposedly no payment in return.

The debenture trustee conveyed an easement consisting of a right for an adjacent landowner to permanently build a sewer line to service thousands of homes to be built by that adjacent landowner. The easement was worth some $800,000 according to papers filed by Mr. Finley based on the fact that the easement allowed the adjoining landowner to avoid the cost of building an extra mile of sewer line if the easement had not been granted.

Mr. Finley contended that the easement which was 30 feet wide and which covered three fourths of a mile in length (over 2.7 acres of the Lacey land) was absolutely unnecessary to the Lacey land because it already has sewer to its southerly boundary without the easement being involved.

Mr. Finley's papers further contend that the easement damaged the Lacey land because it removed the flexibility of assembling property on the other side of the easement if necessary to make a future sale. Representatives of the debenture trustee denied that granting the easement caused any damage, but they also contended that absolutely no consideration was received for granting the easement other than the cost of drafting legal papers.

This "sale" which occurred in the spring of 2003 was not reported in the *Diocesan Messenger* for July or December of 2003. It would be interesting to know why a very valuable asset that could have paid off roughly 10 percent of the debentures was allegedly "gifted" to the adjacent landowner by the debenture trustee and the Diocese. And why was this transaction concealed?

In the midst of the offers and counter-offers, none of which have been disclosed by the Diocese, there has been reporting on the ongoing cost of carrying the Lacey land and in paying for the litigation expense. In the July 2003 *Diocesan Messenger*, Vern McLeish reported that for calendar year 2002 there were extraordinary expenses relating almost exclusively to the Lacey land in the amount of $2,394,940. More recently, the debenture trustee and the Diocese have asserted in documents filed with the court that the actual cost of carrying the Lacey land is in the range of $900,000 (US) per year.

ICN has reviewed tax and assessment records, the ongoing interest charges accruing and legal expenses reported consistently by the Diocese. It appears that the actual cost is close to $1,050,000 (US) per year with over $200,000 annually going to pay the lawyers. And it should be noted that in calendar year 2003 the Diocese additionally paid over $700,000 (US) in back taxes and special assessments against the property.

In their most recent appearance in court in late November the lawyers for the Diocese and the debenture trustee asserted their contention in writing that *"the entire process will last approximately two more years – through late 2005 – and will cost [the debenture trustee and the Diocese] millions of dollars in interest and other costs."* And that is only to resolve with finality the claims against the debenture trustee.

The case against the Diocese would still have to be tried, with the possibility of further appeals. Realistically, the litigation could last much longer and cost much more. That would be devastating to both the Diocese and the debenture holders.

Another critical piece of information relates to the appraisal reported to the parishioners in the July 2003 *Diocesan Messenger*. Vern McLeish informed the parishioners that a new appraisal of the Lacey land had been obtained at a value of $11.5 Million (US). He also added, however, that *"unfortunately the on-going legal and holding costs tend to off-set the increase value."*

But in order to offset the carrying costs we now know from the court documents filed by the debenture trustee and the Diocese that the property would have to appreciate at over $1 Million (US) per year just to cover carrying costs, and there is no assurance that the Diocese will not have to pay substantial damages to Mr. Finley.

Consequently, the appreciation in value becomes very closely linked to whether a decision to sell the Lacey land at any particular time is or is not prudent. ICN has learned that a new appraisal has just been completed, and that the value of the Lacey land has in fact decreased rather than increased over the past year.

ICN has learned through Mr. Finley that the value not only decreased, but that the range of values furnished by the appraiser make both of the two offers rejected by the Diocese over the past few months appear reasonable considering the current value. It is significant to note that Vern McLeish's update in the December 2000 *Diocesan Messenger* fails to even mention the updated appraisal.

3.

As outlined, ICN also has learned of a ruling in a Washington Superior Court case in King County by Judge Suzanne Barnett that calls into serious question the conduct of the attorneys that have been representing the Diocese for the duration of the litigation with *Corporate Business Park* and Mr. Finley.

Judge Barnett, in a 20-page Memorandum Opinion imposed sanctions on Richard Clinton and Todd Fairchild and their firm Dorsey & Whitney in the amount of $400,000 (US) for unprofessional conduct – harassing tactics and making unsubstantiated claims.

Judge Barnett also imposed sanctions against their client in the amount of $100,000 (US) for complicity in the improper conduct of the attorneys. Clinton and Fairchild are the same two attorneys assigned to handle the litigation for the Diocese with *Corporate Business Park* and Mr. Finley.

Upon perusal of the Judge's ruling, parallels with the *Corporate Business Park* civil suit immediately spring to mind. Is the Diocese headed down the same path as the other Dorsey & Whitney client? The Diocese has been assured repeatedly by the Washington lawyers that the Diocese would prevail and that the litigation would be over very soon.

Take for example the proclamation of Bishop Roussin on January 26, 2003 that the appeal would be over in less than 60 days. We are at 350 days and counting since that time, and now the lawyers are filing documents in court claiming that the litigation will go on for at least another two years.

It appears that the lawyers are being well paid for their efforts. Has a very serious conflict of interest arisen between the Diocese and its own lawyers where the Lacey land is costing over $1 Million (US) per year while the litigation continues and the lawyers apparently continue to collect roughly $200,000 per year for their efforts? Whose interest is really being served?

4.

ICN is raising these facts and issues again for the benefit of parishioners who have a right to know what is going on in the Lacey land case and who have a right to know how the assets of the Diocese are being spent, perhaps unnecessarily.

The bondholders have been advised that if the Lacey land is not sold by 2006, they may not be paid, or that payment could only come from the sale of important Diocesan assets. How does that square with the Diocese refusing not one but two offers that were almost dollar for dollar enough to pay the debentures in full – now?

The bondholders are well into the fourth year of bankrolling this odd if not tragic drama. Some may well be starting to conclude that they unwittingly have been enabling whatever is going on behind the scenes of this situation that the Diocese claims to be unsolvable but appears, based on recent events, to be just the opposite.

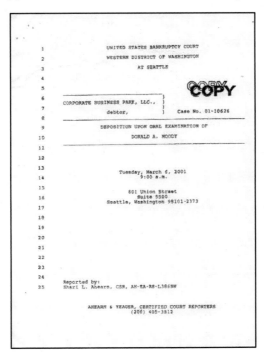

Donald Moody's court deposition proved the most damaging evidence about the diocese hiding the Target Corporation offer.

VP

VICTORIA PROPERTIES, INC.

FACSIMILE TRANSMITTAL SHEET

TO: Devon Haws

FROM: David I. Osmond, President

COMPANY: Nanaimo

DATE: June 20th 2000

FAX NUMBER: 250 714 0525

TOTAL NO. OF PAGES INCLUDING COVER: 8

RE: WASHINGTON STATE PROPERTY

☐ URGENT ☐ FOR REVIEW ☐ PLEASE COMMENT ☐ PLEASE REPLY ☐ PLEASE RECYCLE

NOTES/COMMENTS:

Hi Devon,

Got your voice mail about the Cedar property. Attached is some info on the 160 acres in Lacey, Washington State. We have a listing agreement being signed with Don Moody of CB Richard Ellis - see below.

Donald A. Moody
First Vice President

CB Richard Ellis

CB Richard Ellis inc.
Brokerage Services
Lake Grove

1420 5th Avenue
Suite 1700
Seattle, WA 98101-2384
206 292 6123 Tel
206 292 6033 Fax
206 919 0556 Mobile
dmoody@cbrichardellis.com

" Thanks for your interest.
Dave Osmond

➔ CC: Don Moody

2546 Government Street
Victoria, B.C. V8T 4P7
CANADA
(250) 413-2164, Facsimile (250) 385-6747

JUN 20 '00 11:34   2503856747   PAGE.01

This court document confirmed the acknowledgement that the diocese had been approached by an agent for Target Corporation in the Spring of 2000. That offer would have made the debenture bond issue unnecessary and shown there was no debt crisis as the land value more than covered the so-called indebtedness and only needed to be properly managed to be sold. Dave Osmond served on the Lacey Land Committee for the diocese at the time.

128

Chapter 7 – Roussin Moves On, Is Deposed

Bishop Moves On, Leaves Massive Debt, Rumors of Suppression

Island Catholic News, Volume 17, No 12, January 2004

VICTORIA—On the day of the retirement party of his most challenging clergyman, the same day that an announcement was half-expected of the sale of the controversial Lacey land in Washington, Bishop Raymond Roussin of Victoria trumped the news with the announcement that he has been appointed archbishop of Vancouver with no replacement named for Victoria.

Archbishop Adam Exner, who has served as ordinary of Vancouver since 1991, turned 75 on Christmas day, 2003. His offered retirement was immediately accepted by Rome and on January 9, 2004 Victoria's debt-beleaguered Bishop Raymond Roussin was appointed as his replacement, the result of a process that must have been many months in the making, unknown to ordinary parishioners in the Diocese. Roussin will be the tenth bishop of Vancouver since its creation in 1864.

Bishop Roussin, who came to Victoria from the suppressed diocese of Gravelbourg, Saskatchewan for February 24, 1999, would have been just five years in office next month. With no announced replacement, speculation that the Diocese of Victoria will be attached to Vancouver was the first thought on many people's mind according to the numerous phone calls received at the *Island Catholic News* office in reaction to the matter.

2.

With its usual secretiveness, the Curia (and the Canadian Conference of Catholic Bishops) acknowledged no due process in its bureaucratic machinations of determination for the decisions, leaving people to ponder the radical gap of distance between the official levels and the perceptions on the ground within the church.

At the official level, obviously Bishop Roussin was seen to have done a very good job here with the implied approval of a promotion to a larger area of responsibility. But on the ground in the diocese of Victoria there have always been many more questions than answers about his suitability to lead a progressive people-centered church.

On top of this there is also the permanent legacy of debt he leaves behind and the much questioned ramifications of financial liability engendered in his name by his appointed financial and administrative advisors. This issue reflects a serious lack of balance which affects the Catholic church generally during this era.

All the people who surrounded the bishop in this key area of finances were from a specific narrow sector of society that cannot pretend to represent the wider expression of the makeup of the church.

Island Catholic News has been a constant critic of this financial style since the first public revelations of the *Corporate Business Park* partnership complication in 2000. The handling of the 160-acre industrial property in Lacey, Washington, co-owned by the Diocese may prove a fatal flaw in the legacy of Bishop Roussin.

Sidney

At Saint Elizabeth's Parish, Sidney on Friday evening an exuberant crowd of four hundred sat down to a parish potluck supper and an evening of homespun entertainment at a roasting and fond farewell for Rev. Jack Sproule who retired at age 70.

The pastor for eighteen years in the Saanich Peninsula is legendary in his provocative and progressive theology and pastoral leadership style. Sproule has consistently relied primarily upon the 'people of God' themselves, as incarnated in the parish, to discern and determine and organize their own ministries and pastoral initiatives, with no interference from the priest.

Some fifty organizations thrive in the parish, none of which, he proudly stated, were specifically initiated by 'Father Jack.' In his farewell talk on the theme of gratefulness for the opportunity to serve there in this style, Sproule stated that only the people themselves know and can serve their needs in pastoral ministry.

It is the job of the pastor to keep out of the way, he said, to let it happen strictly by support and encouragement not by exercising any power and control. He says this is no mean feat but called upon all his creative energies especially in the increasingly restrictive atmosphere of the universal church today.

Seattle

In Seattle, Washington, shopping center developer Harvey Simons represented the Diocese in a meeting January 9 with the Madison Project One group which offered to buy the Lacey land property in August, 2003 for $9 Million (US), but was turned down at that time.

Whether this renewed effort to secure the purchase had anything to do with Bishop Roussin imminent departure is only subject to speculation. But the offer, as did another one earlier in the summer of 2003, includes the waiver of claim by Joseph C. Finley, the alienated business partner of the Diocese on the *Corporate Business Park* property.

Concern about the added expense of a major court case with Finley who has charged the diocese with 'constructive fraud' may have been an added incentive for reopening the negotiations before the bishop moves on to the larger center.

Madison Project One offered $9 million (US) in the summer. The most recent appraisal for the land, which places its value at $11.5 million (US), contains an instructive sub text about the Target Corporation depot development on 140 adjacent acres. Target paid $14.3 million (US) in June of 2001 according to the appraisal by Terra Property Analytics dated December 19, 2003. The appraisal also states 'Finally the influence of Mr. Findley's (sic) involvement with the subject makes it much more difficult to sell.'

The diocese would have received an estimated $15.5 million for its 160 acres if it had been open to Target's approach in 2000. Its land was a better fit and large enough for Target at that time. Now at the lower end of the financial cycle, the offers are between 5.3 and 6.5 million dollars lower and not expected to improve for some time due to the soft market economy.

The appraiser, Richard Briscoe of Seattle, says that no offers can be expected for two to three more years due to the downturn in the American economy which effects a shrinking U.S. dollar which substantially reduces the value in Canadian dollars.

On December 24, 2003 Joseph Finley's lawyer issued the deposition list in the 'Bishop v. Finley' case No. 00-2-017830-6, Joseph Finley's 'constructive fraud' case. "Including persons who may be required to attend by subpoena," the list names both Bishops Roussin and De Roo, Muriel Clemenger, Vernon McLeish, Norm Isherwood, David Osmond, Ellis Achtem, Allen Vanderkerkhove and Paul Bundon, all diocesan players in this four-year saga.

Victoria Bishop Named to Head Vancouver Diocese

'not in a dream or a nightmare'

By Ian Dutton, Religion Writer
Excerpted from the January 12, 2004
edition of the *Times Colonist*

Island Catholic News, Volume 18, No 1, February 2004

Bishop Raymond Roussin's voice on the telephone is soft and warm, with a delicate flavour of laughter underlying his words.

Roussin, the new Roman Catholic Archbishop of Vancouver, hasn't had a lot to laugh about in his five years in Victoria. But even his critics agree he has retained his warmth and humanity in trying times.

The former bishop of Gravelbourg, a largely French-speaking community in Saskatchewan, Roussin came to this city in 1998 as a replacement for Bishop Remi De Roo, who was stepping down at age 75 after 37 years as Bishop.

Now, Roussin, 64, will replace Archbishop Adam Exner, who last month turned 75, the mandatory retirement age in the church. The new archbishop said that, other than a few minor complaints, he is in good health.

A date for the handover of responsibilities in Vancouver has not been set, Roussin said. A process to find a new bishop for Victoria is underway.

The new archbishop, who has known of the appointment for about a month, said he's sorry to leave, but is looking forward to the challenges in Vancouver.

"After five years here, it's home now," said Roussin, a Marianist priest who was born in Winnipeg and educated in Switzerland and Quebec.

"I've made a lot of wonderful friends here, and although I already know some people in Vancouver, in many ways, I'll have to start all over again.

"And I particularly like the size of (Victoria). Not that I dislike Vancouver, but it will be an adjustment."

Roussin said the process to replace Exner began in the late summer when the retiring archbishop officially signified his intention to step down.

A list of replacement candidates was created and recommendations solicited from the Catholic family – clergy and laity included, Roussin said.

He learned in October that his name topped that list, which was then forwarded to Rome for examination. A short list of three names was advanced to the Pope for his consideration and ultimate decision.

Roussin said he had never had particular aspirations to be a priest, let alone a bishop or archbishop.

"In the order to which I belong, the Society of Mary, there are lay brothers, some of whom are selected to be priests," he explained. "I would not have imagined anything like this, not in a dream or a nightmare."

In coming to Victoria, Roussin inherited a diocese that faced economic difficulties. As a scandal over land purchases in the U.S. and the investment in show horses unfolded, the bishop devoted much of his energies to administrative and financial matters.

That prevented him from leaving a greater mark on the diocese, his supporters suggest.

"He will be missed, most definitely," said Marnie Buttler, editor of the local *Island Catholic News*.

"In some ways I feel sorry for him, because I don't think he had a chance to be a bishop here. By definition a bishop is a pastoral person, a shepherd for the laity and the priesthood.

"But he hasn't had a chance to implement the programs he wanted, because of the financial stuff.

"I'd say that if you had to guess that he'd be frustrated at his time here, you wouldn't be wrong."

Kate Fagan Taylor, the Catholic chaplain at UVic, said the appointment is good news for Vancouver Catholics.

"This is a very pastoral man, who is aware of people's needs," said Fagan Taylor. "I know he did a lot of good here and he dealt very well with the pressure he was under in this diocese.

"He was a good bishop for us when we needed him and I know he'll do a lot of good in Vancouver."

But Patrick Jamieson, managing editor of *Island Catholic News* and a De Roo biographer, is less certain of Roussin's success.

"I think a lot of the financial problems are to some extent his doing, though he's managed to avoid a lot of that perception," Jamieson said.

"Vancouver could be a good fit for him. It's a very top-down place and he (Roussin) is very much a company man."

Butler said Catholics in Victoria are curious about who the next bishop will be, and that they will miss Roussin.

"There's a general fondness for him," she said. "He's a kind person, quiet and very warm. A lot of people will be sorry to see him go."

Call For Even-Handed Reporting

Island Catholic News, Volume 18, No 1, February 2004

The Editor:

I find the front page of the January issue upsetting. Rumors, innuendo and wild speculation apart, the subjectivity of this piece should have insured its relegation to the "Editorial" page.

For years since Bishop Lobsinger and Brother Hoby died in the plane crash, people of the Whitehorse diocese have been waiting for the appointment of a new bishop. Presently the bishop of Yellowknife administers that diocese, in worse financial straits than our own. It has not been suppressed. At least until now, no one could be found to accept the challenge of being the new bishop of Whitehorse.

A wider viewpoint and even-handed investigative reporting should have been able to put any "Rumors of suppression" of the Victoria diocese into better perspective and also shown the silliness of suggesting that an appointment "out of the frying-pan and into the fire" from Victoria to Vancouver is some kind of promotion.

It takes either a fool or a person of great faith to acquiesce when "Friend, you must come up higher (Lk.14, 10)" is the offer of a heavier cross. No one who knows Bishop Roussin would consider him to be such a fool.

He knows he is loved. He knows he will be missed. This is the reality "on the ground in the diocese of Victoria."

Rev. Phil Smith, OMI
Ucluelet

Who's Got The Secret

The Editor:

I know I am not alone when I say that I will definitely miss Bishop Ray. He was certainly a "man of the people," as well as a man of God; gentle, humble and always approachable. The Vancouver diocese is certainly getting a gift!

But what is it with Patrick Jamieson? He seems to be always "after" Bishop Ray. Has he forgotten that it was Bishop De Roo, who left our diocese in such a financial mess? The latest episode is in the January issue of ICN, where he talks about the "usual secretiveness" of the Curia and CCCB. Surely nothing compares with the secretiveness (deception) of Bishop De Roo in not informing the incoming Bishop Ray of the financial situation that he was inheriting?

And still on the subject of secrecy, Mr. Jamieson appeared to be opposed to Bishop Ray's informing the congregations of the financial situation the church was left with when Bishop De Roo retired; (*Times Colonist* Feb. 29/00). Why?

Perhaps if we had had more openness with the previous bishop, we wouldn't be in this ongoing state. I'm afraid I trust the present financial committee to handle this situation more than I would Mr. Jamieson's "in depth" reporting on the subject.

Elizabeth Vaillant
Victoria

Let's Pray For Him

The Editor:

I read to my dismay in your # 12 paper that our Bishop Roussin is leaving us with an enormous debt. I want to reiterate that this intense good man had nothing to do with the creation of this debt.

We all know who originated this debt. And we all know that our Bishop Roussin tried all the avenues open to him to solve the problems, even to the detriment of his health.

Let us thank our Lord that, as far as is known, his new placement will start on much sounder ground than here.

Let's pray for him

Mrs. Wally de Groot
Sidney, BC

Cancel My Long-held Subscription

The Editor:

A headline in *The Vancouver Sun,* continuing the article "Vancouver Catholics Get New Archbishop" (January 12), boldly states "Islanders Concerned Roussin Was Not More Proactive." Further reading indicates that the only Islander to be named as so concerned is Patrick Jamieson.

It is one thing to be a life-long fan of Bishop Remi, but is another to contrast these bishops so unfairly. You disregard the disgraceful and oppressive financial burden left to Bishop Roussin at the time of his consecration and criticize a man so victimized for having "done nothing new or significant in Victoria," while you praise the dynamism of his proactive predecessor.

Perhaps it is "new and significant" in our present day society that a man, not having been told of the financial situation he was being left with, has never blamed the one responsible. Bishop Roussin has never pointed a finger of blame at Remi nor criticized him publicly.

He accepted the responsibility of this unfair burden bequeathed him, was completely up-front with the people of his diocese as to the amount of their liability, and continued to apprise them of the diocesan situation as he and they worked towards its solution. This he did with the broad-based support of the individual church members, the leadership of a committed group of advisors, and the sale of church property. In the meantime, he lifted up the shocked and discouraged spirits of his people by prayer, encouragement and retreats.

Your own newspaper, with its article "Bishop Moves On, Leaves Massive Debt, Rumors of Suppression" has still more unsubstantiated criticism of Bishop Roussin. One wonders what this holy and completely honest man actually did to be described as casually "moving on" after having (it would seem) purposely left the people of his diocese with "a massive debt" and an atmosphere of "suppression."

"Following Remi," you told the *Sun* reporters, "many people expected (Roussin) to be more dynamic." Following Remi's financially paralyzing legacy, many people were surprised at Bishop Roussin's ability to function at all, to say nothing of the way he handled his episcopate with dignity, discretion and forgiveness.

You ask for comment if one feels that Bishop Roussin "has been wonderful." I believed that he has been, and I look forward to his leadership here in the Archdiocese of Vancouver.

As a protest to your (at best) faint praise and (at worst) detraction of Bishop Roussin, I ask that you cancel my long-held subscription to your paper.

Sister Noreen O'Neill, SSA
New Westminster

Archbishop Raymond Roussin Deposed in Washington Land case

Former Victoria Bishop ordered to make sworn statement in early May

Island Catholic News, Volume 19, No 3, April 2004

Judge Paula Casey of the Superior Court of Thurston County, Washington issued a court order Friday March 12 that former Bishop of Victoria Raymond Roussin must appear before the lawyer of Joseph C. Finley in Seattle, Washington to make a sworn statement about certain matters in the case of Finley versus the Bishop of Victoria.

A second deposition was ordered on the same date for Norman Isherwood, a one-time member of the Diocese of Victoria Lacey land subcommittee. Isherwood is a non-Catholic businessman and real estate developer in Canada and in the USA who was asked to serve as a volunteer on the committee because of his real estate expertise. He was on the committee during 2000, but apparently left the committee in 2001 around the time that Mr. Finley commenced his legal action against the diocese over the handling of the Target deal and other matters.

Finley has charged the diocese with improper behavior in the business partnership, including breach of fiduciary responsibility, use of illegal tactics and defamation of character. This business partnership goes back to 1997 when Mr. Finley and the diocese entered into an ownership arrangement of the Lacey property. The joint ownership, titled *Corporate Business Park*, was originally with former Bishop of Victoria Remi Joseph De Roo.

2.

Finley gained evidence through court records in 2001 that Target Corporation had approached the Diocese with a purchase offer for the Lacey land in June of 2000, although he was not informed of this opportunity at the time. This is a breach of the partnership he claims. He also states he would have worked hard to bring the deal to successful completion if he had been informed. In his hundred page brief to the court dated January, 2004 Finley claims this is just one instance of many where the Diocese breached its fiduciary responsibility to work with him as its business partner and in the process defamed his reputation.

The court case has been going back and forth since 2000 and promises to take a number of years to play itself out. The Diocese of Victoria had been insisting in its diocesan newsletter, *The Diocesan Messenger*, that this is the reason why it has not sold the land while at the same time denying that there ever was a Target offer. Norman Isherwood is expected to be questioned on his acknowledgment to a media reporter of the Target offer. *The Globe and Mail* newspaper picked up on the discrepancy in a story by Robert Matas on September 26, 2002 titled 'Records cast doubt on Victoria diocese cash plea.'

Finley insists there have been any number of offers for the land, all of which have been turned down, but that the Target offer was the key one that would have satisfied the losses and would have made unnecessary the debenture bond offering raised by the Diocese in 2000 and renewed in 2003. In his brief he claims that the debenture bond offering itself was raised in an illegal manner with the Diocese using 'a straw man' corporation to assume the mortgage of the Lacey land, a tactic that is illegal under American law.

3.

Now Archbishop Roussin of Vancouver has been directly drawn into the court proceedings despite being transferred to another canonical jurisdiction. On April 1, 2004 Judge Paul Casey reissued her court order deposing Archbishop Roussin despite pleadings by his lawyers arguing that his new jurisdictional responsibilities within the church changed his status regarding the Lacey land partnership. On May 25, the archbishop will be required to testify under oath regarding the allegations in Joseph C. Finley's January brief.

Judge Casey's decision could have far reaching implications. The Catholic church has organized itself into separate legal entities, such as the Victoria Diocese and the Vancouver Archdiocese. This has helped to insulate the church from some liability in the tort claims arena so far. But the Judge seemed to be focused more on the fact that Archbishop Roussin was the Bishop in charge and the decision-maker in Victoria during all of the relevant periods of the lawsuit, roughly late 1999 through early 2004, and she decided that he could not escape having to testify because he had been sent to the Vancouver Archdiocese earlier this year.

Diocese Clears Legal Hurdle in American Land Dispute

Parishioners closer to repayment

By Kim Westad

Excerpted from the May 15, 2004 edition of the *Times Colonist*

The Catholic Diocese of Victoria is one step closer to ending a lengthy legal dispute with an American lawyer, which means parishioners who bailed their church out of millions of dollars of debt are closer to being repaid.

A three-judge panel of the Washington state court of appeals has unanimously rejected Joseph Finley's appeal concerning a 160-acre parcel of land located outside Lacey, Wash.

Finley, a U.S. lawyer who got involved in business deals in the late 1980s with former bishop Remi De Roo that led to the local diocese being left $17-million CDN in debt, had appealed a lower court ruling concerning the land.

However, the appeal court this week affirmed the validity of a settlement concerning the land that was approved by the diocese and Finley several years ago.

As a result, title to the Lacey land now rests with the trustee for parishioners who purchased bonds from the Catholic Diocese of Victoria to help it out of financial trouble that dates back to De Roo's dealings with Finley.

Finley still has the option of appealing to another court, said Vernon McLeish, financial officer of the diocese. Finley could not be reached for comment.

"It is a very important decision though. We are starting to move to some conclusion here," McLeish said Friday.

If Finley does not appeal, the diocese plans to eventually sell the property. Proceeds would be used to repay bonds purchased by parishioners.

Some 2,100 parishioners came to the aid of the diocese after a financial scandal erupted in 2000. At that time, it was disclosed that De Roo had been involved with Finley in the 1980s in an investment scheme relating to Arabian horses.

The unsanctioned activities resulted in losses of approximately $2 million. Nine years later, De Roo participated in the purchase of the land in Washington state, hoping to turn a quick profit and eliminate the losses on the horse scheme. The land didn't sell, and in December 1999, the diocese had to borrow $4 million from its own bankers to cover interest and property-related expenses on the Washington land.

The payments were too much for the diocese, and AG Capital, which held the mortgage, foreclosed on the diocese, which ended up with the $17 million debt.

The diocese turned to parishioners, asking them to contribute. Some $13 million was raised through a combination of donations and church bonds, which was used to buy out the 18-per-cent mortgage guaranteed with AG Capital on the property.

Investors were promised an annual six-per-cent return after three years. Vancouver Island parishioners contributed most of the money.

De Roo, a well-known social justice advocate, retired in 1999 after 37 years running the diocese.

Unpublished Letter to the *Times Colonist*

Newspaper Continues to Distort Coverage of Lacey Land Saga

Island Catholic News, Volume 19, No. 5, June 2004

I found Kim Westad's May 16/04 article titled 'Diocese clears legal hurdle in American land dispute' confusing in its construction, if not a tad mischievous in nature. As someone who continues to closely track this court case, I have to ask what is the purpose of the piece?

The only real news in the front page article is that an appeal was lost, but the headline indicated that some development to do with the substance of the court case was to be revealed. This appeal rejection does not directly affect the main issues of the case, which will go forward May 31 when former bishop of Victoria Raymond Roussin will make a sworn statement in the law offices of Joseph C. Finley's lawyer in Seattle.

This was ordered by Judge Paula Casey on March 12 and re-ordered a few weeks later when Roussin's Vancouver lawyers tried to halt it on the basis that he had transferred canonical jurisdictions within the Catholic church from Victoria to Vancouver.

Main Case Just Beginning

In her piece Kim Westad did not bother to explain in detail the nature or facts of the appeal that Finley lost. More importantly, the main trial has not yet begun. Finley has been arguing that it is the Diocese of Victoria that has not shown good faith over the five years since Bishop Remi De Roo left office in 1999.

This is the essence of the court case itself, that the Diocese since that time has not kept him, as their business partner, properly informed of potential offers on the land (breach of fiduciary responsibility) and has squandered opportunities that would have made the debenture bond offering unnecessary in the first place. He is also charging the diocese with defamation of character and using illegal procedures in how it set up the debenture bond offering on the Lacey land.

Actually if the diocese had lost this latest appeal, it could have been a crucially bad sign for the Diocese's side of the case because Finley has been making most of the positive progress in the substance of the case. Archbishop Roussin being ordered to make a sworn deposition was a credibility enhancement for Finley's side. His unsuccessful appeal could have been undertaken in the flush of this encouragement; just as Vernon McLeish's obvious jubilation at its rejection reveals a relief born of anxiety at what another negative court order would augur for his side.

Upon analysis, it seems to me that the Diocese of Victoria's strategy all along has been to break him financially and drive him off the case so that they don't have to deal with the substantive issues of the case where they are particularly weak.

If it comes to court, Finley will probably win. The Diocese knows it needs to stop him from getting that far no matter what the cost. I also have some ideas about the motivation behind the lack of co-operation with Finley; who is benefitting from that. As ICN goes to press, Finley and his lawyer are in Victoria taking a sworn statement from Norm Isherwood, a former Lacey land sub-committee member of the Diocese.

Need Objective Reporting

I really don't understand why the *Times Colonist* continues only to report one side of this case, and only what the Diocese wishes it to print. Westad's article is transparently an effort to put a positive spin for the church's side while at the same time ignoring the actual substantive new developments such as Roussin's ordered deposition and the facts of the case from Finley's point of view.

After all no one has ever argued that Finley is not a legitimate business partner of the diocese (or else there would be no standing in the court for the main case) so why not cover it as you would any business dispute, something from both sides and an atmosphere of balance instead of the shadow projecting the *Times Colonist* coverage has always maintained?

It's very strange. The church in this context is just one more social organization, why not treat it as such with objective coverage and neutral balance so that we can all get to know the truth behind this strange and abiding issue.

Contrary to what is claimed in the piece, the appeal loss does not bring the debenture holders any closer to resolution or pay back. Only the main case itself can do that and the longer it takes the more unlikely it is that anything will be paid back if only due to the millions of dollars that are going to fighting the case, the lost opportunities due to lack of co-operation between partners and the upkeep costs of the property itself.

As reported, ICN has learned that there are new environmental impact issues that threaten to drop the value of the property, while the Diocese turns its nose up at the latest all cash offer that includes Finley waiving his claims if taken.

The *Times Colonist* refuses to look at this side of things because the Diocese doesn't tell them about it. In the meantime the debenture bond shareholders remain equally quiet when they should be demanding accountability for their increasingly squandered investment.

Raymond Roussin at the formal reception following his induction as Archbishop of Vancouver early in 2004. In a newspaper interview he was quoted: "I would not have imagined anything like this, in a dream or a nightmare."

Property that sold for $3.78 (CDN). Converted into condominium townhouses by University Ridge Development. The land was offloaded rather than sub-divided and sold at a higher profit for the diocese to help recover its purported losses.

Christ the King Catholic Church, Courtenay, blessed on June 6, 1992. Two million dollars from the 'surplus land' sold went to repair and restore this 10-year-old building in the Comox Valley. The surplus land was sold to repay the debenture bondholders, but according to court documents none of the $7.3 million raised was used for that purpose.

Chapter 8 – The Allotment Garden

Whatever Became of The Allotment Garden Property In Gordon Head?

Island Catholic News, Volume 18, No. 6, July 2004

An Analytical Reflection

When I heard about the deposition of Bishop Roussin I had already begun working on the 'Lacey Land Saga' in a new direction of pursuit.

My own analysis of the case has been one of incredulity since the start. No matter what Bishop De Roo did or did not do on this matter, the way he was treated by the new administration was out of character with how the institution of the church traditionally has treated its major superior and hierarchical figures; *unless there is a political angle.*

It was clear that Bishop Roussin bore De Roo no ill will, in fact they respected each other immensely; and as brother bishops this would be predominant in their relationship.

De Roo had an impeccable reputation until this 'fall from grace' trumpeted in the front pages of the newspapers. The rapidity of this denouement in itself was dubious. His discrediting was clearly a political act that represented a changing of the guard within the institution of the church.

This happens all the time in institutions a whole lot less political than the Catholic church so while it was certainly hurtful and shocking on some important level, it was not all that surprising if you have studied the history of the Catholic church in Canada.

Smokescreen

These sorts of 'developments' however often form a convenient smokescreen for other activities; or should we say a unique opportunity for other sorts of activities, the sorts of shadowy activities such as Joseph Finley is identifying against the Diocese in his court case. If Joseph Finley is proven correct, as I believe he will be, what could be the purpose of this 'smokescreen.'

For me the very treatment of Finley, who none of the lead characters – lead decision makers of the diocese – knew personally, is a clue to what could be going on closer at hand on Vancouver Island.

His demonization in the media, driven by the financial revelations by the Diocese, serves a convenient political purpose as well. As long as he is effectively depicted as the 'bad guy' by the public, the so called 'good guys' have carte blanche to operate as they will with impunity. For example, they have complete control of the so-called 'surplus lands' of the diocese.

One of the 'benefits' of this 'financial crisis' that was so loudly announced on the front pages of the *Times Colonist* and elsewhere, was that millions of dollars of diocesan land was made accessible to those with the dollars to spend to buy it.

This was land that was accumulated largely during the four decades of Bishop De Roo's era and had increased the value of the diocese hugely from less than a million dollars when he arrived in 1962 to an estimated ninety million dollars when he retired in 1999.

This land naturally was never available for commercial development but rather was held in reserve for future needs. Much of it had been donated by those who wanted to see the church continue and prosper on the Island.

With the financial crisis and the debenture bond offering all this changed. All this so-called surplus land was available for sale, and so was the church property and parish schools and hospital land if you look closely at the fine print of the debenture offering.

Gordon Head

Developers on Vancouver Island must be looking with increasing avarice at the church reserve lands, if only because land is becoming in shorter and shorter supply, especially land in prestigious Gordon Head.

According to the *Diocesan Messenger* figures, properties that were assessed at approximately $15 million (CDN) were sold to help pay back the debenture bond holders. However, less than $8 million was realized from the sale of these properties and none of it was used to pay back the debenture bond holders. Rather they were requested to renew their three year commitment for another three years and 80 per cent did; plus new money came in on the second appeal.

It could also be noted that in a rising real estate market, as experienced during the last few years, actual market sales values are generally considerably higher than assessed values.

There is another very important factor to consider when lower than expected property sales values were received and accepted. The marketing strategy must be questioned. Were professional appraisals obtained to establish market value? To what degree were all potential buyers made aware of the properties that were put up for sale? What alternative sales methods were used to ensure that the highest values were obtained?

When the financial crisis was so loudly and publicly announced, did this not create a fire sale atmosphere resulting in the low sales figures?

This is all just general information that is universally known although no one seems to suspect any incompetence or corruption is at work in the rather curious facts that the once treasured diocesan properties were sold at about half their assessed value, resulting in no apparent improvement in the situation. This legacy is lost forever.

On the other hand some of the people who were lucky enough to get their hands on the sold properties did decidedly better.

Allotment Gardens

Take, for example the controversial sale of the allotment garden properties at Gordon Head next to Holy Cross Church on Gordon Head Road. That land was sold for $3.78 million (CDN) and subsequently subdivided by the purchaser. Luxury homes were constructed on the site, selling for $18 million in total according to the figures available at the Land Titles Office.

If the church itself had been able to do the subdividing and construction, the ultimate profit would have gone a long way toward reducing the debt. Fifteen years ago a piece of church-owned Gordon Head property was subdivided and sold by lottery to help pay off debt on the high school.

But it wasn't a church corporation that did the subdividing, constructed the houses and made the profit. In this case it was University Ridge Development. And who is University Ridge Development? And why should they have been selected for this privileged opportunity?

Why is it that ordinary parishioners are saddled with a huge loss and payback privilege while wealthy speculators can make millions off their collective misfortune. It's a hard one to explain unless you just chalk it up to another victory for capitalist values.

A little bit of research reveals that University Ridge Development is a company set up for this project. It is a company whose principal officers include five directors, a wealthy father and his two sons plus two other directors. All five run companies of their own and these companies serve as members of University Ridge Development.

This is all information that is available from the provincial Registry of Companies and by a visit to the registry office of URD itself, which is housed in the office of a large legal firm Jones Emery Hargreaves Swan on the twelfth floor of the CIBC tower on Fort street. Any citizen is entitled to view this information during working hours according to sections 163 & 164 of the BC Company Act.

I was particularly interested to see who had invested in University Ridge Development to see who precisely had gained by the church's loss.

Who Makes Up University Ridge Development?

The principle principal is Robert MacAdams, owner of Pacific Beach Investments, a company which owns Island Hall in Parksville and manages various other similar sized tourist industry facilities. To give you a sense of this man's wealth, the loan from the Western Canadian Bank for the $3.78 million purchase was for $4.28 million, the extra half million dollars indicating it was being guaranteed by someone with deep pockets.

I kept digging around in the obvious locations to see who University Ridge Development included. I did not run into any obvious conflicts of interest in my cursory research. The benefitting members of the company only included companies owned by the principal officers and the directors.

One company, for example, was owned by one son, Brad MacAdams, another by the other Darren. These companies had the names Riptide Holdings and Sonoma Holdings continuing the Pacific beach motif of their father's firm. The other company Carolyn Developments was jointly owned by the other two principals, James Henderson and Russell Stubbs.

But in a small community such as Victoria, there does not have to be formalized or legalized bonds to facilitate spin-off benefits. In its 'you scratch my back and I'll scratch yours' atmosphere there can be future unspecified benefits to tipping a well-off associate to a good deal like the allotment garden property. It's called cronyism.

The Court Case

It's another thing however to be found out to have created a situation where such a good deal can be arranged. The court case in Washington will likely get into this aspect of things in its effort to prove malice aforethought.

My investigations consisted of the obvious cursory and predictable search path. Whether the court case in Washington will turn up any revelations that throw this in a different light is a more important question.

In my view the whole 'Lacey Land Saga' was created to allow this sort of thing to happen.

What I mean by this is the so-called financial crisis was worked up into an unnecessary catastrophe and this allowed certain business transactions to happen that could not have occurred without it. Joseph Finley contends that the whole debenture bond issue was unnecessary or only necessary if the Target offer was refused. Thus the logic of turning away if not down Target's higher offer for the land.

The debenture bond issue caused the sale of surplus lands to take place and this has sunk the diocese deeper and deeper into debt, paying lawyers to fight Finley who was a legitimate business partner, plus paying ongoing costs to maintain the property in Lacey.

The latest development there adds to the catastrophe. The State of Washington is requiring new regulations regarding storm water drainage on such properties, so if the land is not sold in the immediate future and development started by the middle of 2004, the value of the property will drop by 25-30 per cent.

The Diocese by dragging its feet on the sale of the property, by fighting with Finley instead of working with him, has lost more money. If Finley wins the case, and it looks like he will at least on the facts, there will be more huge reparation costs on top of that plus legal fees and damages.

The Garden

Editorial by Marnie Butler

Island Catholic News, Volume 14, No. 9, October 2000

Well, it seems to be a 'done deal' – the diocese will sell the allotment gardens next to Holy Cross Church on Gordon Head Road. This three hectare property will sell for about four million dollars, not as agricultural land, but as re-zoned residential land, and it will be developed as such.

I don't know why I was initially surprised the diocese offered this land for sale. Surely it has a high appraised value and, of all properties being offered, it is probably one of the most desirable and the most saleable pieces of land owned by the diocese, which has excluded both church and school buildings for sale.

And this is not the first time the land has been considered for other uses. With its close proximity to the University of Victoria, apparently the location has been suggested for an ecumenical college and a new Catholic high school, and perhaps other related purposes, by the diocese.

Still it seems so sad that the garden property must go. I know it must be a real heartbreaker for the gardeners, even the co-chair of the Diocesan Debt Repayment Plan and avid gardener Ellis Achtem, will lose his plot. Through many hours these folks have nurtured the land, season by season, year by year, some for 27 years. Many people who use the small garden plots would have liked to buy the land or figure out a lease agreement, but given the appraised value of the property, it was impossible.

Communal gardens, such as the one in Gordon Head, offer more than the opportunity to grow delicious produce and beautiful flowers; they are a vital centre for the building of community and connections, in and out of the garden. They are also a functioning green space, so critical to a healthy environment.

Many years ago, I occasionally went with a friend to tend her small garden plot on the property. A novice gardener, she seemed to know everyone there. "There is lots of good, friendly and free advice here," she said, "as well as plant cuttings and the exchange of seeds. I'm learning so much. I'll have my own home and garden one day."

And she does. I wondered then what a young, single, twenty-something woman did with all the vegetables. "I share them with the seniors in my apartment building," explained my friend, who is a nurse. "Some of them are lonely and kind of isolated. I am concerned about them and it gives me a good excuse to visit."

I am sure there are similar stories from many about how the allotment gardens widened their community connections. I spoke to a woman yesterday who likened them to the "Victory Gardens" of England during the Second World War. "After the gardens were built, usually in vacant lots, we met neighbours we had never known before. We caught up on the local news in the gardens; we were all pulling together."

J.E. Cirlot, in *A Dictionary of Symbols*, defines the garden as "the place where Nature is subdued, ordered, selected and enclosed. Hence it is a symbol of consciousness as opposed to the forest, which is the unconscious, in the same way as the island is opposed to the ocean. At the same time, it is the feminine attribute because of its character as a precinct. A garden is often the scene of 'Conjunction' or treasure-hunts..."

This is a useful definition in terms of the diocesan financial situation. Like a garden we must be 'conscious' and 'contained' when it comes to the sale of diocesan property, and also realize that all our 'treasure' can't be measured in terms of money.

Of course, it is necessary to sell property in order to pay off the recent almost $13 million bond issue when the bonds mature in three years. And the sale of all properties is in the good hands of a committee appointed by Bishop Roussin to oversee the sale of properties both here and in Washington State.

However, during this time we can also "stay awake" as it exhorts in the Gospels. We must be in touch with the feelings of loss and regret. We must be as aware as possible of the impact of the sale of these properties will have, both on the diocesan family, the individuals within that family, and on the greater community.

The People of God here on the Island have proved once again, through the successful bond issue, that they can pull together to reach a common goal. May that goal also include the wise stewardship of all diocesan property.

Commission outraged by De Roo's investments

CHURCH *from page A1*

The report also called on Bishop De Roo to issue a letter to the diocese stating that the investments and loans should have received the proper approval.

It also recommended changes in financial reporting by the diocese, including outside annual audits and permission of the Catholic Church's finance committee and the College of Consultors for any extraordinary expenditure over $25,000.

"I apologize again for my errors," implied.

"While I do not entirely agree with all the statements of the commission and its process, I do endorse the lessons that are to be learned from this experience," he said. "In today's world it is almost impossible for bishops to both tend to the spiritual needs of the diocese and at the same time to be first-class business administrators."

His successor, Bishop Raymond Roussin, said he will implement all the changes recommended by the commission.

"I intend to implement even further changes to ensure the patrimony of the diocese can never again be put at risk through the bad judgment of any small group of people."

A scandal came to light four months ago, Bishop De Roo, 76, over

Roman Catholic bishop Remi De Roo got into a spiral of secret investments that cost the Victoria Diocese $17-million. DIANA NETHERCOTT/The Globe a

The inquiry based its findings on interviews with Bishop De Roo, Ms. Clemenger and 12 other Victoria diocese staff and clergy in April. Ms. Clemenger, who retired at the same time as Bishop De Roo, could not be reached for comment yesterday. Her account of the investments was not highlighted in yesterday's report.

from a trust fund set aside for...
The venture, through a Washington state lawyer named Joseph Finley, failed. By 1992, $2-million the nuns' account known a Priory Trust and diocesan had been invested and lost in bian horses.

To recoup the losses, Bishop Roo said he approved of a ...

THE GLOBE AND MAIL

FOUNDED 1844 • FRIDAY, JUNE 30, 2000

Trust fund for nuns wiped out in Victoria

Pension money used to buy race horses

KIM LUNMAN
British Columbia Bureau, Victoria

A trust fund set up by the Roman Catholic Church in Victoria for elderly nuns' pensions was used for secret investments in Arabian race horses that have left the diocese with a crippling $17-million debt.

The fund, known as the Priory Trust and worth an estimated $1.1-million, was wiped out after a failed $2-million investment in race horses in Washington state in the late 1980s.

A church official in Victoria and a chief investigator in Ottawa, looking into the B.C. diocese's financial woes, said more than half the money used for the unauthorized $2-million loan to buy the horses was taken from the nuns' fund.

"The bank account is gone," said Vernon McLeish, the diocese's new financial administrator. "Everything disappeared. Everything went."

Mr. McLeish said he does not know where the remaining money for the $2-million investment came from because there was no record on the diocese's books for the loan, now being blamed for a scandal that has rocked the Roman Catholic Church in British Columbia.

Monsignor Peter Schonenbach, one of three people appointed by the church to investigate the debt, said the nuns' fund is a key finding in the canonical inquiry's report.

The report by Father Schonenbach, Rev. Bill Woestman, a church-law expert at St. Paul's University in Ottawa, and Bill Broadhurst, chancellor of temporal affairs in the archdiocese of Toronto, is soon to be released.

Father Schonenbach said the Priory Trust was used for the loan in the late 1980s to Joseph Finley, a U.S. lawyer and developer, to invest in Arabian race horses.

According to Mr. McLeish, the

Bishop's secret deals 'beyond belief,' probe finds

Church report blasts Victoria's Remi De Roo

KIM LUNMAN
British Columbia Bureau, Victoria

A report on the financial debacle in the Victoria Roman Catholic Diocese found it "beyond belief" that Bishop Remi De Roo would make secret investments that are now costing his flock more than $17-million.

Bishop De Roo told a church-appointed commission that he made the investments in Arabian horses and a U.S. land deal without the required approval because he was sure they would pay off. The investments were made over the past decade before his retirement last year.

"It is truly beyond belief that he would have jeopardized the patrimony of the diocese without extending his consultation beyond that of the financial officer and legal counsel," the three-member commission stated in a harshly worded 10-page report released yesterday.

The report found that only three people — Bishop De Roo, retired financial administrator Muriel Clemenger and a lawyer acting for the Victoria diocese — knew of the investments that have slipped the

Ironically perhaps the wrong bishop was investigated

"I intend to implement even further changes to ensure the patrimony of the diocese can never again be put at risk through the bad judgment of any small group of people." – Raymond Roussin, June 30, 2000.

"In today's world it is almost impossible for bishops to both tend to the spiritual needs of the diocese and at the same time to be first class business administrators." – Chris Considine, QC, attorney for Remi De Roo.

Chapter 9 – Summer Developments

Some Summer Developments in the 'Lacey Land Saga'

Autumn, 2004

This was a confidential memo to the Board of Directors of *Island Catholic News* about information as I had come to know it about the 'Lacey Land Saga' over the summer of 2004. ICN had become implicated in a court order, so these people needed to be properly briefed.

Part One

1. In early June, before I went away for most of that month, former Victoria Bishop, now Archbishop Raymond Roussin of Vancouver, was deposed to make a sworn statement in the office of Joseph C. Finley's lawyer in Seattle. This encounter lead to all sorts of interesting complications.
2. In May, 2004 Judge Paula Casey in the Superior Court of Washington in Thurston County had repeated her March 12th order to have Roussin appear, after his lawyers from the Archdiocese of Vancouver tried to have her instructions changed on the basis that Roussin was now in charge of another Roman Catholic jurisdiction.
3. The week prior to the Roussin testimony, Finley and his attorney, Cleve Stockmeyer of Seattle, WA, had come to Victoria to do another related deposition, this one with Norman Isherwood, another player in The 'Lacey Land Saga' that has been going on since 1997.
4. On May 24th, a colleague and I spent two and a half hours with Finley and Stockmeyer over coffee in the new Marriott Hotel where they were staying; we briefed them on the overall situation as we knew it to be, in the Diocese of Victoria.

5. We probably did not tell them anything I had not already related to Finley over the phone at some point, but this time Stockmeyer was taking close notes.

6. I had been working with Finley on this particular story since I
was introduced to him in August 2002. Finley has proven a useful
source for "the other side of" what I have come to call the 'Lacey
Land Saga.'

7. As former Bishop Remi De Roo's business partner in *Corporate
Business Park*, the ownership of 160 acres of industrial develop-
ment land on Interstate Highway Five near Lacey, Washington,
Finley has become a key player in the financial workings of the
Diocese of Victoria.

8. Significantly, he became increasingly alienated from the succeeding administration after De Roo left office in February, 1999;
to the point where they are now embroiled in a major legal dispute. This is a prolonged and aggravated court case, a civil dispute, and the ordered depositions were part of that process.

9. The day after our briefing, they deposed Isherwood and a
week later Archbishop Roussin appeared in Cleve Stockmeyer's
Seattle office for his turn.

10. Picking up on some of the details we had given them, the
questioning of Archbishop Roussin had started with character
questions about a member of his staff who had a publicly known
history of sexual harassment allegations.

11. Under sworn testimony, Archbishop Roussin made the mistake of: a) denying knowing anything about this person's troubled
history prior to his having been hired by the diocese; b) denying
knowing there were two more incidents after taking office and
being in his employ; and, most directly, c) denying that these two
women had formally approached him as bishop, set up and attended an appointment to inform him in detail about their harassment experience.

12. If Roussin had his wits about him at the time, (or had been
properly coached), he could quite easily have finessed the questions by simply saying that 'yes we knew about that and tried to

do something about it,'– in which case they may very well have moved on and no damage would have been done.

13. But apparently Raymond Roussin is not that sort of player. Why he immediately moved into denial mode about the situation, why he mislead the court, we may never really know. Unfortunately it was a mistake, and it has come to be a new factor in what has been going on with the Lacey land since Remi De Roo left office in February, 1999.

14. As one friend put it, the archbishop seemed to have forgotten the cardinal rule of court, always assume that a lawyer does not ask any question for which he does not already have an answer.

15. Roussin's denials entirely contradicted what had been conveyed to Finley and his lawyer in the coffee shop of the hotel the day before the Isherwood deposition on May 25. Naturally Finley and Stockmeyer came back to us for further confirmation. We had repeated common information that had been offered in a cautionary context, not foreseeing that this seemingly incidental knowledge, picked up through usually reliable sources, could turn out to be so significant.

16. Prior to my leaving Victoria to travel, but after the Roussin deposition, Finley contacted me and I also spoke with Stockmeyer. They wanted to know how solid this information was that I had given them because if it was true the Archbishop had perjured himself around this matter.

17. I had heard these stories from employees at the diocese in 1999, plus other sources. The person's sexual harassment history prior to the time of being employed by the Diocese was, in the words of one closely placed source, common knowledge.

18. My source left the employment of the diocese in the aftermath of the Remi De Roo discrediting debacle. I called the man and his wife answered. I remembered that she had been the first source of this information for my colleagues at the newspaper.

19. I quickly explained the current situation to this woman who had served as a national leader of a Catholic women's organization, since she had also been an early source of this information.

Before her husband came on the phone, she immediately confirmed that she had heard there were two women at the diocese who had been harassed by this same individual after Roussin took over. She then passed me on to her husband who had personal experience of the situation at the Diocese.

20. This man had worked as a development officer during the last five years of the previous administration.

21. My source told me on the phone that it was common knowledge that the employee in question had a history of sexual harassment allegations. The story on the street was that there had been an early leave-taking from a previous position, on account of alleged sexual harassment of employees and had arrived at the diocese with this reputation.

22. An alleged victim from the earlier era was said to have gone to Bishop Roussin to speak to him about the inappropriateness of hiring such a person to work for the church, I had been told.

23. Roussin might not have directly hired the person. Employment was possibly gained through the new committee that oversaw the financial administration of the diocese.

24. Under sworn testimony, Roussin stated that he trusted this group implicitly. It was this misdirected trust that ultimately got him in more serious financial and personal health difficulties; due to the demoralizing effects of the strain of the 'Lacey Land Saga'.

25. By the time Roussin left office, in January, 2004 the debt had risen from 17 million dollars to 26 million in the figures printed in the *Times Colonist*, Victoria's daily newspaper and the *Diocesan Messenger*, its own organ. In March, 2000 the 17 million dollar figure was accepted at face value as the debt De Roo had incurred; but this was based on the fact the Lacey land had not yet sold. If the land had that equal value, there was no actual debt.

26. Why would such an individual be hired to work with the church's financial affairs? On the shadow side, it gave the committee a hold on him or her. Some information they could use for their own purpose. Such a compromised person would obviously be an entirely loyal employee.

27. At any rate, my source felt strongly enough about it that he said he took measures at the time, in early 1999, to warn the staff at the diocese in the lunch room about what he had heard.

28. He told me in early June that he heard that there had been two specific episodes at the diocese after that but he did not know if the bishop had been directly informed about them. I heard the details of how Roussin had been informed from one of the victims herself.

The Actual Incidents

29. I knew the names of the two individuals. I had a passing acquaintanceship with them through *Island Catholic News*. They had both left the employment of the Diocese a few months after the episodes.

30. I didn't have any trouble getting one of them on the phone and quickly explained that her experience was becoming key to this legal case that she might have heard about.

31. She wanted to know more of what it was all about and after I explained she put the phone down for a moment and I could hear her speaking with her partner, saying: "Remember that stuff I told you about when I was working at the diocese, well this is a reporter who wants to talk to me about it, what do you think?"

32. I heard her partner say something like 'go for it, get the truth out,' so she immediately came back on. In brief she confirmed that there had been an extremely unsettling incident. She gave me the details, how exactly and where she had been touched inappropriately and unnecessarily. She said that she had gone directly to Bishop Roussin and that nothing had been done. This was the reason why she left the employment at the Diocese.

33. She said that a similar episode had happened to the other woman a few days later.

34. The two women made an appointment with Bishop Roussin and explained in detail about it, she explained to me.

35. Previously, she said she had put together an harassment policy proposal for the diocese to adopt, based on her research from

the University of Victoria and presented it to Bishop Roussin that day.

36. The following day she did a follow-up memo to the bishop, recalling their meeting and its purpose and content. She had kept a copy from April 1999. While speaking with her I wondered if once she had reflected on the significance of this new development, she might not want to be so forthcoming about it all. But this was not to be the case. Rather she got stronger in her desire to have it dealt with.

37. In the end she met with Joseph Finley and his lawyer in Victoria over a period of five to six hour. I was present during the whole time, as were her partner and one of my work colleagues.

38. Once she knew where her part fit into the story, she then related her experience in detail and signed a written statement for them to use in court, one that basically and unequivocally contradicted everything Bishop Roussin had denied.

39. She also handed them a copy of the memo she made in April, 1999, a copy of which had been given to Roussin on the day following the two women's appointment to tell him about the episodes.

Part Two

40. The day after Archbishop Roussin's flawed testimony in Seattle, his lawyers made an application to the court to have the entire testimony suppressed, naming *Island Catholic News* as they only media in particular which should not be allowed to see the document. So from this time *Island Catholic News* was more deeply implicated in the case because of the reporting it had done over the previous eighteen months; nine stories in 18 issues of the paper between January, 2003 and August 2004.

41. ICN was depicted in the Diocese's application as serving merely as 'a mouthpiece for Joe Finley's interests,' so it was necessary to issue an affidavit spelling out the history and purpose of the newspaper and our particular interest in this case. I did this from Europe.

42. ICN's involvement started as an effort to clarify the situation around the discrediting of Bishop De Roo's name in 2000 when the story broke so sensationally that he was responsible for such huge debt that required draconian measures to recover the loss.

43. As we got into the story over a number of years, but particularly after interviewing Finley in depth, it became clear that we had been correct that there was politics at play in the controversy.

44. I did a fourteen page affidavit that claimed ICN was a legitimate newspaper that had been on this and similar stories of political discrediting since its inception in 1987, in effect, but especially since the mid-1990s when the political climate within the Catholic church had become so divided.

45. I referred to my 2002 book, *In The Avant Garde*, a biographical study of Bishop De Roo which attempted to set the context of his career and discrediting within the historical political framework of the church during the Twentieth Century. This De Roo discrediting in our view is just the latest instance in a long line of such angry politics. In the end, only the sexual harassment section of Roussin's deposition was temporarily suppressed as a result of the Diocese' action.

46. Besides this perjury situation, other related developments had transpired over the summer of 2004. Finley had obtained a sworn statement from Patrick McCourt, a land developer in the Washington State area who had made a publicly reported bid in July, 2001 to purchase the Lacey land.

47. The *Times Colonist* newspaper of Victoria had reported in its July 21, 2001 edition, on its front page that *Barclays Bank North*, a company owned and operated by McCourt had offered 9.6 million dollars (US) for the *Corporate Business Park*. On August 28 of the same year the *Times Colonist* reported that the deal had fallen through. This was reported on the lead page of the second section of the newspaper.

48. The significance of this is in what McCourt reported he wanted to do with the land if he got it at less than $10 million (US). His

purpose was to sell it immediately to Target Corporation who were prepared to buy such a size piece for more than $14 million (US).

49. In his sworn statement McCourt claimed that he made that bid solely on the knowledge that he could turn right around and sell the property to Target Corporation who he knew were looking for warehouse land in that area.

50. When they could not get the *Corporate Business Park* land, Target did buy a slightly smaller piece immediately adjacent to the *Corporate Business Park* site for $14.4 million (US). This was a piece of land that did not suit their purposes as well as CBP but since they could not get the Diocese to take any interest in selling to them, they had to settle for the smaller less desirable piece of property for their purposes. Earlier than the McCourt statement, this had been outlined in Finley's hundred page statement of claim in his suit against the Diocese of Victoria.

51. Finley as the diocese' business partner, would have benefitted from such a sale. He was claiming that Target had made a purchase offer and that the Diocese had refused to pursue the offer thus costing him his share of the profit. This had been the original arrangement with De Roo, that after an original debt of two million dollars was paid and the diocese had recovered its further investment, that the profit would be shared between the two partners. The Target deal would have made the debenture bond offering of the year 2000 redundant and kept the so-called surplus lands of the diocese safe from the fire-sale prices.

52. Because it did not make sense for the diocese to turn down such an offer, it could not be true. This was the logic of the chief business writer of *The Vancouver Sun* when I presented him with the contradiction. It may have reflected the rationalization of many other presumably intelligent observers. We spoke via telephone.

53. In David Baines' expressed view, Finley was a dubious character, he had seen so many like him before, a hustler at best who wasn't going to con him too. I was dumbfounded by his attitude, why he would assume the church's business partner was like this. Evidence was mounting that both sides can play this game. His

attitude did not make any sense to me. Baines' reputation was as a crack investigative reporter who had broken the Vancouver Stock Exchange story when it was at risk of losing its registration.

54. Baines did say that if there ever was any confirmation that there had actually been a Target offer, he would like to know about it. As it turned out, he was just kidding. When I got back to Baines about the Patrick McCourt statement, he said "So what?"

55. The story began and ended for him with Remi De Roo's foul up, he said. What did it matter if anyone was interested in this piece of land, which was way out in the boondocks anyway? Such cynicism shocked me, even in an informal conversation.

56. I started to wonder what was going on. There was lots of evidence that Target was interested. *The Globe and Mail* reporter Robert Matas had written it up in *The Globe's* September 26, 2002 edition. Matas' attitude and article were the exact opposite of Baines'.

57. Finley had a sworn statement dated March 6, 2001 from Realtor Don Moody of CB Richard Ellis realtors saying he brought the Target offer to The Diocese of Victoria, who had failed to inform Finley as their business partner about this prospect. Finley was able to convince a jury of his case.

58. Finley outlined all this in detail during the famous Public Library meeting of November 26th, 2002. This meeting attended by 60 interested clergy, bondholders, parishioners, citizens and the media was videotaped for distribution and formed the basis of a special edition of *Island Catholic News* dated January, 2003.

59. The Diocese' reaction to this edition formed the basis of the defamation case that is also a key part of the case Finley is pursuing against the diocese. A letter was distributed to all parishes under Bishop Roussin's signature saying that the whole edition was full of falsehoods as was Finley's claim. Roussin admitted in his deposition that he had not written, had hardly even read this damaging statement.

60. This letter, which was published by ICN along with Finley's refutation of its allegations, (see **Chapter 5**) plus an offer of mediation to solve the problem, resulted in *Island Catholic News* being

removed from most Catholic parishes on Vancouver Island, certainly the larger ones, particularly Holy Cross, Sacred Heart and Saint Andrew's Cathedral in Victoria. These had always been previously liberal-minded parishes that took an interest in ICN's justice-oriented critical edge style.

61. This action by the Bishop cost *Island Catholic News* half its annual income, all of its larger advertising and sales and distribution through the parishes, its normal channel of distribution. The advertising stopped because all Catholic businessmen were expected to get on side with the Diocese's claims about the situation against De Roo. When ICN refused to buy it, it was punished in the way business men deal with such political situations, All Money Ends Now – AMEN.

Part Three

62. Besides these developments, there were other related matters. In the July edition of ICN I published a story I had ready before going away on holidays, about the former allotment gardens at Gordon Head, next to Holy Cross parish. It got into the details of how it had been sold as 'surplus land' for 3.78 million dollars Canadian to a wealthy realtor/developer whose sons had grossed eighteen million dollars on the sale of the subsequent housing units erected on the site.

63. This had been a piece of property that served a social purpose, a common good project where people from the parish and the neighborhood could grow food together. Bishop De Roo had resisted the idea of selling it commercially. It was the first land to be sold under the debenture land offering as though someone had their eye on it for a long time.

64. If it had to be done, I wondered why the diocese could not do such a development itself, gain the profit for the debt situation. It had been done before in the 1980s, in the same area -- Gordon Head. All the advisors who surrounded Roussin in the financial administration of the diocese had this sort of expertise and experience.

They did it every day for themselves so why could they not apply their trade for the good of the church they were always claiming to be so concerned about while blaming De Roo for the troubles. So naturally many of us wondered who was gaining behind the scenes and how?

65. Norm Isherwood called to say that he had stumbled upon the Allotment Garden story – he had not read any of the previous eight segments in the series – so he was shocked and hurt that anyone could take this sort of perspective on what he had assumed was just a bunch of honest brokers bringing their talents to bear to help the church out of a difficult situation, not of its own making.

66. He revealed to me that he had been the one, a non-Catholic -- who had been instrumental in selling all the so-called surplus lands of the diocese, including the allotment gardens in Gordon Head. We had a lengthy chat where he threatened to call a lawyer for what was implied. I assured him that he was not who I had in mind with my suggested allegations. In the end he seemed calmed down enough.

67. All the time I was speaking with him, I was thinking about what I knew about Norm Isherwood himself, some of which he must have known was public knowledge. A private investigator had been set on his case and found that the *Times Colonist* of May 25, 2002, (byline Gerard Young), reported that a new building had gained approval for the 844 View Street property, one of the so-called surplus lands of the diocese. Norm Isherwood was listed as a principal in the purchase of the property, and the property was among that listed as surplus land sold by Isherwood himself to purportedly pay off the debenture bond holders.

68. He had sworn in his deposition that he had not gained from the surplus land he helped to sell. I knew Isherwood was a member of the original Lacey land subcommittee and that he and Finley had met a number of times in Seattle at the time of the revelation to Finley of the Target offer in spring, 2001. We had carried all that documentation in the Special Lacey Land Edition of ICN,

January 2003. (see Chapter 4, Finley's chronicle towards approach to Target)

69. In terms of the Lacey land, I heard that an offer is still on the table despite the Diocese' denial about any number of them. Madison Project One is offering $11.3 million (U.S.) and the Diocese was asking 11.6 but the offer still has not been accepted despite the fact that this amount would pay back the debenture bond holders.

70. $13 million (CDN) was raised from over a thousand bondholders. They were to be paid back with interest at 6 per cent after three years but this did not occur, rather the bonds were voluntarily renewed in 2003 to 80 per cent, with more new money coming in at the time of the renewal. The Diocese considered this a great success.

Part Four

71. The court ordered the Diocese and Joseph Finley into mediation to try to solve their problem. While that negotiation is on, the sexual harassment section of Roussin's deposition is suppressed. Finley has made an offer of $10.5 million (US) which is calculated to be enough to pay off the debenture bond holders and leave a little something for the Diocese itself. But now the debt has risen to $26 million (CDN) and the Diocese is showing no interest in Finley's offer.

72. They decided not to sell Finley the Lacey land. That sale would not have taken care of the risen debt figure. It was said all along that no actual church or school property would be sold, just the so-called surplus lands, such as the allotment garden land.

73. The Isherwood revelations indicate some irregularities and the obvious cronyism of the Gordon Head Allotment Garden development.

74. What is the Western Canada Bank's role in all of this? It is the bank of record of the Diocese since Roussin took over and all the property sales and developments such as the allotment garden, the View street property that Isherwood says he did not buy, have

been worked through that bank. It held the Lacey land appraisal and is the bank connected to the Fisgard Capital assumption of the mortgage of the Lacey land, the so-called arms-length arrangement that Finley calls a straw man.

75. All this needs to be investigated by a competent journalist and a major newspaper that has the resources to properly do so. But we have seen both the attitude of David Baines at The Sun and how The *Times Colonist* in Victoria has operated since the word go; when they featured De Roo on the front page thirty times in six months in 2000 and have not investigated any other sides of this irregular story.

76. So the question becomes, will the new bishop in Victoria, Richard Gagnon, the former vicar general in Vancouver, be able to take an independent look at all the curious contradictions and self-serving attitudes. It's the key question to the recovery of the financial health of the Diocese of Victoria. Realistically it is not very likely as he is still surrounded by the same 'advisors'.

Joseph Finley with Cleve Stockmeyer at the Marriott Hotel in Victoria, May 24, 2004. They were in the city for the Norman Isherwood deposition.

Chapter 10 – Joseph Finley

Why Won't the Bishop of Victoria Deal with This Man?

Island Catholic News, Volume 18, No. 10, November 2004

Why the Diocese of Victoria will not properly relate to its business partner Joseph C. Finley is still the question plaguing the sale of the church's Lacey land property especially when two more offers have been refused, ones that would involve enough money to 'pay all the debentures in full,' according to Finley.

Finley is the Diocese' business partner on *Corporate Business Park*, (CBP) a hundred and sixty acre industrial development property since 1997. CBP is situated in Lacey, Washington and the Diocese has been trying to divest Finley of his interest since 2000 with a series of court actions to which he has responded.

This action and reaction scenario has resulted in a major civil court case with charges by Finley of fraud, defamation of character, breach of fiduciary responsibility on the part of the Diocese; plus use of illegal tactics such as the creation of 'a straw man' to assume ownership of the mortgage of the property.

Latest Developments

In the latest developments in the case, in September Judge Paula Casey of Thurston County Superior Court, Washington ordered the two partners into mediated negotiations to settle the dispute, whereby Finley made an offer of $10.5 million (US) to take full ownership of the property.

Finley states that this figure is based on the appraised value of the land and is enough for the debenture bond holders (who loaned the diocese enough money to buy back the mortgage) in the Catholic Diocese to receive their investment back plus something left over for the Diocese.

Due to all the costs of the legal battle with Finley over the past four years, the debt listed by the Diocese has risen much higher than the original figure of $17 million (CDN) said to be the cause of the financial crisis when first announced.

More than a thousand debenture bond buyers provided $13 million (CDN) in 2000 (and renewed in 2003) for Fisgard Capital to purchase the mortgage of the property away from the debtor. This is the ploy Finley charges is 'a straw man' structure, illegal in the United States. Finley is claiming that Fisgard is not really an arm's length body, but one controlled by the Diocese.

The situation has grown so estranged and acrimonious that the two partners can hardly agree to disagree, resulting in the almost automatic refusal by the diocese of any offer associated with Mr. Finley, or that he is in agreement with.

Since the summer, the Diocese has refused Finley's $10.5 million dollar (US) offer and another related one for 11.3 million (US) by Madison Project One who Finley brought to the table and with whom he was prepared to work with on the subsequent development of the property post-purchase.

Finley said he was then prepared to waive his legal claim and drop his law suit if the offer was taken. He was still prepared to drop his action if his 10.5 million dollar offer was taken (which he claims is the equivalent of a $11.6 million all cash offer from a third party because of specific savings which he outlines in his letter).

The Diocese' Thinking

The Diocese of Victoria refuses to deal with Finley, firmly believing it will prevail in the end. In the meantime the debt rises, questions about the debenture bond holders ever getting their return persist, and the Diocese feels forced to sell its surplus land at approximately half its listed value.

ICN examined one such property in its July 2004 Edition, that of the Gordon Head Allotment Garden next to Holy Cross Church on Gordon Head Road, near the university.

That property was sold for $3.78 million (CDN) and the subsequent development of town houses on the property sold for over $18 million. In response to this story (which raised the question of who was benefitting behind the scenes and why the church itself had not done the project to make the needed profit to pay down the debt), ICN received a call from the agent who claimed to have sold all the so-called surplus lands.

This individual, himself a land developer, who volunteered to help the church committee overseeing the situation, expressed dismay and hurt at the suggestions in the story, that anyone was improperly benefitting either directly or indirectly from these sales.

Conflict of Interest?

The call was from Norman Isherwood, a property developer in Canada and the United States. Prior to the phone call, ICN only knew Mr. Isherwood as a member of the Lacey land committee who had been part of negotiations with Mr. Finley in 2001 when Mr. Finley tried to work with the Diocese to sell the Lacey property to Target Corporation who wished to build a huge warehouse in the Lacey area.

That potential deal fell flat due to lack of co-operation of the Diocese with Mr. Finley. Nevertheless Target did buy a smaller piece of adjacent property although it did not suit their purposes as well as *Corporate Business Park* would have. Target paid $14.4 million (US) for the smaller piece of land. All the details of this Target offer form a significant section of Mr. Finley's claim against the Diocese.

He states in his letter dated September 28, 2004 that the judge has presently advised the Diocese it will "have to go to trial on the claims for fraud and breach of fiduciary duties."

Mr. Isherwood and former Bishop of Victoria Raymond Roussin were each deposed to make sworn statements in the court case. These were ordered by Judge Casey in May, 2004.

As part of his statement Mr. Isherwood stated on page 41 of the transcript from the court record that he did not buy any of the surplus land sales (which would have consisted a conflict of interest).

Research into the matter in the pages of the *Times Colonist* for 2002, however, revealed him listed as a principal for the purchase and development of the 840 View Street property that was part of the surplus land sales to pay back the debenture bond holders.

According to the *Times Colonist* article dated May 25, 2002, under the byline of business writer Gerard Young who has been following the Lacey land story since it first broke in the pages of the *Times Colonist* in March, 2000: "The property is owned by the Roman Catholic Bishop of Victoria, as head of the diocese. It is one of the properties the church offered for sale on Vancouver Island after former bishop Remi De Roo put the diocese $17 million in debt with failed horse and land investments."

"Developer Stan Sipos, who along with Rob Hunter and Norm Isherwoood are principals in the building to be known as the Stafford, said the sale price is about $1 million."

Finley's Latest Offer

In the cover letter to *Island Catholic News* regarding his latest offer to purchase the *Corporate Business Park* property Joseph Finley explains that the "way this offer is structured is the equivalent of an all cash offer from a third party for $11.6 million (US)."

He states elsewhere about his relations with the Diocese: "I confess to being mystified by the collective group that is advising/running the Diocese. They have caused the Diocese to lose many millions of dollars over the last four years for their unbelievably ill-advised decisions relating to the Target deal and subsequent events. They have lately proclaimed in open court that the Washington property is worth $11.5 million (US) and stated that they want to sell, but when presented with an offer, they balk, refuse to negotiate or simply run and hide...

"One could ask how decisions are getting made. Why turn down a solid offer for the true value of the property... I would rather not spend another year of my life righting the wrong that took place here, but I am not afraid of the battle and not afraid of the outcome. I have nothing to lose...

"The people running the Diocese, Archbishop Roussin and their lawyers made a gross miscalculation when they decided to try to take the property for themselves and not live up to their obligations. They made another gross miscalculation when they thought I would not be able to fight them."

Cover Letter Detailing All-Cash Offer

"None of the diocese' committee members would run their successful businesses that way – they would go broke."

September 28, 2004

Island Catholic News:

I am attaching a copy of an offer that I recently made to the Diocese and the Debenture Trustee. They made a letter offer, also attached, that was received after mine was made to them, and I authorized a response from my attorney, which is attached as well.

The Diocese and their lawyers think that the Washington Supreme Court will not accept my Petition for Review, and we expect a decision in October. This has their sails full again, but even if the Petition is not accepted it does not end the case. All it would do is allow the debenture trustee to sell the property.

The next battle will come over where the proceeds of any sale would go, and we already have a motion pending before the Court to require all sales proceeds to be held pending the outcome of our jury trial against the Diocese next May.

The Diocese's attorneys moved to dismiss all of my claims, and they lost. The judge denied their motion and advised them that they would have to go to trial on the claims against the Diocese for fraud and breach of fiduciary duties.

I confess to being mystified by the collective group that is advising / running the Diocese. They have caused the Diocese to lose many millions of dollars over the last four years for their unbelievably ill-advised decisions relating to the Target deal and subsequent events.

They have lately proclaimed in open court that the Washington property is worth $11.5 million and stated that they want to sell, but when presented with an offer, they balk, refuse to negotiate or simply run and hide.

My offer to the Diocese is for $10.5 million (US), all cash in 120 days or less. It is backed up by $300,000 (US), non-refundable, as earnest money. In addition, I will pay for a site plan for the property at the cost of $150,000. If for any reason I do not close, they get the benefit of the site plan.

The way this offer is structured is the equivalent of an all cash offer from a third party for $11.6 million (US): 1) because a settlement is involved, there is no excise tax. Otherwise on the sale of the property to any other party this alone will cost them $200,000; 2) no broker commission is involved – a saving of $575,000; 3) I offered to pay the cost of a special assessment on the property for roads and sewer, $322,000. An arms-length commercial buyer will not agree to do that.

And, the above is conditioned on a full and complete settlement of all claims among the parties. When those claims are settled, the case is over. If I do not close on the property, the claims do not come back. Stated otherwise, the worst consequence of my not buying the property as proposed is that in 120 days the Diocese would have $300,000 (US) in cash. They would have a site plan for the property at no cost to them. And they would have no further litigation expense or exposure.

They refuse to agree to the settlement structure either out of ignorance or based on a desire to be punitive to me. I get very little from this deal, but the tax structure is valuable to me, and neither the Diocese nor the Debenture Trustee can use it. One never knows where they are on price. During the recent mediation they threw out numbers as low as $10.1 million and they have been as high as $11.5 million.

What is known is that absent a settlement, we are going after the sale proceeds if need be and we are going after damages in excess of $6 million (US) at trial in May. Based on the way the Diocese's lawyers bill for their time, I expect that they will run up well over another $500,000 between now and the end of the trial.

One could ask how decisions are getting made. Why turn down a solid offer for the true value of the property and get a settlement in the bargain when the litigation risk and expense is well into seven figures? It is obviously in the lawyers' best interest to keep the case going, but it is hard to see how the Diocese comes out ahead on that type of decision-making.

I am confident that we will prove a constructive fraud and breach of fiduciary duties by the Diocese at trial. (This will be a two-week jury trial and will no doubt get a lot of media attention given the nature of the claims.) I believe that the damage award could be well into seven figures, maybe as high as $6 or $7 million. *(Actual award was $8.167 million (US).)*

I would rather not spend another year of my life righting the wrong that took place here, but I am not afraid of the battle and not afraid of the outcome. I have nothing to lose.

The people running the Diocese, Archbishop Roussin and their lawyers made a gross miscalculation when they decided to try to take the property for themselves and not live up to their obligations. They made another gross miscalculation when they thought I would not be able to fight them.

They have invested well over $1 million of Diocesan funds in legal bills in those miscalculations, and they have cost the Diocese at least another $6 million by squandering Diocesan property at distressed prices to support their endeavor, not to mention that they have a total loss of their prior $3.5 million investment in the Washington land. That is at least $10 million lost for no discernible reason whatsoever other than malice and ego and bad judgment. *None of the Diocese's committee members would run their successful businesses that way – they would go broke.*

Now they have a chance to make another decision. Let's hope for everyone's sake that they start to choose more carefully.

Very truly yours,

Joseph Finley

P.S. Please note that this offer is for enough money to pay all of the debentures in full and have $300,000 or $400,000 left over.

ICN & The 'Lacey Land Saga'
– *Framing Gospel Values* –
Editorial

Island Catholic News, Volume 18, No. 11, December 2004

It seems well past due to explain why *Island Catholic News* takes the editorial posture it does regarding the 'Lacey Land Saga' of the Diocese of Victoria; now three bishops later.

In a recent letter to a supporter who feels conflicted by the newspaper's editorial position, we wrote to her in reply: "We feel that it is the job of the newspaper to urge, cajole and badger the diocese into doing the right things because they have transparently lost their way both financially and morally, confusing gospel values with the world's."

So, what are these gospel values which ICN claims it knows so much about? Justice and fairness, obviously, and compassion and forgiveness and not holding a grudge. ICN believes the gospel of Jesus Christ requires that we not view life in this world as an alien adventure but as an invitation to transformative values and an ample and abiding opportunity for grace.

The Lacey land situation has reduced things to an 'us versus them' situation with all its attendant acrimony, grudge bearing and unnecessary loss.

Unfortunately, this is the common plight of many dioceses, caught as they are with the twin challenges of preserving an aging institutional framework with a dwindling budget, (and buying into the capitalist scheme to do it). But none of this is any excuse for sidelining the primacy of the gospel call.

That the Diocese of Victoria has gotten lost financially is no secret, we are more concerned with the moral compassing.

On the surface their explanation is that the diocese does not wish to deal with its alienated business partner, but the cost of this is getting somewhat ridiculous and prohibitive to the diocesan parishioners, particularly the debenture bondholders.

Diocesan statistics published in the *Diocesan Messenger* state there are less than 8,000 weekly regular donor in the parishes, (i.e. envelope users) so this is quite a high percentage of the weekly Catholics. On the other hand, the Canadian Conference of Catholic Bishops use the Statistics Canada census figure of nearly 100,000 people who identify themselves as Roman Catholic on Vancouver Island. At least three quarters of these numbers of people no longer identify with the local Diocesan Church yet still consider themselves Catholics. So the question in this context becomes where is the Catholic church? Or better, who makes up the Catholic church – Catholics or the institution? This tension goes a long way in explaining *Island Catholic News'* attitude towards the Diocese of Victoria. Is the institution always correct?, or do the 80 percent who have voted with their feet and walked away have something relevant to say?

2.

Since January 2003, ICN has published a series of articles examining the ongoing financial crisis in a certain light. The reaction has been two-fold. Some, like our letter writer, are not appreciative of airing the church's dirty laundry in public and feel the situation requires complete loyalty to the institution of the church as it muddles its way through. Our sort of 'disloyalty' can be baffling if not infuriating to these people.

On the other hand, ICN has experienced a renewal through the support and interest of others who feel this story needs to be told in just the way we have been doing it, from the other side of the ledger – if only to rectify some sort of balance to the public perception of the situation.

This attitude is accompanied by a distaste for the sort of 'power and control model' they see in the church generally, but particularly around this issue.

There are any number of possible explanations as to why the situation has devolved so drastically; and therefore requires ICN's vigilance around moral compassing.

One explanation is that somehow a moral blindness has become built into the makeup and structure of the administration and that due to this the diocese has projected its shadow energy onto its alienated business partner and as such feels it cannot in good conscience deal with the devil.

This is a normal moral problem and is actually the 'positive' explanation. The simple grace of forgiveness and reconciliation between the partners could take care of this. As such this is actually a positive situation, in that it is simply remedied if there is a good will on both sides.

This explanation is predicated on the fact that the financial-administrative team is made up entirely of wealthy, elderly, white, males who think a certain way which is making it worse in effect.

More balance needs to be brought to the perspective. More community and communion through the rectifying presence of non-white, non-elderly, non-male, non-wealthy people – in other words, ordinary people with more common sense.

You can be certain that if ordinary people were running the show with this Lacey land situation, it would not be dragging on for five years, or be nearly half the mess with the estimated debt now reach 25 million dollars according to the *Diocesan Messenger*.

Let's give the people of the diocese – especially the debenture bond holders – a present this Christmas, see some common sense and settle the situation to the satisfaction of all. Until it is straightened up, you can be sure ICN will be watching with its eye fixed on what we call gospel values and their attendant transformative grace.

Small Paper Persists Despite Theft of Distribution Boxes
Island Catholic News, Volume 19, No 4, May 2005

VICTORIA—*Island Catholic News*, Vancouver Island's independent Roman Catholic newspaper, has been hit with persistent theft of its distribution boxes throughout the region.

According to Patrick Jamieson, managing editor of the monthly newspaper, now in its nineteenth year of publication for 'Vancouver Island and the Gulf Islands,' eight distribution boxes have mysteriously disappeared over the past number of months.

"Two were taken from the Oak Bay village area, one in Sidney, two most recently in Saanich. Another three have disappeared overnight in Victoria, one on Blanshard Street near St. Andrew's Cathedral," Jamieson stated. "It's mysterious because they are placed beside the other community papers and ours are the only ones that disappear so consistently."

Jamieson says he doesn't really know who or why they have been stolen, whether it is vandalism, or actually aimed at the little independent newspaper which has consistently taken many controversial positions on social, political and Catholic issues.

"The latest was the same sex marriage issue in March," Jamieson stated, "two boxes were taken at that point."

"We have taken an independent stand on that issue since the late 1990s. We have also contradicted the official line of the Diocese of Victoria on the controversial Lacey land issue since 2000 when you might say the paper's troubles started."

As a result the newspaper has become highly unpopular in certain official circles within the Catholic church on Vancouver Island to the point of being removed from the Catholic parishes in Victoria.

"We were officially removed from many parishes and most of our major large Catholic advertisers have pulled their ads, due to the Lacey land contretemps," Jamieson stated. "Our income has been cut by more than half. In its heyday the paper had a budget of $70,000 dollars annually, now it hovers around thirty thousand due to these punitive actions, just because we dare to step out of line on certain issues."

"This filters down to the general Catholic population and many of them don't know quite how to react, I sense from the response I receive on the street," Jamieson explained.

"I suspect some of these thefts and destruction are the result of that translation to the level of individual Catholics who feel they should take some drastic action to do something about the situation, but we don't really know. We are reduced to such speculation unless we get hard information from the public at this time." The municipal police have been informed but to no effect, the thefts continue.

The newspaper has flourished spiritually under the new era of alienation from the Diocese, Jamieson claims. "Many new people have come forward with fresh energy, like-minded sorts who feel you can be Roman Catholic and independent adults in your faith development process. The age of censorship is over, so Catholics who are mature in their faith identify with the little newspaper as a sign of that," according to the ICN spokesperson.

ICN is a provincial non-profit society and a registered federal charity and is supported by donations, subscriptions, 'donations in kind' as well as advertising which is slowly being built back up due to the hard work of board members, Jamieson explained. "Admittedly, it's a new approach to running a church paper, created in response to an extraordinary situation," the founding editor stated,

"But I personally find it energizing, similar to the original start-up period in 1986."

"We are busy with a new distribution strategy which involves the use of these boxes so we definitely cannot afford to lose them. We are having a new type built for us. The ones that have been stolen were actually originally designed for inside placement in the parish churches, so they are not strictly suitable for outdoor use unless under a sheltered cover.

"Because they are so small they lend themselves to being easily carried away. The new ones are designed for better visibility and security purposes. We need help with this."

"If we could get some clues as to who took any of them, it would help us with the profile of the nature of the problem, and how to prevent it," Jamieson said.

"It may just be simple street vandalism, or it could be targeted for theological reasons by misdirected souls. We are certainly losing patience with the situation and are prepared to exercise the full extent of the law in the matter. The telltale sign is that only ICN boxes go missing."

"The boxes are worth a hundred dollars each at least, so it is adding up to major theft. They were originally built by the Saint Vincent de Paul Society in the late 1980s as a gift but we will have to find the money for the new ones."

SECTION S · OBITUARIES, S8 · CLASSIFIED, S9

Globe B.C. & Sports

THE GLOBE AND MAIL ■ CANADA'S NATIONAL NEWSPAPER ■ GLOBEANDMAIL.COM ■ TUESDAY

Retired bishop Remi De Roo, shown in 1999, was caught in the changing political tides of the church, says Patrick Jamieson, managing editor of the Island Catholic News.

Bishop De Roo vindicated

Washington State jury backs land deal cleric made in U.S. with church funds

BY ROBERT MATAS, VANCOUVER

Months after Roman Catholic Bishop Remi De Roo retired in 1999, church officials shocked the country with accusations that the popular theologian had misspent millions of dollars from a nuns' trust and buying land in the U.S. for a quick flip.

Six years after the explosive allegations were made, a jury in the Superior Court of Washington has vindicated the bishop.

Contrary to allegations by church officials, the jury decided the bishop, who was head of the Victoria diocese, had made a solid investment. During the 2½ week trial in Olympia, the state capital, the court heard that the land at the centre of the controversy may have increased in value as much as fivefold since its purchase.

The church had no grounds for violating its contract with U.S. businessman Joseph Finley after Bishop De Roo retired, the jury found in a vote of 11 to 1.

The jury awarded $8.2-million (U.S.) to Mr. Finley for damages caused by breach of contract and $4.2-million for breach of fiduciary duty. A date has not yet been scheduled for a judge to confirm the jury's verdict and set the payment that Mr. Finley will be entitled to receive.

"They have exonerated him. The decision validates [Bishop] De Roo's financial judgment," Patrick Jamieson, managing editor of the Island Catholic News, said yesterday in an interview. "This judgment proves he was not such a bad administrator."

Mr. Jamieson said the controversy arose from church politics. Bishop De Roo was well known for his liberal views on gays, married priests and women in the church. The Catholic Church has become more conservative in recent years, Mr. Jamieson said. "He was caught in a backtide."

Church officials who did not support the former bishop on church issues were too quick to accuse him of fiscal mismanagement, Mr. Ja-

mieson added. None of the church leaders in Canada spoke to Bishop De Roo's defence when allegations of fiscal mismanagement first surfaced. The land deal would have worked out if the church had honoured its deal with the U.S. businessman and had not attacked the former bishop in public, he said.

Bishop De Roo, 81, was not available for comment yesterday. He apologized publicly in June of 2000 for his "errors." Recently, according to his website, he has been lecturing and holding retreats.

See CHURCH on page S3

Jury Backs De Roo

"Six years after the explosive allegations were made, a jury in the Superior Court of Washington has vindicated the bishop … the church had no grounds for violating its contract with U.S. businessman Joseph Finley after Bishop De Roo retired, the jury found in a vote of 11 to 1. The jury awarded $8.2-million (US) to Mr. Finley for damages caused by breach of contract and $4.2-million for breach of fiduciary duty."

184

Chapter 11 – Trial Results in 'Vindication'

Lacey Land Partnership Trial Scheduled for Olympia, Washington

Island Catholic News, Volume 19, No. 5, June 2005

The long awaited business partnership trial between the Diocese of Victoria and Joseph C. Finley, an American lawyer and land developer started Monday May 9 at the Superior Court of Thurston County, Washington at Olympia and is expected to last between two and three weeks.

This is the court case that has threatened since 2000 when the Diocesan administration decided to attempt to end the partnership with Mr. Finley around *Corporate Business Park* (CBP) in Lacey, Washington.

CBP was the jointly owned tract of heavy industrial land entered into by former Bishop Remi J, De Roo in 1997 with Mr. Finley in an effort to make a profit that would eradicate an earlier loss in a business deal with Mr. Finley.

In the earlier failed business deal, dating from the late 1980s, the Diocese lost one million dollars on a short term bridge financing loan to Mr. Finley's Arabian show horse business Swiftsure Farms, also located in the State of Washington. This was at a time when the federal tax structure in the United States effecting show horses was altered reducing the worth of show horses to five percent of what they had been.

Conflict between the two parties began immediately after Bishop De Roo left office in February, 1999 but came to a head a year later when the Diocese publicly announced a huge financial crisis due to the arrangement. At that point the Diocese took legal steps to gain control of the land, cancel the partnership and justify the situation.

Mr. Finley co-operated to a certain degree but eventually launched a court action to prove that there had been a breach of fiduciary responsibility on the part of the Diocese due to their actions. The current trial, more than five years on, is the culmination of that legal procedure.

The trial is by judge and jury and a key witness for Mr. Finley is expected to be former diocesan financial administrator Muriel Clemenger who served in that capacity with Bishop De Roo during the time of the Swiftsure loan and the *Corporate Business Park* venture.

Mr. Finley is claiming that there were a number of high level offers for and interest in the *Corporate Business Park* land that were ignored, refused or unattended to by the Diocese costing him his share of the profit from the partnership.

The Diocese which successfully gained control of the property after buying back the mortgage from the original lender recently accepted an offer to sell the land. Mr. Finley is expected to argue it was a low-ball offer that was deliberately below the threshold under which he could make any profit. Finley also claims that there were any number of larger offers which were deliberately ignored, some of which he facilitated himself in his role as a partner.

The Diocese has maintained all along that *Corporate Business Park* was not a sound investment from the start and that Bishop De Roo did not go through the proper church channels to start the deal; and that they are simply trying to make the best of a faulty situation.

The result of the trial will go a long way at establishing the permanent record of the affair, determining whether Bishop De Roo was a sound fiscal manager, whether CBP was a sound business investment, and whether he or his successor caused the diocesan losses.

If Mr. Finley wins a settlement, this will add further cost to the diocese' much publicized financial woes and cast a shadow on the financial decisions made under the subsequent bishop Raymond

Roussin who followed De Roo into the Office of Bishop and is now the Archbishop of Vancouver.

Archbishop Roussin was already deposed to make a sworn statement in the proceedings, This in itself became controversial when his lawyers moved the next day after his testimony to suppress the testimony from the media in particular naming *Island Catholic News* which has been attending to the story closely since 2002.

Only part of Archbishop Roussin's testimony was allowed to be suppressed in June, 2004, but it all is expected to play a part in the trial which started in earnest May 9.

Bishop De Roo Vindicated

Washington State jury backs land deal cleric made in U.S. with church funds

By Robert Matas
Excerpted from the May 31, 2005 edition of
The Globe and Mail

VANCOUVER — Months after Roman Catholic Bishop Remi De Roo retired in 1999, church officials shocked the country with accusations that the popular theologian had misspent millions of dollars from a nuns' trust fund buying land in the U.S. for a quick flip.

Six years after the explosive allegations were made, a jury in the Superior Court of Washington has vindicated the bishop.

Contrary to allegations by church officials, the jury decided the bishop, who was head of the Victoria diocese, had made a solid investment. During the 2 ½ week trial in Olympia, the state capital, the court heard that the land at the center of the controversy may have increased in value as much as fivefold since its purchase.

The church had no grounds for violating its contract with U.S. businessman Joseph Finley after Bishop De Roo retired, the jury found in a vote of 11 to 1.

The jury awarded $8.2-million (U.S.) to Mr. Finley for damages caused by breach of contract and $4.2-million for breach of fiduciary duty. A date has not yet been scheduled for a judge to confirm the jury's verdict and set the payment that Mr. Finley will be entitled to receive.

"They have exonerated him. The decision validates [Bishop] De Roo's financial judgment," Patrick Jamieson, managing editor of the *Island Catholic News,* said yesterday in an interview. "This judgment proves he was not such a bad administrator."

Mr. Jamieson said the controversy arose from church politics. Bishop De Roo was well known for his liberal views on gays, married priests and women in the church. The Catholic church has become more conservative in recent years, Mr. Jamieson said. "He was caught in a back tide."

Church officials who did not support the former bishop on church issues were too quick to accuse him of fiscal mismanagement, Mr. Jamieson added. None of the church leaders in Canada spoke in Bishop De Roo's defence when allegations of fiscal mismanagement first surfaced. The land deal would have worked out if the church had honored its deal with the U.S. businessman and had not attacked the former bishop in public, he said.

Bishop De Roo, 81, was not available for comment yesterday. He apologized publicly in June of 2000 for his "errors." Recently, according to his website, he has been lecturing and holding retreats.

Victoria Bishop Richard Gagnon said yesterday the Catholic Diocese of Victoria plans to appeal the jury's decision.

"The diocese does not agree with the decision by the jury. . . . The diocese believes an appeal will lead to a reversal of the verdict and dismissal of Mr. Finley's claims," he stated in a prepared statement sent to *The Globe and Mail* in response to a request for an interview.

Bishop Gagnon did not comment on the possible impact of the court award on the diocese.

However, Mr. Finley's lawyer, Randy Gordon, said Mr. Finley is not looking for the church to sell assets to pay out the court award.

The church's obligation could be met without interrupting its good works, Mr. Gordon said.

The sale of the property at the center of the controversy for its true value may be more than enough to take care of the court award, he said.

Mr. Finley would like to work with the church to reach a settlement, he said.

"Our goal is not to hurt the church, just to have [it] fulfill its legal obligations." However, if the church pursues its appeal in the court, "all bets are off," Mr. Gordon said.

The land at the center of the controversy is a 65-hectare industrial site in Lacey, Wash., a community of about 30,000, outside the state capital Olympia. The land was bought at a foreclosure sale for $5.3-million in 1997 by a partnership formed by the Victoria diocese and Mr. Finley.

Mr. Finley put the deal together; the diocese provided 100 per cent of the financing.

The partnership took out a mortgage on the property for $7.5-million in 1998 and anticipated reselling the property within 24 to 36 months for about $15-million.

But months after the bishop retired in 1999, his successor, Bishop Raymond Roussin, said the diocese did not have funds to make the mortgage payments. He tried to break up the partnership and accused Bishop De Roo of financial mismanagement.

After the diocese defaulted on payments, the mortgage holder imposed severe penalties, accelerating the debt. The diocese eventually raised $13-million (Canadian) from parishioners to pay off mortgage holders.

The Washington state jury received two appraisals of the land. Mr. Finley's lawyers called an appraiser, who said the land was worth $28-million (US).

The diocese appraisers valued the land at $15.5-million to $20-million.

American Court Vindicates Bishop De Roo's Record & Reputation

Editorial
Island Catholic News, Volume 19, No. 6, July 2005

A May 27 court judgment in Olympia, Washington has vindicated the financial acumen and administrative record of Bishop

Remi De Roo, and gone a long way toward redeeming his personal and pastoral reputation. This report in a lead story by Robert Matas in *The Globe and Mail,* May 31 features a banner headline (under a large color photo of the bishop) which reads: 'Bishop De Roo Vindicated.' Five years earlier Bishop De Roo seemed to be under a permanent cloud, after a glowing career.

Discredited

Remi Joseph De Roo served as Bishop of Victoria for thirty seven and a half years retiring in February, 1999 with a stellar record as a leading proponent of the laity-enhancing dimensions of the Second Vatican Council. De Roo was the surest advocate of the social justice model of liberation theology adopted by the Canadian Catholic church during his long tenure as chairperson of the Canadian Bishop's social affairs commission in Ottawa. He was one of the youngest Council Fathers at Vatican II in 1962, the year of his appointment as bishop.

One year after his retirement, his previously impeccable record was severely tarnished by headlines across Canada that he had made bad if not foolish-looking land and show horse investments in Washington State. He was said to have built up huge debt for the small diocese and broken canon law in the process. "Six years after the explosive allegations were made, a jury in the Superior Court of Washington has vindicated the bishop," the *Globe and Mail* article reads.

The American jury awarded De Roo's former business partner Joseph Finley $8.2 million (US) for breach of contract by the Diocese of Victoria during the era of De Roo's successor Raymond Roussin. Roussin's administration was also found guilty of breach of fiduciary responsibility, which means that they would not properly cooperate with their inherited business partner. This lack of cooperation was judged to have cost Finley his share of the profit from the land sale deal. Roussin, a former bishop of Gravelbourg, Saskatchewan was appointed Archbishop of Vancouver in January 2004.

Background

Finley was loaned two million dollars in the late 1980s by the Diocese of Victoria in an effort to save his Arabian Horse farm at the time when the federal US government changed the tax structure around show horses so that their value was decimated. That two million dollars was lost. Finley insisted the Diocese keep that debt on the books and he would endeavor to bring a redeeming deal that would make it good. The Washington land deal was his effort at redemption of the debt in 1997.

Appraised at nearly $15 million (US) the diocese was able to buy it for $5.3 million with the understanding that 160 acres of heavy industrial land would require 2-3 years to sell. Prior to that time line expiration, De Roo retired and Roussin replaced him as Corporation Sole Bishop of Victoria, the legal and corporate designation of the Diocese. Finley's contract was with the 'Corporation Sole B of V.'

Bishop Raymond Roussin's financial advisors took a dim view of the arrangement, as well as its sponsors Finley and De Roo, and refused to work proactively on the deal. Finley proved to the satisfaction of the jury that this resulted in breach of contract and breach of duty to a partner. He also successfully established the value of the land as $28 million (US) which determined the amount of the judgment against the Diocese of Victoria in favor of himself. The actual value of the land had been a contentious issue as Finley only gained a profit under the contract if it was over a certain threshold.

Debt Occurred Under Roussin

The $8.2 million judgment adds hugely to the debt incurred under the Roussin regime. This includes the sale of debenture bonds worth $13 million (CDN) to buy the mortgage of the property. These have to be paid back from the sale of the actual property. Along the way the Diocese divested itself of fifteen million dollars' worth of surplus property, but at fire sale prices. It was largely sold to local

191

developers at 50 cents on the dollars, reaping only 7.5 million in return. None of this money went to pay back the debenture bond holders who renewed in blind faith at a rate of 80 percent in 2003.

Finley argued in court and in the media that none of this debt was necessary if the Diocese had cooperated with the many deals he brought to the table only to have them all spurned between 2000 and 2004. The judge and jury agreed that had the deal been left to properly mature and sold on schedule all sorts of money would have been made all around. The court was convinced by his case and concluded that the deal was originally sound and as a consequence De Roo's judgment that the property was a good deal was vindicated.

Property Value Increase

It was largely 'political factors' that clouded the situation at the time and De Roo had been severely mistreated in the process and in the media in 2000. As Robert Matas reported in the *Globe and Mail*: "Contrary to the allegations by church officials, the jury decided the bishop had made a solid investment. The court heard that the property at the center of the controversy may have increased in value as much as fivefold since its purchase."

Ironically, Bishop De Roo, who refused to defend himself or speak publicly during the entire six years debacle (except to apologize generally for whatever errors he might have made and for whatever damage these may have caused) was the author of an investment which can still redeem the entire situation because it has increased so radically in value.

This is in spite of all the mounted debt caused by the subsequent decisions. Unfortunately the same people are advising the latest Bishop of Victoria, Richard Gagnon, a former Vicar General of the Archdiocese of Vancouver. In his first year as bishop, Gagnon has announced that the diocese will appeal the decision, a decision that threatens to cost an estimated two more years of court time plus lawyer's fees estimated at a further three million dollars.

A further complication is that the land in question was actually sold for $14 million (US) in January, 2005. However, there is a saving technicality.

Happy Ending?

If the new bishop would cooperate with Finley even at this juncture, the day could be saved because the January sale is not closed and the Diocese has the final closing option, as explained by Cleve Stockmeyer, a member of Finley's legal team, in an ICN interview on May 29. If rescued, the land could be sold for its proper value of $28 million (US). The new purchaser could be bought out at a half million dollars. Time is running out though and the hard feelings that lead to the 8.2 million dollar judgment seemed to be far from being resolved. Expensive emotions.

The Lacey Land Fiasco
Where Does it Go From Here?

Island Catholic News, Volume 19, No. 6, July 2005

Was any of it necessary?

From the start, observant Catholics were asking why could not the two bishops – De Roo and Roussin – and their two administrators – Clemenger and McLeish – sit down quietly and work out a continuation of the strategy that had generated the *Corporate Business Park* partnership in the first place? Why did it have to become acrimonious? Why did it have to go public at all? Could not all of this expense and animosity be spared?

At the time, in the spring of 2000, Bishop De Roo was widely castigated for the investments and yet the court in awarding the Diocese's business partner $8.169 million (US) for breach of contract and breach of fiduciary responsibility on May 27, 2005 has shown that the investment was a sound one, now worth $28 million (US).

This court-determined value is the figure upon which the court order is based.

Bishop De Roo did not make 'a bad investment,' a 'shaky land deal' as it came to be called repeatedly in the pages of the *Times Colonist*. It was a very good deal that has turned a piece of property originally obtained at a bargain price of $5.3 million (US) and now valued more than five times that.

As Muriel Clemenger, De Roo's administrator at the time of the deal, recently stated in the pages of the *News Group* coverage, the land was always very valuable and Bishop De Roo knew that.

So what was it all about? Now the focus of responsibility has shifted to Bishop Roussin, De Roo's successor who listened to people with apparently other agendas rather than the financial soundness and security of the Diocese of Victoria. Interestingly these advisors cannot be held fiscally responsible for the decisions made by the 'Corporation Sole, Bishop of Victoria' due to the antiquated corporate structure of the diocese. This is the point of both Gregory Hartnell and Jack Sproule's reflections on the issue, printed elsewhere in this edition.

The real problem is that the new bishop Richard Gagnon who now bears sole responsibility for the Diocese of Victoria as Corporate Sole is still being advised by the same people who have lead him down this costly path. The big problem is that they are suggesting the Diocese appeal the judgment, even though overturning jury verdicts is nearly unheard of. It is at best a twenty per cent hope and this promises to cost millions more in lawyers' fees, court costs and property maintenance.

Other voices are saying that these Washington based lawyers need to be sued by the Diocese for malpractice, as they have been by clients in a similar situation.

The light at the end of the tunnel for the Diocese and the debenture bond holders is that the land could still be sold for the proper amount, $28 million (US) rather than the mere $14 million (US) which the Diocese did in January. The Diocese wisely kept the closing option to itself, so can buy out the present purchaser for the half million dollars already put up. This is the way to go, not appealing the May 27 court verdict.

The Diocese under Bishop Gagnon must take hold of the situation in a sensible manner. Now is his moment of truth. Up until now it could be reasonably explained that he is the victim of earlier poor judgment but now his own judgment is under scrutiny. The next moves will be fully his. Now is the time to get new advisors, listen to other people, get rid of the earlier lawyers and turn this fiasco around.

This will put an end to speculation that there are 'behind the scene' reasons for keeping this fiasco going.

All Three Bishops Blamed

Excerpted from the June 10, 2005 edition of the *Saanich News*

Bishop Richard Gagnon seems determined to follow in his predecessors' footsteps by surrounding himself with legal and financial advisors who are giving him very bad advice ("Former bishop vindicated in eyes of some Catholics," *Weekend Edition*, June 3).

As a practicing Roman Catholic Christian I pray he changes his mind.

The initial errors committed by former Bishop Remi De Roo were compounded by his successor, former Bishop Raymond Roussin. Bishop De Roo apparently heeded advice given to him by Muriel Clemenger to invest in show horses and rural land in a foreign country. Bishop Roussin, instead of pursuing less costly and contentious out-of-court mediation with Bishop De Roo's disgruntled business partner, apparently allowed local Diocesan properties to be sold for less than their true value, and pursued costly litigation that has dragged on for more than five years.

None of this very worldly activity advances the good news of the Gospel. In fact, contrary to assertions now made by Patrick Jamieson, the recent jury decision in the Washington state court, far from vindicating Bishop De Roo, only proves what a disastrous decision he made in the first place. Had Bishop De Roo's supposedly "very smart investment," as Mr. Jamieson calls it, been such a wonderful thing,

195

one wonders why it was made in a covert manner, with only Ms. Clemenger and Bishop De Roo's American lawyer friend privy to it.

Bishop De Roo was well known as an armchair socialist who often pushed the envelope of Church teaching. It's hard to see how his idea of social justice was furthered by all this nonsense, but Mr. Jamieson seems determined to put an optimistic spin on these latest events. It seems obvious that the good bishop's conscience was troubled by this whole business, otherwise he would have made the investments with the full and open support of his Diocesan staff.

Bishop Roussin was properly concerned that something was amiss, but rather than pursue the matter in a conciliatory manner through mediation, his advisors counseled him to take the costlier, more contentious, and frankly, less Christian way.

The result is that the propagation of the Gospel in this diocese has suffered a considerable setback in recent years, and the spiritual authority of all three bishops has become seriously compromised. Some Catholics, thinking it their duty to blindly obey bishops, had been abused by supporting the diocese's bond scheme. Because of the failed financial and legal strategy undertaken by Bishop Roussin, they are still waiting to be paid back.

Bishop Gagnon should fire the legal and financial advisors he inherited from Bishop Roussin, humbly admit that the diocese has made some very grave mistakes, and seek out-of-court mediation with Mr. Finley, before more time, energy and money is squandered. Diocesan finances should be taken out of the hands of these bishops, so that these funds are no longer a source of temptation to them.

Gregory Hartnell,
Victoria

Bishop Gagnon Should Avoid Legal Challenge

Excerpted from the May 31, 2005 edition of *The Times Colonist*

Re: "Judgment may force Catholics to sell land," May 30, *Times Colonist.*

Sad news for the diocese – but fair is fair. You printed a picture of Bishop Remi De Roo but not one of Bishop Raymond Roussin. While Bishop De Roo made the first mistake with Arabian horses, Bishop

Roussin under advisement made what I believe was the bigger one in not settling with Joseph Finley out of court and without the huge legal costs for which the diocese is now responsible.

Bishop Richard Gagnon would be well advised to forget appealing this judgment (with its further legal costs) and sit down with Finley (as he suggested) and discuss out-of-court solutions. Further legal challenges would only serve to burden an already wounded diocesan financial situation.

Paul Gawthrop,
Victoria

Mean Spirited Tarnishings

Island Catholic News, Volume 19, No. 6, July 2005

The Editor:

I was very pleased to see the prominence *The Globe and Mail* gave to the story which affirmed former Bishop De Roo's judgment in investing funds near the end of his tenure. The way in which his reputation was tarnished at the time was mean-spirited. Those brought in to administer the diocese seemed anxious to publicly humiliate him.

At the same time, it is necessary to highlight that the *Island Catholic News*, and its managing editor Patrick Jamieson, were also the victims of the controversy around the issue. In trying to shine light on the facts of the case and the questionable actions of the diocese, the paper came under attack and was banned from distribution in many parishes. The street distribution boxes were vandalized repeatedly.

Mr. Jamieson, and former editor Marnie Butler were taken to task as "unfaithful" members of the church. Some public apologies are in order from diocesan officials I think.

The question *The Globe and Mail* story begs now, however, is what is the quality of financial management of the diocese at this point? With the former partner in the deal offering to settle in light of the court judgment, the diocese says it will appeal. This will undoubtedly mean more money paid to lawyers and further delays in disposing of the land. Maybe the media should follow this continuing saga.

Kevin Simpson
Vancouver BC

Some Justice & Truth Emerging

Island Catholic News, Volume 19, No. 6, July 2005

The Editor:

Hurray for justice. The post-Bishop Remi De Roo Catholic leadership in the Victoria Dioceses has suffered a severe blow with the court judgment regarding the Lacey land investment. The Catholic faithful of the Victoria Dioceses have been deceived. The truth has prevailed.

The land Bishop De Roo bought for $5.3 million (US) is now worth possibly $28 million (US) and the American jury determined that the deal was sound as an investment from the word go. It determined that it was not Bishop De Roo's administration but his successors who made all the poor decisions that have cost the diocese yet another $8.2 million (US) in addition to earlier losses due to bad faith decisions.

Some Western Catholic newspapers have contributed their share in misinforming the public and vilifying Bishop Remi by insisting that this investment was related to race horses. The truth is that the first investment was show horses, not race horses, and the second, the Lacey land investment. In my mind the whole debacle was initiated at the highest hierarchical level to discredit Bishop Remi and it has backfired.

The Victoria Diocese attempted to cut Joseph Finley, the partner, out of the investment profits but found by the court judgment that the Victoria Diocese was in breach of contract and fiduciary duty. Subsequently, they must pay Finley $10 million (CDN).

Island Catholic News, an independent paper on Vancouver Island, has attempted to provide unbiased investigative reporting on the Lacey land Investment. Because the investigative reporting did not coincide with the *Diocesan News*, parishes refused to provide an outlet for distribution of the *Island Catholic News* and cancelled their subscriptions. In addition, *Island Catholic News* issues made available in public places were mysteriously removed. Serious attempts are being made to sabotage the truth and close down the *Island Catholic News*.

I have high regard for Bishop Remi. He ordained me to the priesthood in 1965. He was of great assistance to me in advising and procuring the dispensation to be "reduced to the lay state", as it's typified, in 1975. His understanding of and true Christian action extended to writing a letter to be read in all parishes in the Victoria Dioceses about my situation and thanking me for my ten years of faithful service as a missionary in Peru and assistant pastor in the Vancouver Dioceses.

I don't know of any other Bishop who has treated one of his priests who requested a dispensation in a similar manner. Some of the requests for dispensations are still on their desks, filed or somewhere in Rome. Shame, shame. It is as if they have control of these priests' eternal salvation.

It is for this reason that I have taken a serious interest in the issue of the Lacey land investment. I have attempted to keep informed of the decisions of the post-Remi officials of the Victoria Diocese. I am pursuing justice and detest misrepresentation of the truth and manipulation.

Some right-wing Catholics made it very difficult for Bishop Remi to implement the documents of Vatican II in his diocese. His social teachings followed Christian principles. This did not sit well with some very conservative Catholics in Victoria and throughout Canada. His retirement provided an opportunity for them to focus on and publicize one issue, 'race horses and bad investments' and they attempted to detract from and vilify his reputation.

I clearly welcome an inquiry so that the whole truth will prevail. I recommend that the Victoria Dioceses cut their losses by paying the deserved penalty and get on with their true mandate of the Catholic church which is the evangelization of the People of God.

Joe Gubbels, Volunteer
Catholic Social Services
Guadeloupe, France

Former Bishop Vindicated in Eyes of Some Catholics

Diocese considering appeal of $10-million lawsuit

By Mark Browne

June 3, 2005 edition of *Weekend Edition* of *The Victoria News*

A recent Washington State court judgment resulting in the Catholic Diocese of Victoria losing a $10-million lawsuit is viewed by some Catholics as a vindication for retired bishop Remi De Roo.

The lawsuit centers around a 160-acre chunk of land in Lacey, Wash. When De Roo was the bishop of the Victoria diocese he formed a partnership with Seattle businessman Joseph Finley to buy the land in 1997 for $5.3 million in a foreclosure sale. Finley put the deal together while the diocese put up 100 per cent of the financing.

After De Roo retired in 1999, his successor, Bishop Raymond Roussin, attempted to break the contract with Finley while indicating that the diocese couldn't afford mortgage payments on the property.

The diocese then started defaulting on the payments before raising $13 million from parishioners to pay off the mortgage holders.

At the same time, the diocese under Roussin had accused De Roo of misspending millions of dollars on the land deal.

However, while the matter was tied up in the Washington courts for several years the still unsold land has increased in value fivefold by some estimates. Finley's appraiser valued the land at $28 million while appraisers for the diocese determined the land to be worth $15.5 million to $20 million.

That the land could be worth up to $28 million has *Island Catholic News* editor Patrick Jamieson concluding that De Roo made a good investment.

"It's a very smart investment," he said.

De Roo was known as a left-leaning social activist and Jamieson pointed out that many on the right wing of the diocese considered the former bishop to lack fiscal management skills.

"I found him very frugal, very smart and he knew the value of the dollar," Jamieson said, adding that De Roo is now at the point where he can "recover his reputation."

Muriel Clemenger, who served as the financial administrator for the diocese when De Roo was bishop, also said De Roo knew what he was doing when he entered the partnership with Finley.

"The land is very valuable. The bishop knew it was valuable or he wouldn't have had anything to do with it," she said.

The two-and-a-half week trial into the matter wrapped up in Olympia, Washington on May 27. The jury in the Superior Court of Washington ruled 11-1 that the diocese had no basis for breaking the contract with Finley. The jury then awarded $8.2 million U.S. in damages to Finley.

The diocese is not happy with that decision and Bishop Gagnon said the jury's ruling is not necessarily final.

The ruling in the lower court, he pointed out, is a jury verdict that has not yet been finalized as a judgment of the court, which is expected to take place in a couple of weeks.

"We're waiting to see what the court says," Gagnon said.

As well, the diocese is still waiting for its lawyers to provide a summation of the court's findings so the matter can be discussed further, he said.

All that said, if the court follows through with the jury's verdict, the diocese will likely appeal the ruling, Gagnon said.

"I think there'll be a good possibility for an appeal in this matter," he said. "We don't agree with the decision by the jury and we're confident we have a good case and that Mr. Finley's claims will be dismissed."

SUPERIOR COURT OF WASHINGTON
IN AND FOR THE COUNTY OF THURSTON

JOSEPH C. FINLEY,   )   NO. 00-2-01783-6
)
v.   )   SPECIAL VERDICT FORM
)
BISHOP OF VICTORIA   )
CORPORATION SOLE,   )
_____)

1. Did the Bishop of Victoria Corporation Sole breach its fiduciary duty to Joseph C. Finley?

RESPONSE: YES ___X___   NO _____

If you answer "YES" then answer question 2. If you answered "NO" then skip to question 3.

2. What is the dollar amount, if any, of Joseph C. Finley's damages proximately caused by the Bishop of Victoria Corporation Sole's breach of fiduciary duty?

RESPONSE: $ 4,200,000.00

3. Did the Bishop of Victoria Corporation Sole breach its contract with Joseph C. Finley?

RESPONSE: YES ___X___   NO _____

If you answer "YES" then answer question 4. If you answered "NO", do not answer question 4.

4. What is the dollar amount, if any, of Joseph C. Finley's damages proximately caused by the Bishop of Victoria Corporation Sole's breach of contract?

RESPONSE: $ 8,169,000.00

SIGNED: _Nicole D. Ross_
         Presiding Juror

Jury awards Finley: the jury voted that Finley was cheated as a partner but it was overthrown at the appeal level on a technicality. On the facts of the case, the jury awarded penalties to Joseph Finley in May 2005. It was overturned later, not on the basis of facts, but on a point of law, as explained by diocesan lawyer Paul Bundon. (see pages 216 & 217) who wrote "The Diocese engaged a respected former Superior Court judge... for a successful appeal."

Chapter 12 – Less Than True Value

Diocese Insists Upon Selling
Lacey Land at Half Value
Finley moves to halt 'fraudulent transaction'

Editorial & Analysis
Island Catholic News, Volume 19, No. 9, October 2005

VANCOUVER—Printed below is *The Globe and Mail* story by reporter Robert Matas from September 23, 2005 which reports on the latest legal developments in the Lacey Property situation in Washington State, land owned by The Diocese of Victoria which has become a major headache if not recurring nightmare for the Roman Catholics on Vancouver Island.

In this latest twist, Joseph C. Finley, the Diocese's legal opponent in the seemingly interminable 'Lacey Land Saga' has charged the Bishop of Victoria with authorizing 'fraudulent transactions'. Finley took this action in an effort to halt his former business partner from selling the Lacey property for half its assessed value; half its true market value. This higher market value was determined by previous court decisions in the ongoing battle which started in March, 2000.

Finley won Washington State Court decisions on June 17 and July 8, 2005, totaling $8.2 million (US). He fears that he will not be paid if the land in question is sold at the under-valued price. It underlines the question why the Diocese has always undervalued the land.

The Diocese signed a deal with John Teutsch last January to sell it to J&J Lacey Land Ltd. for $14 million American and is intent on going ahead with that deal in spite of the fact that the land was accepted by the U.S. court as being worth twice that amount. As Robert Matas points out in *The Globe and Mail* article, the diocese's own appraiser valued the land at between $15.5 and $20 million.

Finley's $8.2 million dollar judgment for breach of fiduciary responsibility and breach of contract was based on the land being worth $28 million (US), a professionally assessed figure which the jury in the trial accepted as the true value of the land. The Diocese is appealing that decision but with small chance of overturning a jury trial decision, it seems.

Finley is also afraid that the Diocese is trying to avoid payment on the basis that the Canadian courts will not enforce an American court order. Ironically it is Finley, the supposed enemy of the church on Vancouver Island, who could be best looking out for the interests of the debenture bond holders.

Some thousand Catholic parishioners on Vancouver Island seem to be pacified by a sleepy haze of repeated assurances that they will be paid back in full from the sale of the Lacey land; while it is self-evident that the lower sale price will put them at risk if Finley and the Diocese' lawyers are to be paid in full.

Through Fisgard Asset Management Corporation they own the mortgage of the increasingly valuable real estate. Fisgard claims to be an arms-length independent agency administering the funds raised to buy out the mortgage but Finley, in his formal complaint reiterates his conviction that it is improperly controlled by the Diocese.

Finley doubts Fisgard's objectivity in the process, insisting in his September 19, twelve-page complaint that Fisgard is a straw man entity for the Diocese which has made all the effective decisions around the land despite giving up title.

De Roo Exoneration Continues

The Globe and Mail article continues the stream of reporting on the controversy that is slowly shifting the blame from Bishop Remi De Roo's administration to Archbishop Raymond Roussin of Vancouver "who succeeded (De Roo), decided the purchase was ill advised. He stopped mortgage payments, tried to break up the partnership and accused Bishop De Roo of financial mismanagement. Earlier this year, a US court awarded $8.5 Million [sic] to Mr. Finley for damages caused by breach of contract by the church in Victoria," according to *The Globe and Mail* reporting.

This not so subtle shift of 'blame' promises to lift the mantle of culpability from Bishop De Roo, who in the view of the jury trial decision in June, made a sound investment – one that had nothing to do with horses or race tracks. In the view of the court if the Lacey Property had been left to properly mature, its sale would have gained the Catholic church on Vancouver Island a very useful profit. That profit, according to Finley, is still available to the Diocese and the debenture holders if the court will halt the sale action at the low-ball price.

Tragically, because Bishop Roussin when he was Bishop of Victoria between 1999-2004 decided to intervene in the investment process, the diocese is losing money unnecessarily and threatens to throw away even more in a questionable strategy.

For the Diocese of Victoria to sell the Lacey property for half its value on the slim hope that the award to Finley is not enforceable in Canada seems cynical and short sighted, and certainly against the spirit of the gospel.

Finley's Complaint

There are some revealing sections in Joseph Finley's formal complaint filed in the U.S. District Court in Tacoma Washington against The Bishop of Victoria Corporation Sole on September 19, 2005:

Section 19. "The Bishop of Victoria had a disincentive to sell the Lacey Property for its true value. A sale at true market value would have been highly probative of Finley's claims against BVC, and would have proven an increased amount of damages. By selling the Lacey property for less than true value, BVC and Fisgard created misleading evidence that was introduced at trial. This was done knowingly, willfully and intentionally."

22. "The Lacey property was contracted for sale to J&J Lacey for far less than true market value in a sale that was improperly motivated by concerns other than achieving anything remotely close to true market value."

Significantly for the debenture holders who are at risk of not being paid back in full is this section:

23. "BVC and Fisgard intend to use the proceeds of the sale to J&J to pay back the debentures that BVC owes in preference to Finley's judgment even though the debenture holders do not have any security recorded against the Lacey Property and even though the debentures holders are substantially over collateralized by real properties in Canada. Unless these fraudulent actions of BVC and Fisgard are prevented there will be no funds from the sale to J&J to apply to Plaintiff's Judgments. A sale at true market value could have realized sufficient funds to pay Finley and to substantially retire debentures."

28. "BVC and Fisgard were under no immediate need to sell the Lacey Property since the debentures are not payable until August 2006."

31. "By contracting to sell the Lacey Property for less than true market value to J&J, BVC and Fisgard would make it impossible for both the debentures and Plaintiff's judgments to be paid out of the sale proceeds."

Finley's complaint closes with the request that the proceeds of the sale be applied to Finley's judgment; the sale be enjoined or the judge cancel the contract for the sale. He also wants an injunction against further disposition of the Lacy land by Bishop of Victoria Corporation Sole, to stop the Diocese from further similar efforts at lower than true market value sales.

B.C. Ex-Bishop's Real Estate Deal Sparks U.S. Lawsuit

Church evading payment of $8.5-million in failed land deal, businessman alleges

By Robert Matas, Vancouver
Excerpted from the September 23, 2005 edition of
The Globe and Mail

A controversial real estate deal that tarnished the reputation of Bishop Remi De Roo has now sparked a lawsuit alleging that the

Catholic Diocese in Victoria is fraudulently trying to avoid paying $8.5-million (US) [sic] ordered by the court.

In a formal complaint filed this week in the U.S. District Court in Tacoma, Wash., American businessman Joseph Finley alleges that the Victoria-based diocese is selling real estate in the state of Washington at a bargain-basement price to avoid having to make the court-ordered payments.

"The plan is to not pay [Mr. Finley] fully out of the sale proceeds," Mr. Finley's lawyer, Samuel Elder, said yesterday in an interview.

If the church does not intend to pay its court-ordered debt from the sale proceeds, Mr. Finley wants the court to cancel the sale or take other actions to ensure he receives payment, Mr. Elder said.

Mr. Finley also started a court action this week in B.C. Supreme Court to have the U.S. court order enforceable in Canada.

Neither the Catholic Diocese of Victoria nor its lawyer responded to requests for an interview.

At the center of the controversy is an industrial site outside Olympia, the Washington State capital.

Bishop De Roo, as head of the Victoria diocese, had arranged to buy the property in partnership with Mr. Finley for $5.3 million in 1997. Mr. Finley assured the bishop that they could sell the land within 24 to 36 months for almost three times the purchase price.

However, Bishop De Roo retired before the land was sold. Bishop Raymond Roussin, who succeeded him, decided the purchase was ill-advised. He stopped mortgage payments, tried to break up the partnership and accused Bishop De Roo of financial mismanagement.

Earlier this year, a U.S. court awarded $8.5 million [sic] to Mr. Finley for damages caused by breach of contract by the church in Victoria. During the court case, an appraiser called by Mr. Finley's lawyer said the property was worth $28 million. The diocese appraisers valued the land at $15.5 million to $20 million.

However, the church is currently in the process of selling the property for $14 million (US), lawyers for Mr. Finley state in the document filed in court. The church has indicated the proceeds from the sale will go mostly toward repaying parishioners who contributed $9 million (US) by buying debentures used to pay off the mortgage-holders.

"We do not think it is appropriate to pay the debenture-holders before paying the [court] judgment owned by the church," Mr. Elder said.

The court has been told that the diocese, as of June 1, 2000, owned surplus properties worth $70 million. Mr. Finley's lawyers also stated that the church did not have a current appraisal of the property before signing a contract to sell the land for $14 million.

However, based on the number of offers and the offering prices being received from real estate developers, the church ought to have known the land was worth far more than $14 million, the lawyers stated.

The lawyers said that the church "knowingly, willfully and intentionally" sold the property for less than its true value in an attempt to lessen damages in the breach-of-contract lawsuit. The property was contracted for sale "for far less than true market value in a sale that was improperly motivated by concerns other than achieving anything remotely close to true market value," they said.

Diocese Debenture Difficulties Threatens More Land Giveaways

10 to 20 bonds require resale to survive due to deaths of holders, according to media reports

A Reflective Report

Island Catholic News, Volume 20, No. 4, May 2006

For the first time, The Diocese of Victoria in its current debenture bond renewal campaign has threatened the sale of schools, churches and diocesan buildings if the renewal level is not met.

Early indications are that it will be difficult if not impossible to achieve the 80 per cent renewal level of the previous renewal in 2003. At that time fresh money also came in which again seems less likely to occur due to a shift in attitude by parishioners and bond holders.

Deaths of 10 to 20 bond holders threatens to make the 80 per cent level nigh impossible. In what some parishioners consider a crass approach, the diocese has offered these post-mortem bonds to new purchasers.

There are other factors which make the implicit threat of sale of formerly untouchable properties a probability. These include a perceived lack of momentum and a further disenchantment with the management or mismanagement of the Diocese fortunes, both financial and legal.

A tone of anguish colours the proceedings for a second renewal that was promised would be unnecessary three years ago.

The threatened sale of further diocesan properties also raises the question in the minds of parishioners whether the land will be sold at fifty cents on the dollar. This was the near giveaway prices to hungry land developers in both the earlier efforts of sale of surplus lands and the Lacey land property itself, which is at the hub of the debenture bond renewal program.

Background

Debenture bonds were sold in 2000 to buy the mortgage of the *Corporate Business Park* property after the Diocese stopped payments on the land.

CBP was a Lacey, Washington land purchase agreement between the Diocese of Victoria and its business partner Joseph C. Finley started in 1997, three bishops ago.

In May, 2005 Mr. Finley was awarded $8.2 million (US) for breach of contract and breach of fiduciary responsibility by the Diocese of Victoria in a Thurston County judge and jury trial in the State of Washington.

No mention of these difficulties are made in the covering letter from Bishop Richard Gagnon, ordinary of the Diocese of Victoria, or in the attached explanatory material. This less than entirely forthright attitude has caused some bond holders to decide not to renew their bonds but to cash in.

One bond holder explained to me over coffee after Mass on the Sunday of the diocesan-wide pitch that the original purchase had been more less a gift to help out the previous bishops.

He said the first renewal had followed naturally enough, but now after six years of incessant difficult news around the issue, it was time to get out and stop propping up questionable management decisions.

How widely held this thinking is will be apparent from the renewal news.

These decisions include the recent decision to appeal Finley's court victory with the extra legal fees and costs that involves. Questions have been raised about continuing to trust the same legal team and the same strategy in the expensive court battles.

Another undermining factor is the ongoing atmosphere of uncertainty resulting from blaming previous bishops that has ensued and the dividedness within the Diocese due to the overall ongoing seemingly endless situation.

Less Enthusiasm

I attended an evening liturgy at the cathedral on the weekend when the pitch was being made for the renewal and perhaps it was the time of day or my own admittedly jaundiced attitude but I did not feel the energy or enthusiasm for the chase I sensed three years earlier.

Contacts in other parishes report how a major push is being made by the main players on the Diocese' financial and administration team. This indicates the seriousness with which the administration is taking the possibility of an inadequate renewal. Official assurances are being made that there will be no difficulty in reaching the goal.

My own gut evaluation is that the Diocese will be lucky to get sixty per cent renewal this time and as little chance of fresh money.

The direct admittance that schools and churches will be on the block if and when it fails is worrisome given the diocese' record of reaping only fifty cents on the dollar with land sales.

Fifty Cents On The Dollar

In 2000-2001 period, at the time of the announcement of the sale of bonds, court records show that the Diocese sold over fifteen million dollars of land (CDN) for approximately half its value, the largest piece going for 3.8 million dollars, a prize piece of real estate formerly known as the Allotment Gardens in upscale

Gordon Head. This went to a wealthy developer who did the sub-dividing where all the profit is made.

According to *The Globe and Mail* reporting, the diocesan lands are worth only $70 million (CDN) compared to $90 million when De Roo left office in 1999. Some $20 million has been lost by the church's decision to fight Finley instead of cooperating with him. And this is only the land value losses.

The Diocese is currently bogged down in its effort to sell the Lacey land property for half its court determined value, at $14 million (US).

Joseph Finley's award of $8.2 million (US) was determined by the value of the land being accepted by the court at an appraised value of twice that amount. Finley has temporarily halted the low-ball sale through court action arguing that neither he nor the debenture bond holders are likely to be paid if the Lacey land is not sold at full value.

It is obvious that land in Greater Victoria is now at a premium because the region is approaching maximum development capacity. In other words there is little left to buy and develop except land in preserved property like the church reserves which developers are very eager to get their hands on, especially at fire sale values.

This has been a major disadvantage to the Diocese of the financial crisis strategy they announced in March 2000. A blind spot has arisen in the Diocese strategy where well-heeled developers can pick up property at bargain values with little or no benefits coming to the parishioners.

For example, none of the 7.8 million dollars gained in 2000 from the sale of surplus lands went to pay back the debenture bond holders directly. Rather the money was used to pay down other debt, maintain the Lacey land property and fix up the poorly constructed Christ the King Parish in the Comox Valley.

Two million dollars went for that repair job on a ten-year-old church building in Courtenay. The former pastor of that parish at the time of the problems is now rector of the Cathedral. There his extreme precautions at fiscal accountability and security would serve to indicate there is little to no chance of a repeat of such difficulties in his new areas of responsibility.

Ethical Guidelines

If and when there is a need to sell schools and churches and other diocesan buildings and land, there needs to be the establishment of a procedure to avoid any hint of conflict of interest which the public record has also indicated occurred in the past around the sale of properties.

It gives the wrong impression if business associates and cronies are seen to be benefiting from the sale of lands. Legal work done for the purchaser of the Allotment Garden property and the purchase of the View Street property have been seen as a little too close for comfort in this area of ethics.

An arms-length arrangement needs to be established for any further sale of land to avoid such perception of conflicts of interest. Most of the team making up the Diocese financial and administrative decision making process are wealthy real estate developers and business men as well as lawyers specializing in such dealings.

These are all very successful older men, much admired and thus their invitation to serve in a voluntary capacity for the good of the church.

These are capable men who are most successful in their own business decisions but have been making costly decisions for the diocese in their strictly volunteer capacity on the key diocesan committee.

As members of that key decision-making committee they have no actual liability given the Corporate Sole structure of the Diocese, where the Office of the Bishop provides the sole figure who wears the crown of responsibility and liability for all the decisions taken on the sound advice of such invaluable advisors.

The Crown And The Head

One calculation of the overall ongoing costs of the Lacey land fiasco comes in at $43 million (CDN) made up of the following factors: legal fees at over $4 million; lost surplus land value at $7 million; tax, assessment and interest invested in Lacey land $5 million; owed to debenture bond holders $15 million; owed to Finley judgment $11 million and projected ongoing legal fees $1 million.

How will selling the land at $14 million (US) take care of these facts. Heavy the crown that wears the head.

Catholics Again Urged to Invest in Debentures as Legal Battle Continues

By Cindy E. Harnett
Excerpted from the April 6, 2006 Edition of the *Times Colonist*

The Catholic Diocese of Victoria is pleading with parishioners to again renew debentures they bought in 2000, to donate, or at the very least pray.

About 2,000 people bought debentures to help the diocese, which otherwise would have been forced to sell 15 per cent of its approximate $80 million in assets, including schools and churches. The diocese's debt is the result of a failed investment by former bishop Remi De Roo that has resulted in a costly and protracted legal battle.

"We're inviting people to continue the initial commitment that they made six years ago," Bishop Richard Gagnon, said in a phone interview from Kamloops.

The church is encouraging new investors "to replace the debenture holders who have died" since 2000. Vernon McLeish, at the diocese pastoral centre, said "roughly 10 to 20," of the original investors have died.

Parishioners were called on to renew their debentures in 2003. Last week, a letter went out from the bishop asking parishioners to renew one more time before the debentures are due for payment Aug. 31. Otherwise, "The diocese has no recourse but to sell property," Gagnon said.

The letter suggests investors extend debentures another three years; donate the interest; donate some or all of the debentures' proceeds if cashed; make a straight donation, or buy a debenture for the first time. As a sixth option, "Offer prayers on a frequent basis for the successful extension of the debentures."

To sell schools and churches "is the last thing we want to do," Gagnon said.

The financial predicament started when the diocese, in an attempt to recover losses from an investment in Arabian horse breeding, invested with Joseph Finley, of California, in a 65-hectare property in Lacey, Wash. The diocese guaranteed a $12-million mortgage on the land and entered a joint agreement with Finley. After De Roo retired in 1999, then-Bishop Raymond Roussin stopped monthly payments of $180,000. The diocese was already in debt for $3.5 million on mortgage payments and legal fees.

In June 2005, a Washington state superior court upheld a jury's $8.2-million judgment against the diocese for breach of contract. The next month Finley was awarded an additional $290,000 in lawyer's fees.

The diocese is appealing the U.S. court decision.

A trustee who was to sell the Lacey property has said the money from the sale will be used to repay the debenture holders. But in September 2005, Finley filed a statement of claim in B.C. "seeking an order in the nature of enforcement of a foreign judgment," his Vancouver lawyer Mike Bertoldi told CanWest News Service at the time. According to the story, Finley claimed the church has an ownership interest in the land. Finley refused comment when contacted by the *Times Colonist* on Thursday.

Paul Bundon, lawyer for the diocese, said in a statement that "The bishop's position is that the U.S. courts have previously ruled that the trustee is the owner of the Lacey land and the sale proceeds may be used to pay the debenture holders."

Gagnon told parishioners in a March 24 letter that the land could have been sold in September for $14 million but Finley's litigation "prevented a potential buyer from obtaining adequate title insurance and this stopped the sale of the land."

Diocese Nearly Neatly Outfoxed Again

Diocese lawyer reveals cynical strategy

Editorial and Analysis

Island Catholic News, Volume 20, No. 7, August 2006

In a clever legal maneuver, on June 23, 2006 Joseph C. Finley the alienated business partner of the Diocese of Victoria attempted to call the Diocese' bluff by making a bid for the Lacey land property which would pay off the debenture bond holders who hold the mortgage on the land, execute his judgment against the diocese and place the property in his hands for profitable resale. The creative motion was rejected by the court but revealed some of the inner dynamics of the relentlessly ongoing struggle.

Court Documents filed in the Superior Court of Washington For Thurston County on June 23, 2006 tell the story.

The Lacey, Washington property has been an issue of major contention between the two parties since 1999 when the Diocese moved to dissolve *Corporate Business Park,* a business partnership between the two parties. In this latest motion Finley himself would have paid off the debenture bond holders and bought the property for a price in the range of what the Diocese insists is the true value of the land.

Knowing from his court experience that the value of the land is much more, Finley reasoned that he could pay off the debenture bond holders and reap enough profit to make up his previous losses at the hands of the Diocese. It was an outside chance that did not pay off in the end as the court dismissed the motion for such a writ of execution on his $8.2 million judgment of September, 2005.

The court has been reluctant to force the Diocese to pay Finley until the debenture bond holders are properly taken care of. Their funds were raised to buy back the mortgage on the Lacey land property when the investment was at risk after the Diocese stopped payments in late 1999.

The Diocese has been insisting that the Lacey land property is only worth half the value that the court determined when it issued its judgment in favour of Finley in September, 2005. His $8.2 million award was based on the real estate appraisal that the land was worth $28 million (US) not the $14 million that the diocese is willing to accept for it as determined by a sale to John Teutsch, an American developer.

Knowing better the actual value of the land, Finley was prepared to take it off their hands at their insisted upon value and at the same time relieve the debenture bond holders of their risk by immediately paying them off at full value during the month of July 2006.

It was a clever ploy that failed when the court dismissed it on June 23 but it did reveal the weaknesses of the Diocese arguments in the ongoing case. The Diocese was insisting in its pleading on this matter that it was simply Finley's way of avoiding the appeal hearing which should be settled in the next few weeks.

Finley won an $8.2 million (US) judgment against the Diocese approximately one year ago on the basis of breach of contract obligations and breach of fiduciary responsibility toward a business partner. The Diocese in its appeal to have the judgment overturned insists there never was a proper business partnership between the Diocese of Victoria and Mr. Finley though the Judge and Jury trial in Thurston County, Washington decided otherwise.

Lawyer Reveals Ultimate Winning Strategy

Paul Bundon, attorney for the Diocese revealed its strategy in the case during the debenture bond renewal campaign when he wrote to a tax lawyer inquiring as to the Diocese eventual capacity to pay back the debenture bond holders if it keeps losing huge judgments such as the $8.2 million of 2005.

Piqued by the impertinence of the questioning from a source presumed to be unconditionally loyal to the Diocese' fortunes come what may, Bundon wrote: "as to the pending appeal on the monetary judgment entered against the bishop, the appeal is based on questions of law rather than an effort to overturn facts.

The key legal point is that when a business venture has failed, as this one did, and the partnership documents provided that neither party had a duty to invest further money in the business, as these documents did, and the two partners then agreed as they did here that the property was to be transferred to a third party (in this case, Fisgard) in satisfaction of the partnership debt, neither partner can then claim to have been damaged by the agreed transfer. This is a very clear legal matter and even common sense will tell you that our legal position is correct."

Bundon continues: "It is perhaps worth noting that after the jury verdict was entered against the Bishop, the Diocese engaged a respected former Superior Court Judge to analyze the potential for a successful appeal. The former judge agreed to represent the Diocese in the appeal, and the Diocese is confident that its position is well supported."

It is noteworthy that Bundon admits the merit of the case proven to the satisfaction of the judge and jury but hopes to overturn the decision on a legal technical matter, that the case should not have been heard in the first place.

In other words, the moral weight is with Finley and that while the facts show he was hard done by, the moral self-righteous tone of the Diocese will be upheld that he was not a worthy partner nor opponent which has been the tone of the Diocese' attitude all along,

Bundon states that the case will not be decided on facts but on a point of law. While the facts were obviously on Finley's side, that when you sign a thirty-six page legal contract it does have some obligations which the Diocese did not honour, no matter what you privately think of your partner, how morally unworthy he is deemed. It's an odd twist in an odder case.

The Diocese did get its second renewal of the debenture bond extension when $10,700,000 of $13,000,000 were extended according to a table issued by the Diocese. Only at Saint Andrew's Cathedral were some thirty per cent of the bonds not renewed. Overall a million and half dollars (CDN) was withdrawn by debenture holders, but at 88 per cent renewal, the crisis was settled, for now.

Victoria Diocese Throws Away $15 million (US)

Diocese Sells Lacey Land at Half Price; Compounds Woes

Analytical Report

Island Catholic News, Volume 20, No. 11, December 2006

The Diocese of Victoria seems to have sold its Lacey land property for $14.875 Million (US), according to a November 15 report in the *Times Colonist*, Victoria's daily newspaper. I say 'seems to' because when you analyze the situation closely, it would be better if they hadn't – not at half its actual value as they have done.

While the bishop and the debenture bond holders who started receiving payback cheques expressed a certain amount of 'happiness' in reporter Louise Dickson's page one article, the glee could be short lived if the Diocese does not win its appeal of the $8.2 million dollar judgment in favour of the Diocese's aggrieved business partner Joseph C. Finley.

Mr. Finley was judged to have been cheated of his share of *Corporate Business Park*, the partnership behind the whole 'Lacey land Saga' which dates back to 1997.

Finley was able to convince the American court that the land is now worth twice the value for which the Diocese has sold it. In 2005 values it was assessed at $28 million (US), so now could be assumed to be worth upwards of thirty million, twice the sales value the diocese received. Why would the Diocese do this? How does throwing away $15 million make any real sense.

Not The First Time

This is the second time the Diocese has sold its real estate assets for fifty cents on the dollar. $15 million dollars of so called

218

surplus lands were sold for half that value in an earlier effort to pay back the debenture bond holders. Debenture bonds raised $13 million (CDN) in the year 2000 to redeem the mortgage on the land after the diocese under Bishop Raymond Roussin stopped payments on the property at the end of 1999. This poor decision was taken out of a pique about previous Bishop Remi De Roo's business practices.

These business practices of De Roo have been subsequently vindicated by the Finley judgment according to the May 31 headline story in *The Globe and Mail*, a national newspaper reporting on the 2005 Washington State court judgment.

None of the original $7.5 million gained from the sale of the 'surplus lands' was used to pay back the debenture bond holders. Court records reveal none of it was put aside for that purpose although that was the reason given for selling the land at half its assessed figures. Usually the assessment figure is lower than the actual sale price, not more as in these cases.

"'I'm happy,' Victoria Bishop Richard Gagnon said yesterday," the *Times Colonist* story reads. "The diocese is grateful that the land sold and that the debenture holders can see their investment realized over six years, it removes a certain liability,"

One has to wonder if it hasn't actually raised the liability, on the financial front at least.

On another note, Archbishop Raymond Roussin appeared November 23 & 25 on a Catholic television program about his clinical depression which has debilitated his reign in Vancouver. Roussin made no mention of the original cause of his problems back here in Victoria, the financial losses he incurred by problematic decision making and the moral complexities brought to bear on his transparently fragile spiritual sensibilities.

Brinkmanship

Selling the Lacey land at this time does nothing to improve the Diocese's financial liabilities. The Diocese has thrown away fifteen million dollars (US) just when it could least afford to do so.

It is actually a very strange time to sell the land in terms of the Diocese financial fortunes. The bonds were successfully renewed for the second time in the summer so there was created a three year window to get a better price for the property.

Yet within months of the successful renewal, the diocese sells the property for such a low figure. It does not make sense logically. Why go through all the effort of renewing the bonds at that time?

If the Diocese loses the appeal, which at present is the most likely prospect, it is a debt that cannot be blamed on any earlier administration. There are prayers at the parishes these Sundays for 'a favourable decision' – not for justice and fairness but for a favourable decision.

If the Diocese loses the appeal before three American judges, the people of the Diocese may well wish the Diocese had settled with Finley long ago; or at least sold the land for its true value rather than continuing this grudge battle which Catholics on Vancouver Island cannot afford financially or spiritually.

Documented Offers

The Bishop was grateful that the land sold, he said, but there are nearly a dozen documented sale opportunities over the past seven years that the Diocese has spurned; all of which would have brought in more money – Safeway, Target (twice), Barclays Bank North (some reported in the *Times Colonist* and others documented by court records according to *The Globe and Mail* reporting).

There were many other offers that Finley cobbled together so that the business partnership could be amicably and successfully concluded. The court decided he had been cheated of $8.2 million (US) because the Diocese consistently turned up its nose at the deals he consistently brought to the table.

These were reported duly in the *Island Catholic News* in the years between 2003 and the present.

The *Times Colonist*, on the other hand, has consistently refused to challenge the conventional wisdom of its original reporting on the story, as though following a pre-set agenda.

As a result we are still treated to this fictitious version of the affair that the *Times Colonist* follows assiduously at the bidding of the Diocese. The people of the diocese deserve better.

Alternative Perspective

Island Catholic News has produced a DVD comprised of segments of three interviews with myself over the last year and half since the Finley judgment. It is available for anyone who wishes to look more deeply at this strange saga and all the unanswered questions it leaves begging.

The DVD is structured logically, historically and thematically so that people who have given up on the story out of confusion over the details, can get a clear picture of the story and the issues it raises.

It is all factually based on the court records, original research plus the mainstream media reporting but also takes into account the difficult issues behind the scenes such as the reasons for the half price sales, the acrimonious attitudes toward Joseph Finley and the political theology at play in the current Catholic church.

Only Connect

Editorial and Analysis
Island Catholic News, Volume 21, No. 3, April 2007

Part of the purpose of *Island Catholic News* is to assist people to connect the dots in the bigger picture of what exactly is going on behind the scenes in the church today.

The stories we are reporting on this month may seem disconnected on the face of it but the common thread that connects them is just beneath the surface.

The soup kitchen expulsion at St. Peter's in Nanaimo, the difficulties at Holy Cross and the further legal action taken by Joseph Finley shown in the legal document reproduced on this page are an apt example of how we just need to 'only connect' in the words of a famous English novelist.

The Connections

At a recent Voice of the Faithful meeting in Sidney, the speaker attempted to make connections between some of these stories and it was objected to that there are no relevant connections and that each issue must be dealt with separately and be 'gotten over with.' These are not the sort of stories that are going to soon go away, even by a force of will.

In fact their resolution, if resolution is desired, will only come when the pattern that connects them is more widely recognized and the root causes ameliorated.

Mr. Finley's persistence in taking his court case to the final arbitration, for example, is not rooted in his perverse nature as the other side would have us believe but (from what I have discerned from working on this story since the year 2000) by an innate sense of injustice. By any account, the best description of the situation is that the game is tied at one all and it is going into overtime.

The overtime will be decided by golden goal so best expect it to end quite quickly, thus ending the legal aspect of a long and twisted saga. The Diocese had but twenty days to respond which ended on March 28. One can expect a quick decision. The pastoral ramifications could go on for decades.

The Legal Situation

In summary fashion, Finley by the facts of the case, in round one was able to prove that he was cheated. In round two the Diocese got the three judges of the Court of Appeal to agree that the case should not have gone to court in the first place, that the partnership was already dissolved. Mr. Finley thinks he has spotted a fatal weakness in that judgment. We shall soon see.

Far from a spectator sport, the Catholics on Vancouver Island are radically affected by the cost and outcome of all this. Ironically it is Joe Finley who wanted to save the people money by being prepared to avoid the costly and deadly court proceedings all along.

In November 2002 he spoke at the Victoria public library urging immediate mediation which was turned down. *Island Catholic News* has put that public meeting on DVD from the taping we had professionally done at the time. Anyone can have an unedited copy for their own viewing.

The offer for mediation was turned down by the bishop of the day, and a priest who was at the meeting was reprimanded for endorsing the idea publicly on the CBC broadcast of the news of the event.

It is the same pattern at Holy Cross where a good and valued pastor was treated miserably for speaking his truth. It is a different bishop in charge now but the same treatment, the same pattern. What or who is the common factor? Where do these wrong- headed strategies come from? Who is advising these bishops in such transparently ill-conceived manners?

This is where the real story lies in all these episodes. The bishop is not consulting widely or deeply enough on any of these issues. The same is being revealed on the closing of the soup kitchen at St. Peter's. Why and how has a small band of financial and administrative advisors – who cannot be held accountable under the corporation sole structure of the diocese – gained control of the overall management of the diocese with no opportunity for other voices to be heard.

At Holy Cross, the laity got themselves well organized to take proper charge of the situation. Otherwise, years of sound pastoral development would have been lost to an ill-conceived coup by ultra-traditionalists who cannot reconcile themselves to the progressive nature of the parish.

ROCK or Restoring Our Church with Kindness has been the resulting concerned Catholics organization to emerge and sensibly they have issued a connecting statement about the common pattern with the St. Peter's Situation.

Only Connect

The great English novel *Howard's End* by E.M. Foréster has as its theme 'Only Connect'. The novelist was similarly concerned with the two Englands that were emerging; one a hard bitten commercially efficient vision of the empire, the other a kindlier and truer version of the original principles and values that the country represented.

Catholics today on Vancouver Island are faced with a similar sort of decision about their version of the Catholic church; and through the media and the internet the world literally is watching.

How Much Actually Lost on Lacey?

By Gregory Hartnell, Victoria
Island Catholic News, Volume 21, No. 3, April 2007

Almost ten years after the *Corporate Business Park* partners, Bishop Remi De Roo, and his American lawyer friend Joseph Finley, borrowed $5.25 million (US) to buy suburban property in Washington state, longstanding questions of accountability still persist with respect to the Lacey land fiasco.

According to an article by Victoria-based writer Steve Weatherbe in the February 12 edition of the *B.C. Catholic* ('Victoria diocese wins U. S. appeal'), 'the property was finally sold for $14.875 million (US) far from enough to recoup the diocese's losses."

Despite the fact that Bishop Richard Gagnon is quoted in Mr. Weatherbe's article as 'expressing his pleasure' in the court finding that the Diocese does not owe Mr. Finley $8.2 million (US) as indicated by a jury about a year ago), there is no mention in the Bishop's statement that that sale was insufficient to cover those losses.

Rather, Bishop Gagnon, as quoted by Mr. Weatherbe, said: "the position consistently taken by the diocese over the last eight years has been upheld. I am hopeful that we, in the Catholic community on Vancouver Island, can soon put this unfortunate incident behind us and move forwards [sic] together to carry out the Church's mission in this diocese."

Implicit in this interesting statement seems to be an unacknowledged subtext that, in fact, 'this unfortunate incident' is not quite over, and that the Church's mission in the Victoria Diocese has been seriously impeded if not completely interrupted while it continues to plague us.

Bishop Gagnon's statement is misleading in three ways. By calling it an 'unfortunate' incident, he betrays a kind of pagan fatalism that the whole matter was simply a bit of bad luck over which the Diocese had no control.

By omitting to acknowledge, as Mr. Weatherbe candidly does, that the property sale was 'far from enough to recoup the diocese's losses,' he persists in maintaining a longstanding intransigence with respect to the true costs to the Diocese of these misguided speculative real estate ventures in that foreign jurisdiction.

By omitting to mention that Mr. Finley still may avail himself of further legal options, he leads the faithful to believe that it is completely over, when, in fact, those options are still available to his adversary, as Mr. Weatherbe candidly admits: "it is as yet unclear whether Seattle businessman Joseph C. Finley, the diocese's legal adversary and onetime partner in property speculation, will challenge the judgement."

One wonders how much the Diocese really did lose on the Lacey land fiasco? To give Bishop Richard Gagnon the benefit of the doubt, I am prepared to entertain the notion that perhaps Mr. Weatherbe is privy to financial information that has been kept hidden from the good Bishop.

The Latest Developments

Editorial and Analysis

Island Catholic News, Volume 21, No. 5 & 6, June/July 2007

The collision course seems set. In Toronto six new Roman Catholic Womenpriest priests and deacons were ordained on May 27 including Victoria's Jim Lauder who came back full of a profound enthusiasm from his anointing as a deacon. He says a major highlight was the fact that all those in attendance directly laid hands on him as part of the process.

One of the people in the congregation attending told me that this was the highlight for him as well. He said that after seventy years as a Catholic, attending many ordinations including his own relatives, this is the first time he had such a direct involvement, was even invited to lay hands on the newly ordained, and that it held a profound empowering effect.

Across the pond, at Vancouver, Rome announces Archbishop Roussin's replacement by appointing a coadjutor Bishop with the right of replacement. This is no surprise given Bishop Roussin's health issues that date back to his time in Victoria. All this in a swirl of speculation that Vancouver is so important now it may very well warrant a cardinal to do the job.

The new appointee is transparently an ultra-orthodox Vatican bureaucrat with plenty of ambition. The impact upon Vancouver Island can expect to be significant. Gone now is any speculation that Victoria's Bishop Gagnon may be getting that promotion. Instead he has a new near neighbour to keep an eye on things over this way, an eye trained and focused by Rome. Despite the recent presumably final court victory in the Joseph Finley-Lacey land case, the Holy Cross rebellion against his authoritarian style may have cost the former vicar general from Vancouver his chance at being promoted to the bigger job back home.

The official church's reaction to the Toronto ordinations, fundamentally that of implausible denial, underlines that gap between the two solitudes that the Catholic church has become. One side pretending that everything is normal (if all fouled up), the other going straight ahead as though inspired by the Holy Spirit to create new religious and spiritual options.

The irony is that the progressive traits of the reform groups are always what the church has pointed to historically as evidence it is the one true church.

Clearly Cheated

The Lacey land final court decision was the wrong one in our view. By the facts, Mr. Finley clearly was cheated but that does not seem to worry any one at the Diocese where might apparently means right. They now have the rather uncelebrated problem of making up the fortune they squandered fighting the unnecessary fight with Mr. Finley. Twenty some million dollars Canadian was given away on the basis of this caprice. Fifteen million dollars of surplus land was sold for half that value, losing 7.5 million and the Lacey land itself was sold for half its value at less than fifteen million (US) losing $15 million (US).

This is all in addition to the millions paid in lawyers' fees but I suppose that will consider money well spent since they 'won.' Talk about secular values replacing gospel ones. What ever happened to the milk of human kindness, working things out with your alienated brothers etc. Besides it's a lot cheaper. But the people, who generally have no say in any of these ridiculous decisions, will be expected to pay the bills and swallow the whole line that they will continue to be fed.

The most alarming aspect is that there is an increasing realization that Rome approves of the way all this has been handled. It certainly feeds the concrete idea that the whole exercise since 1999 – including the appointment of the new man in Vancouver who presumably has at least visited Vancouver before – has been to stamp out Remi De Roo-ism and progressive prophetic Catholic theology from the region.

What You Don't Know Can't Hurt You

Editorial and Analysis

Island Catholic News, Volume 21, No. 8, September 2007

Joseph Finley recently took the Lacey land judgement to the Washington State Supreme Court. You won't hear much about that from the Diocese of Victoria. The inside knowledge from his supporters is that his chances are at best one in ten.

Regardless, if he loses he can still take the diocese to court on a civil suit for damages to his character. After all he did prove successfully that the Diocese breached his contract and breached their fiduciary responsibilities to the tune of $8.2 million (US).

The Bishop of Victoria Corporation Sole has won its later rounds on a technicality which Finley is trying to overturn. It will be at least next March before it is settled at this level, longer if the court wishes to hear oral arguments.

So the case goes on and on. Like children squabbling in the school yard and about as mature and useful to boot. In the meantime, the man who it is really all about, Bishop Remi De Roo is travelling around the world trying to light a fire under the moribund church with a re-ignition of the spirit and flame of Vatican II.

Recently he was in China. He seems to have his own program of renewal which is not yet fully revealed. Certainly it is amazing that his spirit has not been crushed by it all, although he is certainly silent on anything smacking of controversy whether inside the church or out. He is missed. Whether he is seriously chastised or simply biding his time is anyone's guess.

At the same time the present pope, as many have come to call him, is trumpeting the traditionalist Latin Mass and other retrograde measures of similar significance. In the face of his modulation in the poorer parts of the world, liberation theology prospers because simply the gospel is about liberation of all sorts.

The church operating under his model believes it no longer has to answer to any questioning of its accountability of gospel integrity. This model brooks no contradiction. The world has to stand to account to the church. The days of dialogue are dead.

'Nothing Illegal'
Diocese Jubilant Over 'Final Victory'
Bare Bones Financial Reporting Calls for Book on Subject

Analysis and Reflection
Island Catholic News, Volume 22, No. 3, April 2008

The Diocese of Victoria hopes its nightmare is over with the higher court decision not to hear Joseph Finley's appeal of their earlier appeal that overturned his $8.2 million (US) judgement in the Lacey land case known as *Corporate Business Park*. The story by Louise Dickson was given prominence in the *Times Colonist*.

The bare bones of the story features the financial skeleton of the saga which goes back eight years in the news and twenty years in the making. Since 2000 the *Times Colonist* has been presenting a skeleton of financial and legal facts which vary at times with themselves.

It's been interesting over the years to contrast *The Globe and Mail* reporting which has been able to get a little more distance from the small town sensationalism and get it in a wider (and more tragic) perspective. A truer perspective.

The difference seems to be that *The Globe and Mail* actually looked at the court documents involved while the *Times Colonist* just went back to its own story file, repeating the same limited perspective.

Only One Conclusion Possible

It was always clear it would likely end this way if only because so little of the other side was ever presented. As former *Island Catholic News* editor Marnie Butler often stated privately, unless Bishop De Roo spoke his side, there was only one conclusion that was possible in the minds of everyday Vancouver Island

Catholics. Many people wondered why he never spoke up but stayed behind his lawyer's voice.

Raymond Painchaud, the videographer doing a life of the bishop, says that it was other people's job to defend the bishop, but as Marnie Butler implies, only Bishop De Roo knows what really went on and he among the last three bishops is the only one who has the eloquence and sheer intelligence to sort it through and communicate it properly. He owed it to us to defend himself.

That has all been lost. Ms. Butler washed her hands of the whole affair years ago, as have many other keen players and close observers. There is a boon in it, of course. Perhaps this stage of closure opens the way for that moment when the whole body of truth, its political and psychological truth can be told. Perhaps now we can get away from the distracting chess game of dollars and legalities and get at the bigger picture.

This is a story, from my tracking, of alarming hints, compelling indications and actual evidence of mis-behaviour at the higher levels within the church, of perjury by high ranking officials, of suppression of pertinent facts by the court, of harassment, of cover up and denial of these facts. It is a story of the rich using church property to enhance their own position, of conflict of interest. It's a changing of the guard within the church, of a closing of ranks, of land sold at half its value. It's a story of the local media playing the story to the pleasure of the church establishment who controlled the release of information.

It goes on and on. It is scandalous and unbelievable to most ordinary Catholics. It is also standard business practice to work things to one's own benefit. It seems the takeover of the church by right wing business practices. It involved the destruction of Joseph Finley's reputation and as such the Diocese must be holding its breath in the realization that a libel suit may well soon follow.

After all he proved by the facts that he was cheated, maligned and mistreated (to the tune of $8.2 million US) and it was only by a technicality that the diocese was able to reverse this decision. But the facts proven in court still stand to be used if he has the will, energy, health and finances to go the extra mile. Lawyers involved have said to me that the court trial contained many facts not known by the parishioners that would influence their opinions in this matter.

Needed De Roo To Step Up

If in the beginning Bishop De Roo had stated publicly his version of the facts (without fear he would be seen to be fighting publicly with another bishop), things could be much clearer, and on an entirely different footing from what we have now. More of the actual truth would be on the table instead of just one side.

It is interesting that the other side had no hesitation to be seen to be smearing his name in public. Such consideration for fair play by the Bishop has not served us well in terms of the truth he always praised so highly when he was in office.

As with most nightmares of our own making, the Diocese of Victoria is far from out of the woods with this situation. No amount of reducing it in the compact language of Richard Gagnon will change the deeper realities.

He has continued with the same advisors who took the very decision after De Roo left office that created the mess, that sold the surplus land for half price, that sold the Lacey land for half its assessed value, that run the diocese as though it is their princely fiefdom, accountable to no one outside the inner circle and transparent only in their own eyes.

Court Drops Curtain on Diocese's Land-Venture Saga

Decision likely ends appeal process over Washington land deal gone awry

By Louise Dickson

Excerpted from the April 4, 2008 edition of the *Times Colonist*

The financial saga of an Arabian horse venture and a high-risk land project that left the Catholic Diocese of Victoria mired in $17 million in debt is finally over.

On Tuesday, the Washington State Supreme Court decided not to hear an appeal by Seattle lawyer Joseph Finley against the diocese.

"We believe it's the end of it," Bishop Richard Gagnon said yesterday. "We don't think there is anything that can go forward from here. I don't want to make any assumptions on the part of Mr. Finley, but we really feel this will bring a prompt conclusion to the situation."

Between 1988 and 1992, Bishop Remi De Roo of the Victoria diocese invested about $2 million in the Arabian horse deal with Finley. About $1.5 million came from a trust fund – the Priory Trust – set up after a Vatican-ordered sale of assets. The investment deteriorated and the money was lost.

In 1997, De Roo became involved with Finley again, guaranteeing a $12-million mortgage on land near Lacey, Wash.

The plan was to make a quick profit by flipping it to buyers who wanted it for a racetrack. But the land didn't sell and interest charges continued to mount.

When De Roo retired in 1999, his successor, Bishop Raymond Roussin, stopped paying the $200,000 monthly interest on the debt.

In February 2000, De Roo's questionable business practices were made public. A few months later, the diocese asked for parishioners' help and announced a fundraising plan to issue bonds at six per cent interest to raise cash to pay off the U.S. lenders.

The plan raised almost $13 million. By August 2003, the debenture holders were paid interest on their investments. Most renewed their contracts for a three-year term.

232

In the meantime, Finley sued the diocese for breach of contract when it stopped making payments on the debt and the land went into receivership.

In May 2005, a Washington state jury awarded Finley almost $8.2 million US.

The diocese was also found guilty of a breach of fiduciary responsibility, meaning it had not co-operated with its inherited business partner. The diocese was fined $4.2 million.

But in late January 2007, the judgment against the diocese was overturned by the Washington state Court of Appeals.

Finley sought a further appeal in the Court of Appeals and lost again.

He then appealed to the Supreme Court, who declared Tuesday they would not hear the case.

"The court shows clearly there is nothing illegal happening here in terms of our relationship with Joseph Finley," said Gagnon. "We're happy about it. We're now able to go forward and look to the future without this problem hanging over us as it has for the past decade."

The lesson the diocese has learned is that it needs to continue to function within its guidelines and canon law, said Gagnon.

"It's an unfortunate business deal that was entered into, that should not have happened. We all learned by these unfortunate circumstances. It was not something that was intended to cause so much damage, but this was a whole process that happened over a decade," said the bishop.

Gagnon has not spoken to De Roo, who is retired and living on Vancouver Island, since the appeal was denied.

The debentures were paid off in the fall of 2006.

Received from the Catholic Diocese of Victoria and Bishop Richard Gagnon

The Catholic Diocese of Victoria, BC was advised on April 1st that the Washington State Supreme Court declined to review the lower court decisions in the legal dispute between Joseph Finley and the Diocese. In 2007, the Diocese of Victoria was successful in its appeal of the $8.5 million judgment when the Washington State Court of Appeals unanimously confirmed that the Diocese had not violated any duty to Joseph Finley. The Supreme Court's ruling means that the Court of Appeals' decision is final, and requires that the matter now be remitted to the Trial Court, where the Court of Appeals' decision rejecting Finley's claims is to be put into effect.

Bishop Gagnon is pleased with the decision and looks forward to a prompt conclusion to this unfortunate situation. He expressed his thanks to the legal team, his advisors and all those who supported the Diocese in prayer and action during this difficult time.

Richard Gagnon welcomed by Remi De Roo at his 85th birthday party at the University Club in Victoria. Many thought this was the first informal step to a formal reconciliation but it wasn't to be. The much heralded May 31, 2009 "Reconciliation" ceremony at St. Andrew's Cathedral was 'postponed' at the last hour with no explanation given. (photo courtesy of Kevin Doyle)

Chapter 13 – The Reconciliation That Wasn't

New Bishop Bans Old Bishop Talking About Vatican II

Preferential Option for Vatican I: Turning Back the Clock on Vancouver Island

By Phil Little, Cedar, BC

Island Catholic News, Volume 22, No. 2, March 2008

During 2007 there have been groups forming to celebrate the original call for Vatican II. On January 25, 1959, the great Pope John XXIII first announced he would be calling an Ecumenical Council of the whole church. During the course of the year, things were proceeding on course. Ideas for speakers and events and courses were being visualized and identified. A Victoria group started and one in Nanaimo. Bishop Remi De Roo, a Father of the Council itself, 1962-65, spoke at both locations to motivate and clarify with his vision.

Then things began to go slightly off the rails and it started to feel like a Marx Brothers comedy, if not a Kafkaesque labyrinth. Permission had been sought from the official church, the Diocese of Victoria was asked to co-operate and The Castle, in Kafka's terms, said no; not unless we are in charge and seen to be in charge. All the usual nonsense. No wonder we needed a Vatican II.

Phil Little has written about the situation that would be funny of it did not seem more like a tragedy.

When you think you might have seen it all, the church on Vancouver Island continues to bewilder and amuse both Catholic and non-catholic observers. The still somewhat rookie bishop, Richard Gagnon, was parachuted into the diocese to help clean up some of the mess left by Ray Roussin in the legal disputes surrounding the Lacey land investments.

Early into his new career as bishop, Gagnon was embroiled in a dispute at the university parish of Holy Cross in Victoria. In late 2006 the bishop ordered the parish priest to fire a lay employee because of a complaint that this person was 'gay'. The parish priest refused to do this on the grounds that such an action was unethical; and also illegal. The priest himself was then removed from the parish and put on leave. The bishop made some decisions and public announcements, which caused the priest to state that the bishop had been untruthful to the parishioners. The parishioners formed a group that continues to advocate for openness and truth in their church.

In 2007, the bishop again stepped into another parish dispute. A newly imported eastern European priest decided that the soup kitchen ministry in the main parish of Nanaimo was attracting the wrong type of people to the church (the usual poor, homeless, hungry types that need soup kitchens). This ministry began with the support of the parish priest in 1985 but was always a ministry of the lay people who in the spirit of Vatican II were encouraged to be 'church' and to respond to the signs of the times. The parish and subsequent clergy over the years provided very little support other than providing the use of the parish hall and kitchen facilities.

The lay people did the fundraising to provide for the upgrades to the parish kitchen facilities and they still had to pay rent. The new parish priest began legal proceedings to evict the soup kitchen ministry. Bishop Gagnon supported his clergy and the ministry was shut down and is still currently looking for some other facility where this service can be renewed.

This program offered a morning breakfast to more than 200 people including over 50 school age children. The parish no longer has to contend with this 'undesirable' rabble hanging around the church for their daily bread while a handful of the devout dribble into the church for 'perpetual adoration'.

Once again Bishop Gagnon has stepped into the limelight to distinguish himself as the regressive prelate of the year. Back in January 2007 the Living with Christ booklet (Vol. 13, No. 1), published by Novalis and found in the pews of most Canadian churches every Sunday morning, reminded people that on January 25, 1959 Pope John XXIII did the unexpected and called for a gathering of the world's bishops for what later came to be known as Vatican II. The article asked the question 'How can we observe this anniversary?' There are few of the council fathers still alive, but the one John XXIII referred to as his 'Benjamin' (the youngest of the group) is none other than retired bishop Remi De Roo of Victoria.

A group of lay persons on the Island responded to this invitation found in the Novalis booklet and began to spin ideas on what could be done not only to commemorate this 50th anniversary on January 25, 2009 but to prepare for this event with a renewed study of the significance of Vatican II.

To this end, a group of parish regulars in the town of Parksville with a long history of dedication and work in lay ministry invited Bishop De Roo to speak on Vatican II during the scheduled Adult Education program during Lent of 2008. The organizers were so confident that this would be well received that they sent notice to the diocesan office asking that a small notice of the series of talks on Vatican II be included in parish bulletins throughout the Island.

The response of the bishop was a letter in early February 2008 to all the clergy forbidding them from supporting the planned series on Vatican II. Furthermore the bishop instructed the parish priest at the Church of the Ascension parish in Parksville that he was not to allow the adult education program on Vatican II to take place. Consequently the very hot and controversial reminiscences by retired bishop De Roo titled 'personal reflections and experiences of Vatican II' were cancelled. (For goodness sakes, Remi De Roo has even been allowed into China to talk about Vatican II!)

Bishop Gagnon has informed the lay education group that he has appointed a committee of ten clergy of the diocese to work on some response to the 50th anniversary of the call for Vatican II. This committee would be open to including some select non-ordained persons in their deliberations. However it is known that during a parish renewal program in 2007, a visiting priest told the parishioners in Nanaimo that it would take 100 years to undo Vatican II but that the work was well under way. The people who have been involved in this effort to promote the 50th anniversary of Vatican II can be forgiven if they might seem to be somewhat skeptical of this announcement that the clergy will decide what if anything will be done.

In the meanwhile, Bishop De Roo can continue to speak about his reflections and memories of Vatican II anywhere but in the diocese he served for so many years.

In 2004 at a lecture in Toronto Bishop De Roo said: "There is structural breakdown in the church, but the breakthrough ideas of Vatican II religious liberty, conscience, activity for justice are more alive and relevant than ever. We need to reclaim that freedom. There is no scriptural basis for a monarchical episcopacy. We members of the church must continue the search for truth in our own culture. There is no other setting for the search."

Apparently the very mention of Vatican II is far more threatening to the church powers than anyone had anticipated.

Remi De Roo's 85th Birthday Celebration
'Circle of Friends' Gathering Calls For New Stage of Development

Commentary
Island Catholic News, Volume 23, No. 2, March 2009

Bishop De Roo's 85th birthday bash at the University Club, organized by Senator Douglas Roche and friends, was what can be called a roaring success. Coincidentally the bishop's birthday fell on Shrove Tuesday, the traditional occasion of Mardi Gras, the last big party before Lent ensues.

A genuine love fest, many were there who had not been in his celebratory company in the ten years since he resigned at the mandatory age of 75. He looks little the worse for wear, giving what was easily the best speech of the evening. He is much practiced in the ten years, still actively lecturing and speaking particularly on the subject of The Second Vatican Council. That great watershed event of the Twentieth Century, which modified Christianity's attitude toward itself, the world and other religions, is much on his mind these years.

His speech exemplified much of that shift. As one of the few still-active 'Fathers of the Council,' Bishop De Roo, who attended all four sessions of Vatican II between 1962-65 as a newly appointed bishop by Pope John XXIII, is an abiding gem, well preserved and still shining. Bishop Richard Gagnon, De Roo's current successor as Bishop of Victoria, was in attendance, taking part in the fun of the festivities, and delivering a welcome and welcoming gracious speech and grace before the meal.

The other speeches by former Premier Dave Barrett, Senator Jean Forest, also an organizer of the evening, and Rev. Harold Coward, longtime Director of the Centre for the Study of Religion and Society at the University of Victoria were informative and excellent in shaping the tone of the event.

Raymond Painchaud's short documentary on the life of the Bishop was a highlight featuring key footage from his long journey which started on a Manitoba farm near Swan Lake, south of Winnipeg.

The evening was the special event that everyone who was invited knew it could be. In the week following February 24th, I had the opportunity to watch a two-hour video presentation of what a wide variety of prominent people have gained from their experience of working with Bishop De Roo over his 46 years as a bishop and 58 as a priest. These included Justice Thomas Berger, former Premier Dave Barrett and David Suzuki.

I came away with the impression that the higher the status of the speaker, the more laudatory the praise. Perhaps it was true, because as one of them stated, such long-term consistent clarity and honesty and truth are so rare in their experience at such a level. As more than one has stated publicly in the past decade, we need to hear more and more from Bishop De Roo on the subjects of the day. Certainly that clear, articulate, balanced, informed and evocative voice was on display at the end of the day that Shrove Tuesday.

Perhaps with the election of Barack Obama and other signs, there is a new moment in the air where voices of visionary hope like Bishop De Roo's will be welcomed and can help to set the emerging agenda.

The birthday party, as excellently executed as it was, was necessarily limited, by invitation only. Certainly I have heard from many since the event, ones who would have liked to have been part of the process.

The thought has occurred to me that maybe a much more grassroots celebration of the Bishop's contribution could be staged with emphasis on being an educational experience. This would mark the 50th birthday of the calling of Vatican II, and the holding of the watershed council. It would take us through 2015, enough time to start to further unpack the significance of the Council; enough time for our gem of a council father to help lead us in a real restart.

The Reconciliation That Wasn't

May 31 'Reconciliation' Event 'postponed' by Diocese at Last Minute Without Explanation

Island Catholic News, Volume 23, No. 4 & 5, June/July 2009

Readers of *Island Catholic News* might have noticed the announcement in the last edition that May 31st there was to be a "Reconciliation Service" at St. Andrew's Cathedral where both the current bishop, Richard Gagnon and Bishop Emeritus Remi De Roo were to be present. This was an event much anticipated throughout the diocese due to the difficult events of the last ten years since Bishop De Roo retired at the mandatory age of 75 in 1999.

In its March 2009 edition, ICN featured the 85th birthday celebrations of the retired bishop, a party held at the University of Victoria and attended by Bishop Gagnon in what many identified as an informal reconciliation between the two eras and their unfortunate overlap.

Unfortunately the second step in the process, the May 31 event, was not to be. The event was 'postponed' at the last moment with no public explanation given. People who had booked flights from distant locations to attend the significant event, in some cases were not only out of luck but out of pocket for their expenses.

Many people in the Diocese were hoping that the event could occur and that an unfortunate era could be brought to a close. Bishop De Roo issued a special letter, to be circulated among friends, associates and admirers, inviting them to attend and bring a friend.

Everything seemed to be moving smoothly only to have the plug pulled at the last moment with no explanation offered. Many fear that the manner in which this was done actually means the whole process is permanently cancelled, not just postponed.

In light of this we should look at where the event came from, what it was meant to accomplish, what the 'postponement' augurs for the future, and what it indicates about the means and methods of the current Catholic church and its style of administration under Pope Benedict XVI.

If the event had been scheduled five years ago, the meaning of the term 'reconciliation' would have been different than today, ten years after the fact. Now it tends to mean making the best of a bad situation, whereas five years ago or even three years ago it might have meant actually getting to the bottom of the facts of the situation.

Too much time has gone by now to hope for an official revelation of the 'truth' of the situation. Too many of the wrong people have spoken out and not enough of the right ones. It is all very clouded and the only hope of clarity will be in informal inquiries such as a comprehensive book on the subject might allow.

241

History will judge that once Bishop De Roo stepped out of office on February 24, 1999, wheels were set in motion that would set the diocese back decades in terms of its previous rate of progress, as well as financial viability and the discrediting of one of the leading lights in the Canadian Church after the Second Vatican Council.

In short the facts were the following: less than two years after Bishop De Roo retired, revelations of financial mismanagement were played out full-blown in the media. This was one of the first cases of the public and willing airing of dirty laundry of such a nature by the Catholic church in Canada in fifty years, since the Archbishop Charbonneau affair.

De Roo had been such a public figure of a left-ward social justice bent that rumours soon flew that this was an effort at public discrediting of his progressive reputation. Close scrutiny of the facts of the matter did nothing to dissuade this notion. *Island Catholic News* followed the details of the story in such a manner that it was punished by the institution of the church financially and politically, but it stuck to the story.

These recent developments around the foiled reconciliation have given encouragement to the idea of releasing the all-but finished book on the story, culled from the pages of ICN since 2000,

Bishop De Roo himself, refused to enter the fray, consistently standing behind his lawyer's advice to avoid public statements except a perfunctory apology for any harm caused.

The subsequent administrations have persisted in a consistent policy which squarely places all the 'blame' for the problems on Bishop De Roo's administration. Close scrutiny of the facts however show that the very damaging decisions were taken by the Roussin administration, his immediate successor, which refused to co-operate with the business partner of the problematic land deal.

This business partner was awarded nearly $8.2 million (US) in damages when he showed the court how he was treated by the Diocese. The Diocese was able to have this decision overturned on

242

a legal technicality at the appeal level, but the business partner had shown that according to the facts the Roussin administration had cheated him of his just due. Another book could be written on the basis of that trial transcript which contained much information that the parishioners of the Diocese of Victoria are entitled to know in detail.

In the meantime a canonical inquiry was held into Bishop De Roo's administrative practices and nothing of any substance was reported. Except, of course, that his reputation was in tatters. The most outspoken churchman of his generation had effectively been silenced and sidelined.

As a consequence of the fuss, he has not spoken on any substantive issue in the past ten years, which would have been unthinkable previously. Former B. C. Premier Dave Barrett and environmental scientist David Suzuki commented publicly on the cost of this loss to the Canadian social dialogue.

Many felt this was the purpose of the exercise anyway, but it came at great expense to the diocese which lost millions due to the foolish policies put in place in reaction to the needless rush of sensational headlines.

With the birthday party celebration, organized by Senator Douglas Roche of Edmonton in February, a corner was felt to be turned in at least recovering some semblance of balance to the ludicrous situation that ensued since 2000.

Senator Roche was able to get Bishop Gagnon to attend and many felt that the May 31st planned event revealed the hand of the Senator at work in an effort to maximise the benefits to the reputation of the bishop emeritus.

Some people on the progressive side of the church felt that the reconciliation might be an example of cheap grace at work, as most of the details of what has been mentioned would not be expected to surface given the process. I myself felt that it was more a stage-of-life exercise at effecting some closure, rather than a full-fledged effort at getting the healing truth to the surface.

It is clear that the orders to cancel the event came from a higher level within the church than the local level. Bishop Gagnon was convinced of the wisdom of the event or it would not have been initially scheduled. Local criticism was obviously taken into consideration and deflected, the bishop having learned something from the Holy Cross debacle of two years back when local reactionary forces painted him into a very awkward corner with their insistence he remove a purportedly gay employee.

Besides all that, the current bishop well knew that the cloud hanging over the diocese since the Roussin era was not of his making. He tried to do something about it but obviously a voice from on high talked him out of it at the last minute, for yet another embarrassing episode which blemishes his historic record.

Bishop Remi De Roo's Open Letter of Invitation to the May 31st Reconciliation Event

Greetings!

March 13th brought consoling good news. Muriel Clemenger, my former diocesan financial officer, contacted me and offered her apology, confirmed later in a letter, part of which follows. This represents a major break-through after ten years of waiting for fuller truth to be made known re the financial problems, much publicized, often misrepresented, which haunted our diocese.

Muriel's words speak for themselves, so I reproduce an excerpt: "There do not seem to be words strong enough to convey to you the distress I felt and continue to feel over the serious damage done to your reputation and your ministry resulting from our business dealings with Joe Finley. The fault was mine. It was a very serious miscarriage of all that is just that you were made to take the blame publicly. As we progressed further into the problems with the Lacey land, I failed to keep you in the loop as I ought to have done. I am deeply sorry. Your generous forgiveness when we spoke of these matters has done much to heal. Thank you. Please share this statement with your family and friends."

Personally, I consider this matter now closed, while maintaining my "no comment" stance with the media so as to avoid reopening old wounds and painful memories. Forgiveness remains the best medicine.

More good news! Our current bishop, Richard Gagnon, has invited me to participate in a concelebration at St. Andrew's Cathedral in Victoria, on Pentecost Sunday May 31st at 3:00 p.m. It is planned as a "reconciliation" service, incorporated into the traditional Sunday Vespers. Liturgically and pastorally speaking, I see this as ideal, for it encourages involvement by friends of various religious persuasions. Some might hesitate to participate in a formal Eucharistic celebration, yet cherish the Sacred Scriptures.

I really hope you will attend this joyous event personally. Do also persuade other friends to come. Join us at the reception that follows at the nearby St. Andrew's Elementary school on Pandora Street. Should that prove impossible, please hold us all in prayer for special divine blessings. God willing, this will help to heal some rifts still hurting our Diocese, while freeing up vital energies for further spiritual growth.

More last minute good news! I just found out that the diocesan officials are cancelling their intended lawsuit against Kevin Doyle, a dedicated lawyer friend of mine who served the Diocese for several years. I rejoice at yet another sign that divine graces of forgiveness and reconciliation are at work!

My health story is also encouraging. After multiple tests, requisitioned by several wonderful and increasingly intrigued doctors, my "exotic/rare" condition (autonomic neurotropy) has been definitively diagnosed. Seems it is a condition in which some blood vessels do not respond appropriately to signals or stimuli from the nervous system. Under some circumstances, fainting spells might occur, so I am cautioned not to travel alone. There is still no known cure. I follow a precise program of "preventive therapy" with daily exercising. I remain fully active and lead a normal life. I will spare you the details, although they might provide occasional entertainment over a cocktail!

Further news from you would be greatly appreciated. Meanwhile, be assured of my best wishes and prayers for continued blessings as we wend our pilgrim way from Easter to Pentecost; good physical health, peace of mind and heart, joy in your soul with refreshment of spirit.

Fraternally yours,

Remi

Victoria's Former Bishop De Roo – Remember?

By Raymond Painchaud

Island Catholic News, Volume 15, No. 7, August 2001

A year ago the name Remi De Roo made front page news in the local and national press. Now, the former bishop is remembered by most as the "gambling bishop." The story must not be permitted to end until his reputation is properly restored as a man of God and a man of the people.

I first met Remi De Roo when I was a student at Collège de Saint-Boniface working as evening porter at the diocesan centre where he lived and worked. I found him to be a compassionate, understanding man.

In the years that followed, I heard of him from time to time: when he was named Bishop of Victoria in 1962; but more especially, about 1983 when he was chairman of the Social Affairs Commission of the Canadian Conference of Catholic Bishops. Their statement "Ethical Reflections on the Economic Crisis" had an essential message that the needs of the poor should come ahead of the ambitions of the rich; the rights of the workers ahead of increased corporate profits. I remember the vicious response of business whose more polite comments were: "Mind your own business." I remember thinking that social and economic justice should become the "business" of the Church. When I met Bishop

De Roo four years ago, he made a brief reference to this episode. After reading one of his books on the subject of that period, I thought that such declarations were needed even more now.

About the time of the conference in 1983, Conrad Black, one of De Roo's harshest critics was "fast-tracked" into the Catholic church with the help of Cardinal Emmet Carter of Toronto.

Between 1986 and 1991, Bishop De Roo organized a diocesan synod in which the Catholics of his diocese were invited to share their concerns and plan a future of hope. It appears that this attempt to give a greater role to lay Catholics (in the spirit of Vatican II) did not sit well with the growing conservative element in the hierarchy of the Catholic church. Locally, many were anxious to see De Roo and his administration replaced, mainly because of his critical stand on big business and his left-leaning social views.

After Remi De Roo retired as Bishop of Victoria, the new diocesan administration seemed to have been quick to release to the national media information about a "financial crisis" in the diocese. Conrad Black's *National Post* broke a story even before the parishes of the diocese were informed. The local paper had many front-page headlines like this one: "Ex-bishop gambled assets from convent" (T.C. May 27, 2000). One of the few articles that was clearly fact-finding was one that appeared in the *Globe and Mail* on June 17, 2000. Kim Lunman suggested that the "crisis" may have been created by the new diocesan administration's reaction to an existing financial arrangement. The so-called "investment in horses" was to be only a "bridge financing agreement" not a long-term investment.

When the new bishop of Victoria, Raymond Roussin, called on the Canadian Bishops' Conference to do a formal inquiry, its General Secretary, Rev. Peter Schoenenbach was soon quoted as comparing De Roo's situation to that of a gambling addict. It appears to me that comments of this kind are made only about political rivals. This leads me to believe that church politics may be at the heart of this "crisis."

What may have been an attempt to discredit the man and the work of former Bishop De Roo came home to his native Manitoba when, in the middle of the "crisis" a group of parents objected to allowing De Roo to preside over the confirmation of their children. The Bishop of Saint Boniface was on his death bed at the time and had asked De Roo to do the confirmation for him.

Most of the so-called "$17 million loss" could be recovered by proper handling of the sale of the investment property. I believe the possible motive behind the "crisis" may succeed if the results of a thorough investigation were not presented to the public in similar headlines in the public press. This has not been done. A press release (June 29, 2000) by the Catholic Commission of Canonical Enquiry made no effort to correct the "gambler" perception of Remi De Roo. It simply stated after its investigation: "The Commission found no evidence that any member of the Diocesan administration has sought or received personal gain at the expense of the Diocese." Remi De Roo's name has not been cleared by those who labeled him a "gambler."

It occurs to me that if a bishop's reputation is primarily based on his financial competence, a diocese should be headed by a financial expert and run as a business.

Remi De Roo would not be the first "victim" of political and economic interests. In the 1950s Archbishop Joseph Charbonneau of Montreal was "expatriated" to Victoria under pressure from Premier Maurice Duplessis because he defended the interests of the workers. There is another Conrad Black connection here. He wrote a rather flattering biography of the former Premier of Quebec.

There is an epilogue to this story. At the present time, the global economic power is in open conflict with the interests of the people, especially the poor. Remi De Roo was an outspoken voice of the people and the poor. The way the Church has treated him here is a clear indication of its priorities; the "master" it is willing to serve. As he tries to understand the reaction of those who call themselves his "brothers in Christ" Remi De Roo might well ask: "Where was Christ in all this?"

APPENDICES

Bishop Announces Diocesan Financial Concerns

The full text of the statement read at Sunday Masses, Feb. 27th in the Victoria Diocese

Excerpted from the March 2000 edition of *Island Catholic News*

Letter from Bishop Raymond Roussin, S.M. regarding the financial situation of the Diocese of Victoria, February 2000.

Shortly after I assumed the position of Bishop of Victoria, members of my staff came to me with concerns about certain financial transactions by the Diocese which they did not completely understand. I started to investigate and when I could not get appropriate answers, I immediately set in place a process to provide me the information I needed in order to take appropriate action.

Investigation Process

I asked Vernon McLeish, formerly a partner in the accounting firm of KPMG and the new Financial Administrator of the Diocese, and Paul Bundon, the senior partner of the law firm of Jawl and Bundon, to be advisors to me.

What I sought was:

1. To determine how much money the Diocese had invested in loans which were not being repaid and in assets which the Diocese was in danger of losing;

2. To determine the amount of any future liability to the Diocese related to these investments, and how that liability might be met or financed;

3. To understand the history of the bad investments, to determine whether any internal Diocesan procedures needed to be changed, who was responsible for making decisions about these investments, and whether it was appropriate that any action be taken against those persons.

I have received a preliminary report from Mr. McLeish and Mr. Bundon and have begun to take action based upon their advice. I have chosen to report to you at this time because both my actions and those of certain lenders and other investors will shortly become matters of public record. You, the people of the Diocese of Victoria, should hear the facts from me and not from some other source.

Financial Situation

Based upon the information available to Mr. McLeish to date, it appears that the Diocese made several bad investments, beginning in the late 1980s, which resulted in losses of approximately $2,000,000.00. In an attempt to recoup those losses, in 1997 the Diocese entered into a joint venture to purchase a piece of development property in the belief that, on a quick sale, sufficient surplus would be generated for this purpose. The Diocese was not called upon to provide any initial cash, however, it was called upon to guarantee the mortgage of $12,000,000.00. Unfortunately, the property has still not been sold and the Diocese, after paying approximately $3,500,000.00 in mortgage payments and legal fees, has advised the lender that the Diocese cannot and will not make any further mortgage payments.

Continuing Liabilities

The mortgage on the property has now been called and the lender has commenced foreclosure and sale proceedings. We are working, in several ways, in an attempt to have the Diocese removed from the legal proceedings. If, however, the foreclosure proceedings run their course and the property, when eventually sold, does not yield enough to pay the mortgage loan in full, the Diocese will be required to honour its guarantee and to cover any shortfall.

I can report that our bankers have sufficient confidence in the management of the Diocese and our handling of this situation that we have been able to arrange a line of credit to cover what my advisors believe to be the maximum potential liability of the Diocese. However, it was a condition of the line of credit that the Diocese refinance existing long term liabilities and sell some properties to pay down the debt of the Diocese. The properties that will be sold will consist only of vacant land and their sale will have no impact on the continuing operation of the Parishes, Schools and the Hospital.

I can also assure you that none of this will affect the Foundation and the Pension Funds (Diocesan and Schools), as these are autonomous bodies operated outside of the consolidated financial affairs of the Diocese.

Responsibility and Action

Work is continuing, to determine how the bad investments could have been made without canonical permissions and without proper consultations within the parameters in place for such transactions.

I do want to make it clear that the present members of the Diocesan staff and clergy were not involved in advising or assisting the Diocese in making the loans and investments that are under investigation.

Mr. McLeish and Mr. Bundon have, however, recommended that I consider forwarding the information they have gathered so far to independent experts in Canon and civil law, for advice as to whether to take action in ecclesiastical and civil courts to hold certain individuals accountable and to seek compensation, where possible. This I have agreed to do.

I also undertake to report back to you from time to time to update you as matters unfold.

I can assure you that, under Mr. McLeish's capable guidance, we have made sure that the errors of the past cannot be repeated, and that the Diocese's investments are now being managed and invested in accordance with the letter and the spirit of Canon Law, and to the highest standards of a trustee under the civil law.

Finally, I ask for your understanding, support and prayers in helping me to make the right decisions for the Diocese.

If you have any concerns you feel may not have been addressed, please write to me directly.

† Raymond Roussin,
Bishop of Victoria

Letters About the Second Target Approach: February 2001

Correspondence referred to in Feb. 6-14 chronicle toward Target completion

Date: January 2003 *Island Catholic News*

February 12, 2001
Mr. David I. Osmond Victoria Properties, Inc.

Re: CPB, L.L.C./Diocese of Victoria/ Debenture Trustee

Dear Dave:

This is the first of two letters I will be sending you today which deal with the potential sale of land owned by CBP and the resolution of an agreement course of action by the members of CBP and the Debenture Trustee for the holders of the AG Capital judgment. This first letter will address the capacity in which you are acting, the handling of the prospective sale of the CBP property to an immediate buyer and the desirability of acquiring the right to relocate the existing easement from the CBP property to Marvin Road. The second will deal with the resolution of an agreed course of dealing if the property is not sold to the present buyer.

I understand that you and Norm Isherwood have been asked to assist the Diocese of Victoria and the Debenture Trustee in determining the best course of action to be pursued in selling or developing the CBP property. Mr. Vern McLeish is the person responsible for representing the Diocese in matters involving CBP, but I am prepared to accept your acting on his behalf and subject to his approval so long as we are in agreement that any action to be taken by CBP cannot be done without the agreement of Mr. McLeish and me. The Debenture Trustee has no right to participate in any decisions even though his consent may be required on some matters for the purpose of clearing title issues only.

CBP (*Corporate Business Park*, LLC) has an opportunity to sell its 160 acre +/- property to Target Stores. The broker for Target approached you or others acting for the Diocese/ Debenture Trustee some time ago, but was advised (incorrectly) that the CBP property was not available. Now, because Target's alternate site in the same area has encountered a number of problems, we have a renewed opportunity to present the CBP property to Target.

We have discussed at length the desirability of having the legal right to relocate our present easement to better serve the Target purchase, and I have negotiated an agreement with the owner of the affected land that would accomplish that. A draft copy as revised is attached for your reference. The benefits to CBP are quite clear. First, we will have an easement in the precise location that Target prefers for accessing the property from Marvin Road, and this access can be immediate, not requiring any delay for condemnation proceedings for public right of way. Second, we do not have to spend any money for road construction or pay any other sums to the adjoining landowner unless we elect to do so if our properly does not sell over the next two years. Finally, with the new easement rights in place, the alternate Target site will not be viable and cannot compete with CBP for the Target purchase. The only burden associated with the easement relocation is that our adjoining neighbor will achieve relative parity with the CBP site at the end of two years if the CBP property has not been sold by then.

I strongly recommend that you obtain approval of the easement agreement by Vern McLeish and any other necessary persons on behalf of the Diocese of Victoria and that you I further obtain approval by the Debenture Trustee. If we do not obtain the easement relocation as presented, it is very likely that our neighbor will elect to sell 20 acres to Target which effectively would kill any chance we may have to secure the sale to Target at any price. Our adjoining neighbor, HP, LLC, will enter into an easement relocation agreement in substantially the form that I have presented to you. Remembering Norm's admonition that we must resolve this matter quickly, I will ask that you and he do everything possible to acquire approval from Victoria immediately. The risk to all concerned is too great to commit this fairly simple, yet critical matter to protracted review and debate on both sides of the border. CBP has an opportunity to sell its property for a real fair market value price to an immediate buyer and will have to hold responsible any party who attempts to obstruct or interfere with that opportunity whether by delay or otherwise. As you know, we must resolve the easement issue in order to be prepared to deal with Target, which could be required by Wednesday of this week.

The final part of this letter deals with the handling of the present sale possibility. I respect your and Norm's expertise, and I value your assistance in this process. At the same time, the duly designated officers of CBP are Vern McLeish and me, and we have retained the services of a capable broker in the Trammel Crow Company. I believe it will aid our progress, therefore if we agree that, henceforth, all communications with Target's broker, Don Moody, be channeled through Trammel Crow, and that any other communications with Target be undertaken only with the joint participation of you, Norm and me. We have further agreed to begin our asking price at $2.75 per square foot, and that we will reduce that price only by consensus and agreement among all of us. I do not believe it is in our best interest to give TCC any figure to work with other than the initial asking price. All other terms and conditions of any sale also will require consensus and agreement among all of us. I further believe that our dealings must be kept confidential, and, to the extent that we enter into an agreement with a prospective buyer or another party, those agreements also must be held in strictest confidence.

I am hopeful that we can implement an overall resolution of the future handling of this matter which will be discussed in the letter to follow, but absent that agreement being reached, both the Diocese and I have a fiduciary duty to CBP to act in its best interest. I believe that entails making the best effort possible to secure the Target transaction for CBP, which in turn requires that we implement a relocation of easement agreement with the adjoining landowner and that we conduct our negotiations through our brokers to secure the best price and terms possible for that transaction. If you are in agreement, please sign in the space provided below and obtain Vern McLeish's signature as well.

Very truly yours,
Joseph C. Finley

Mr. David I. Osmond
Victoria Properties Inc.

Re: CBP, L.L.C./Diocese of Victoria/ Debenture Trustee

Note: The following letter contains a proposal that could be interpreted as a compromise and settlement of disputed claims and is therefore inadmissible in any proceedings where any of the claims or matters discussed may be involved.

Dear Dave:

This letter will present an outline of the basic terms that I believe we have agreed to and other terms that I would like to incorporate in an overall resolution of the above matter. I will not recite any factual background or history of dealing. Everyone involved is familiar with the circumstances and prior course of events and relevant documents and agreements.

1. The Diocese of Victoria and the Bishop of Victoria Corporation Sole will agree and acknowledge that the amount they will accept from Joseph C. Finley and *Corporate Business Park*, LLC is the sum of $3.4 million U.S. and that they will execute a covenant not to bring any legal action to recover any greater sum from either of them. The Diocese and Bishop of Victoria Corporation Sole will further agree that the sale proceeds from

the sale of the *Corporate Business Park* property will be the sole source of payment.

2. The Debenture Trustee for the holders of the AG Capital Judgment will agree and acknowledge that the amount owed by *Corporate Business Park*, LLC, Bishop of Victoria Corporation Sole and Joseph C. Finley is the amount of $ (limited to actual cost) US plus interest accruing from and after ___ (date of purchase)___ at six (6%) percent per annum.

3. Joseph C. Finley will agree to an amendment to the Operating Agreement of *Corporate Business Park*, LLC that will require the formal appointment of ___ (to be agreed upon) __ as a co-manager and that will clearly designate Joseph C. Finley as a co-manager only. The amendment will delineate the items that require joint agreement of the co-managers and specifically will include the following. The filing of a petition in bankruptcy for the company; selling all or any portion of the company's assets; encumbering the company's assets; commencing or settling any litigation; or receiving or disposing of any proceeds from a sale or legal settlement or re-financing or otherwise.

4. Joseph C. Finley will agree that *Corporate Business Park* shall have 18 months from the present to obtain a sale of its property in a sum sufficient to pay the debenture holders that own the AG Capital judgment. At the end of 18 months if a sale has not been agreed to which can be closed before the expiration of another 6 months according to its terms for an amount sufficient to pay the debenture holders, Finley will join in delivering a quit claim deed to the trustee for the debenture holders by *Corporate Business Park*, agree that the trustee shall have no obligation to account to *Corporate Business Park* or Finley thereafter and that both *Corporate Business Park* and Finley will have no right to participate in any sales proceeds from a subsequent sale of the *Corporate Business Park* property. The Trustee will cause to be vacated the judgment previously entered against Joseph C. Finley and *Corporate Business Park* in favor of AG Capital. Upon implementation of this agreement, a quit claim deed will be executed and delivered in escrow with appropriate instructions to implement the intent of this paragraph. ***PROVIDED HOWEVER,*** IF *Corporate Business Park* and/or Finley obtain a credible offer from a third party within thirty days from the date hereof to pay and satisfy in cash the amount owing to the debenture holders as agreed to above, then the Diocese of Victoria agrees to relinquish in full its interest in *Corporate Business Park*, LLC and will accept in return a pledge of Finley's then remaining interest in *Corporate Business Park* and its real property (provided

such interests are reasonably adequate to discharge Finley's and *Corporate Business Park*'s remaining obligation to the Diocese of Victoria and Bishop of Victoria Corporation Sole in the amount of $3.4 million US assuming a sale of the *Corporate Business Park* property for its fair market value).

5. All of the necessary parties will execute mutual releases of all claims not previously covered and will execute such other documents and agreements as are necessary to effectuate the purpose of the agreement outlined in this letter.

Please respond as soon as possible.

Very truly yours,
Joseph C. Finley

February 14, 2001

Joseph C. Finley
Bellevue, WA

Dear Joe:

Your letters of February 12, 2001, directed to Dave Osmond, have been passed on to me and the contents discussed with our lawyers and at Diocesan meetings. I wish to firm the following:

1. Messrs. Isherwood and Osmond are volunteers who are giving assistance to Bishop of Victoria with respect to the Lacey land. They have no authority to bind Bishop of Victoria, and no authority except to report back to me with their recommendations.

2. The proposals for settling debt, quit claiming your interest, and mutual releases are not acceptable to the Bishop of Victoria.

3. Bishop of Victoria will not sign, nor consent to *Corporate Business Park*, LLC signing, the easement agreement at this time. Our position is that you have placed *Corporate Business Park*, LLC in bankruptcy. Now that you have done this, I believe it is inappropriate for *Corporate Business Park*, LLC to enter into business transactions that it does have the financial resources to perform.

4. You advised Bishop of Victoria that you had entered into a listing agreement with Trammell Crow for the *Corporate Business Park* property. We have never been notified of this arrangement with Trammell Crow. We note the agreement is for 480 acres which would indicate it is not

limited to the property owned by *Corporate Business Park*, LLC. Under these circumstances, I believe that you are in a conflict of interest as you are not acting in the sole interests of *Corporate Business Park*, LLC

As you are aware, in order to repay the mortgage and the monies advanced by the Bishop to *Corporate Business Park*, LLC and to you, the Bishop of Victoria wishes to have the *Corporate Business Park* property sold for the highest and best price possible. The Bishop of Victoria will support a sale of the *Corporate Business Park*, LLC property that will maximize the return to the Bishop.

Yours truly,

BISHOP OF VICTORIA
Per: Vernon McLeish, Financial Administrator

March 13, 2001

Mr. Vernon McLeish
Diocese of Victoria

Re: *Corporate Business Park*, LLC

Dear Vern

I have reviewed your letter today to Marc Stern. Please understand that I share your position that Mr. Stern should take no action to the detriment of *Corporate Business Park*, LLC. Mr. Stern was retained to look after the best interests of *Corporate Business Park*, LC, and you may rest assured that I have not asked him to do anything to the contrary.

After you and your attorneys knowingly concealed from the company the existence of a buyer for over eight months, after you further concealed that fact from your debenture holders, after you further directed the buyer to seek property elsewhere, after you filed a motion for the appointment of a receiver without disclosing that information, after you supported a motion for relief from stay by the Indenture Trustee who is not an independent third party, but merely the Bishop's alter ego, and once again concealed the prior sequence of events involving the buyer, and after having supported the filing of an appraisal of value for exactly ½ the amount that you know the buyer was offering to pay, I am really not terribly interested in hearing from you or your attorneys on the topics of conflict of interest, ethics or self-serving instructions attempting to charge Mr. Stern with a duty to look after the best interest of *Corporate Business Park*, LLC.

As Messrs. Clinton and Fairchild are not authorized to accept legal process, I will ask Mr. Stern and my attorneys Stanislaw & Ashbough, to have you served as necessary in Victoria, and we will ask the Court for reimbursement for the cost of doing so. You need not worry about Mr. Stern accepting any instructions from me that would not be in the company's best interest. I cannot say the same about instructions that may be exchanged between you and Messrs. Fairchild and Clinton.

Very truly yours,
Joseph C. Finley

Chronology of Significant Events 1997- 2002
The Diocese of Victoria and its Washington Land Investment

Originally published in January 2003
Special Edition of *Island Catholic News*

1. June 30, 1997. Bishop of Victoria Corporation Sole becomes a co-venturer in *Corporate Business Park*, LLC (CBP) along with Seattle attorney Joseph Finley. CBP purchases 160 acres of industrial land in Lacey, Washington. Acquisition cost was roughly $5.5 million (US). Contrary to the published statements of the Diocese of Victoria made after the retirement of Bishop De Roo, the purchase was made pursuant to an appraisal on the property of over $14 million (US), and the appraiser expressly stated that a marketing period of up to 30 months could be expected for a property of this type. According to court documents, the purpose of the venture was to return to Bishop of Victoria Corporation Solve (BV) funds loaned in the late '80s and early '90s that could not be repaid due to the default of an investment-banking firm in Toronto. The venture provided for repayment of the funds previously loaned plus a return to BV ahead of any distribution of funds to CBP or Mr. Finley. *The purchase was completed virtually 100 percent with funds borrowed by the venture – i.e., not Diocesan funds nor Priory funds.*

2. July 1, 1998. The *Corporate Business Park* property was refinanced through AG Capital Corporation for $7.5 million to cover ongoing interest costs and other expenses. A new appraisal in excess of $14 million

supported the new financing. The Diocese was not a guarantor. AG Capital required that Mr. Finley and the Bishop sign the loan as principals being equally liable. But the venture did not appear in any jeopardy and *only a small amount of Priory funds were invested at that time.*

3.   March, 1999. Bishop De Roo retires. Court documents show that the new staff at the Diocese stopped paying the AG Capital loan without notice to CBP or Mr. Finley. *Staff and lawyers, principally Paul Bundon and Vernon McLeish demand that Mr. Finley sign an amended agreement as a condition of BV continuing to support the venture. Mr. Finley signed, but BV failed to make required debt payments – loan goes into default.* (By this time the loan reserves for CBP had run out, and by understanding and agreement, BV was making the loan payments on the CBP property.) An effort is to be made by the Diocese to refinance the CBP loan to 'lower interest costs.' This was never done.

4.   December 1999 – January 2000. Documents confirm that Diocese agrees with Finley and lender to bring loan current through 1999. This is done. Then Diocese notifies Finley that it will not make any further payments. Bundon and McLeish told Finley and CBP's lawyer that Mr. Allen Vandekerkhove was prepared to purchase the property for $7.5 million or ½ of value. This would not have retired the old debit, and it would have lost in addition, all funds advanced by the Diocese for *Corporate Business Park.* Mr. Finley refused to cooperate, ostensibly for those reasons. It does not appear that other alternatives or proposals to solve the problem of ongoing debt service are offered.

5.   February-March 2000. Diocese makes public disclosure of the investment in the Washington land. The public reaction is so negative and so strong that the Diocese makes an offer to contribute $2 million (US) to the debt to gain a release. This would have been a further loss to the Diocese. However, the negative atmosphere created by the entry of the AG Capital judgment that the Diocese permitted apparently precluded any refinancing at that time.

6.   May-June 2000. The Diocese and its staff, lawyers and advisers create a scheme to attempt to take the land away from *Corporate Business Park* and Mr. Finley. The only problem is that the scheme may be illegal under Washington law. The Diocese decides to issue bonds to parishioners in order to raise money to purchase the judgment from AG Capital. The offering was structured in such a way that, although the borrowed funds were under the control of the Diocese, the indenture trustee would be used to "purchase" the judgment because if the Bishop of Victoria Corporation Sole

purchased the judgment directly, it would have been satisfied and paid under Washington law, and the funds used would have been treated as a capital contribution to *Corporate Business Park*. In an attempt to avoid this result, the indenture trustee was used as the nominal "purchaser." However, according to a Washington lawyer familiar with such matters, Washington law does not honor transactions where the nominal purchaser is not the real party in interest. This matter is in litigation in Thurston County, Washington, and an adverse ruling against the Diocese will wipe out the judgment. The result of such a ruling would be that the Diocese would not have the ability to sell the Washington land to repay debentures. However, it has been learned that the Diocese, its lawyers and staff had a solution that made the debenture offering unnecessary. It is alleged that in May/June 2000, *the Diocese was approached by a broker on behalf of Target Corporation and made an offer to buy the CBP land for $14 million (US). This was enough money to cover all funds owed to the Diocese by CBP or Mr. Finley and return the profit the Diocese was entitled to under the CBP agreement and with Mr. Finley and would have left some $3 million as the rightful profit of CBP. The Diocese staff, its lawyers and advisers elected not to tell Mr. Finley or CBP or the prospective debenture purchasers about the prospective Target offer. Instead they proceeded with the debenture offering that had become unnecessary.* If this occurred as reliable sources and court documents indicate, it was a gross dereliction of duty and breach of fiduciary responsibility to the Diocese and the bondholders, and perhaps constituted securities fraud by concealing a material fact from the bondholders.

7.   September-November 2000. The debenture offering is completed and BV purchases the AG Capital judgment through the indenture trustee. Next, court documents show that the Diocese moved for the appointment of a receiver for CBP who would have had powers to strip the land from CBP and award it to the indenture trustee. This was countered by Finley who filed a Ch. 11 Bankruptcy petition for CBP. When Finley filed the Ch. 11, rather than proceeding with the Target transaction and sharing the proceeds with CBP, BV's staff, lawyers and advisers told Target to look elsewhere because they allegedly could not "delivery clear title" to the property. There apparently was no basis in law or fact, nor any other justification for this position.

8.   February, 2001. Finley learned that Target was attempting to purchase 142 acres adjacent to the CBP property through a representative to one of the owners. Unaware of the prior dealings with Target, Finley

notified Vernon McLeish and Paul Bundon, but they refused to meet with him. Instead, Finley was told to meet with two committee members who were advising the Diocese on a volunteer basis. *Finley explained to the volunteers that the Target sale could be saved because one of the owners of the 142 acres did not really wish to sell and was willing to cooperate so that Target would come back to the CBP property.* Finley later attended a meeting with Vernon McLeish and Paul Bundon in Victoria on or about February 10, 2001. Finley proposed that the parties cooperate to bring the Target sale back to CBP. The staff and lawyers later refused to do so. *The Target deal was lost as a result, and Target purchased the adjoining 142 acres in an all-cash $14 million (US) sale in July 2001. If the Target sale had been done, the bondholders and the Diocese would have been paid in full in July 2001 and all litigation between Finley and the Diocese assumedly would have ended then.*

9.   March 2001 through May 2002. Finley and the Diocese have been battling in court since March of 2001. A potential sale of the property to a land speculator/developer was implemented in May 2001 for $9.5 million with Finley, the indenture trustee and the Diocese battling over the funds. The sale did not close. *In the course of pursuing litigation, the deposition of Vernon McLeish was taken in May 2002. During that deposition, McLeish admitted that the debenture offering provided that surplus lands in Canada had been earmarked for sale to retire the debentures. In fact the debenture offering contains a promise that the Diocese would sell those lands and use the proceeds to pay the debentures.* The debenture offering contains a representation that the surplus lands were worth $15 million (CDN). In his deposition McLeish testified that all but about $2 million of the surplus lands had been sold but that only $6 million (CDN) had been realized from those sales. McLeish testified that none of the $5 million had been paid to debenture holders. Little of those funds were held in reserve. Instead they had been used to retire other bank debt and for other purposes. This was directly contrary to the terms stated in the debenture offering. The Diocese has an argument that funds could be used to retire other debt. *The Diocese could have taken the second opportunity to sell to Target and solve the entire problem. It chose not to. Accepting that solution would have negated any justification or necessity for selling surplus land.*

10.   August 2002. The Diocese and Joseph Finley are mired in litigation with no end in sight. A lawyer familiar with court procedures in Thurston County where the matter is pending, indicates that it could take another 6-9 months to go to trial, and appeals could take another 1-2 years. So long as that continues, the Washington land cannot be used to

repay the debentures, and proceeds of the sale of the "surplus land" are not available. There does not appear to be a ready source for repayment of the debentures.

It appears that previously published reports claiming that the Diocese has "lost millions" on the Washington land investment may have been unfounded and possibly misleading.

When All is Revealed Bishop Remi De Roo Will be Vindicated

By Joe Gubbels, Edmonton

Excerpted from the January 12, 2003 edition of *Prairie Messenger*

The Editor:

Your report on Bishop Remi De Roo's anniversary (PM, Jan. 8) appears to contain a back-handed slap, with the comment in the last paragraph.

With your lack of accurate investigation, you have become caught up with those who wish to denigrate and vilify Bishop Remi after his retirement.

Your controversial parting words in your report refer to "race-horses," "$17 million in debts" and "high-risk investments."

Perhaps, a thorough reading of the "A Special Edition: Lacey Land Revisited" which appeared in the January issue of *Island Catholic News* and other investigative reports in public newspapers would have provided you with the "other side of the story."

The highlights of the Special Edition and other public newspapers point out:

- that Arabian horses are show horses, not race horses;
- that the Lacey land is the disputed investment, not the show horse investment;
- that the assessed value of the Lacey land, at the time of purchase was $14 million US, but was purchased for $7.5 million US;
- that the Lacey land investment was a wise investment, if it was left to mature;
- that the present value is estimated to be much more than the initial assessment;
- that there exists a sworn declaration indicating that there was a purchaser for the Lacey land (at a price of $13.9 million US) prior to the diocesan public issue of debentures;
- that the $17 million CDN debt appears to include all diocesan debts not just the Lacey land;

- that there is grave danger of foreclosure on the Lacey land by the end of May 2003, due to unpaid $1 million CDN in land taxes;
- that there are many questions regarding the recent sales of diocesan "surplus" lands at lower than assessed value.

It seems to me that when all the facts are known, Bishop Remi may well be vindicated and the real villains may be exposed.

About the Author

Patrick Jamieson says to understand Remi De Roo's fall from grace, you must understand Catholic Church politics.

The keeper of the faith
By Mark Browne

Saanich Weekend Edition, September 7, 2001

Former Victoria Catholic Bishop Remi De Roo was the darling of the Canadian left. He was at the forefront of pushing for change through progressive causes. But shortly after his retirement, a financial scandal tied into his leadership of the local Catholic Church tarnished his reputation. Now, the former editor of Island Catholic News is trying to rehabilitate De Roo's reputation in a new biography which argues that to

understand De Roo's fall from grace, one must understand the internal
politics of the Catholic Church.

Patrick Jamieson has had an ongoing fascination with retired Victoria
Bishop Remi De Roo and the politics of the Catholic Church.
When De Roo found himself under fire last year over poor investments
(made on behalf of the Victoria Catholic Diocese before his retirement in 1999),
Jamieson came to his defence. Speaking to the *Weekend Edition* in June 2000,
the former editor of *Island Catholic News* argued that the right wing of the
Catholic Church was out to get De Roo because of their opposition to his left-
wing social views.
It's a topic Jamieson clearly can't get enough of, given his new book *In the
Avant Garde: The Prophetic Catholicism of Remi De Roo (and Politics Within the Catholic Church)*.
"He's a very important Canadian figure," says Jamieson of what prompt-
ed him to write the book.
Jamieson covers a wide range of issues in his biography of De Roo, including: the investment scandal in which the Victoria Diocese lost money on an
investment in Arabian horses in Lacey, Washington, the way that De Roo and
other left leaning Canadian bishops have been discredited, the conflict between
De Roo and newspaper baron Conrad Black and how De Roo began challenging the Canadian establishment in the 1980s.
"Basically, I'm trying to raise a lot of questions," Jamieson told the *Weekend Edition*.
Regarding the horse investments which are at the heart of De Roo's fall
from grace, Jamieson maintains that the major decisions related to the investment (and which led to the deal going sour) occurred after De Roo had already
retired as Victoria Bishop, as such decisions were made by the financial administrator of the diocese that took over after his retirement.
He points out that De Roo's signature is not on any of the documents that
were part of the horse investment deal and that Muriel Clemenger, who was
the financial administrator at the time, signed the papers.
Jamieson says that Clemenger also signed documents for a subsequent
land deal in Lacey – one that the diocese had invested in hoping to recoup money lost in the horse deal.
At the same time, Jamieson suggests that if the strategy employed by
Clemenger regarding the land investment had been left in place, it might very
we have paid off and got the diocese out of debt.
He notes that when the diocese's new financial administration took over
after De Roo's retirement, they stopped payments to creditors – and the matter
wound up in the courts.

Jamieson says he made a point in his book of criticizing the inquiry that the Catholic Church held into how the Victoria Diocese became embroiled in financial troubles in August 2000.

He insists that the inquiry was prejudiced from the start, pointing out how the committee chairman described De Roo as a "gambling addict" to the media.

Jamieson says that much of his book deals with how De Roo became a controversial figure within the Catholic Church after the right wing of the church gained more power in the 1980s.

"With the changing of the guard in Rome, he was like a mouse thrown into a room full of cats," he says. "It wasn't a big plot and conspiracy; it was just a poisoned atmosphere against what he stands for."

Jamieson notes in his book that former Montreal Archbishop Joseph Charbonneau and Father Eugene Cullinane of Saskatchewan were thrown out of office in the 1940s for their left-wing social views.

He argues that Father Bob Ogle, also from Saskatchewan, was removed from office in the early 1980s for being seen as leaning too far to the left of the political spectrum.

De Roo's heated relationship with Black is also addressed in the book. When De Roo expressed his views regarding what he felt needed to be done to ease unemployment in the early 1980s, those views didn't go over too well with the media baron who had converted to Catholicism several years previously.

Jamieson also writes about De Roo's early life in Manitoba during the depression. He suggests that the tough economic times of the 1930s had a significant impact on De Roo's character and the views that he expressed later in his life when a Bishop.

Jamieson asserts that there were attempts within the higher echelons of the Catholic Church to silence De Roo, after he had made it clear to the *Weekend Edition* in 1999 (when he was about to retire as the bishop) that he planned to continue as an activist on social issues. "Shortly after that, he was silenced for the first time. I think what Rome is afraid of with him is that he's so articulate and he's such a progressive symbol for church reform – and what I call progressive theology – (and) that's what go him into trouble," argues Jamieson.

A Victoria diocese staff member contacted by the *Weekend Edition* said that neither the current Victoria Bishop Raymond Roussin nor anybody else within the diocese' administration were prepared to comment on Jamieson's book at this time, since they have yet to review a copy.

Selected Reporting On Post-Retirement Year 2000 Financial Saga

Browne, Mark, *Victoria News Weekend Edition, Crisis rocks the church*, Friday, March 3, 2000, page 2; *The keeper of the faith*, September 7, 2001, pp. 1, 5.

Dickson, Louise, *Times Colonist, Loan plea upsets churchgoers*, Monday, May 15, 2000, pp. A1-2; *Former bishop silent on debt, Borrow to cover interest and expenses, Roman Catholic Church properties listed*, Tuesday, May 16, 2000, pp. A1, 4; *De Roo offers three-sentence letter of apology*, Sunday, May 28, 2000, pp. A1-2.

Di Cresce, Greg, *Winnipeg Sun Police Reporter, Uncomfortable pews, Parishioners protest controversial bishop*, Friday, May 26, 2000, p. 5; *Mountain out of a molehill, Church official defends B.C. Bishop*, Saturday, May 27, 2000, p. 4.

Ian Dutton, *Times Colonist, Catholics raise cash to ease debt, Campaign nets almost $13 million to undo burden left by Bishop Remi De Roo*, Friday, August 4, 2000, p. B1.

Foot, Richard, *National Post, Bishop retired as an 'unremitting reformer,'* Tuesday, February 29, 2000, page A5.

Harnett, Cindy E., *Times Colonist, De Roo's apology not enough for Roussin, Successor says he's acting fast to improve church accountability*, Sunday, May 21, 2000, pp. A1-2.

Henderson, Larry, *Challenge Magazine, An Afterword*, column, September, 2000, p. 28.

Jiminez, Marina, *National Post, Victoria diocese bought 64 hectares to develop racetrack, $3.5M spent in legal fees and mortgage payments*, Tuesday, February 29, 2000, page A5; *Victoria bishop lost gamble on Arabian mares*, Wednesday, March 1, 2000, pp. A1-2; *Bishop's high risk deal not on the books: Successor, National Post*, Friday, March 3, 2000, pp. A1, 12.

Lunman, Kim, *The Globe and Mail, A blessed pitchman hits up the flock, Victoria parishes hear plea to bail out diocese, The Globe and Mail*, Saturday, May 27, 2000; *Trust Fund for nuns wiped out in Victoria, Pension money used to buy race horses, The Globe and Mail*, Monday, May 29, 2000, p. A3; *The lawyer, the bishop and the money pit, The Globe and Mail*, Saturday, June 17, 2000, p. A11; *Bishop's secret deals 'beyond belief,' probe finds, church report blasts Victoria's Remi De Roo, The Globe and Mail*, Friday, June 30, 2000, pp. 1.

Matas, Robert, *The Globe and Mail, Real-estate deal gone bad divides church supporters, Social activist Bishop De Roo criticized for poor financial management of diocese, The Globe and Mail,* Thursday, March 2, 2000, p. A5.

Paterson, Jody, *Times Colonist, Church land deal raises issue of ethics,* Wednesday, March 1, 2000, p. A3.

Roussin, Raymond, *Island Catholic News, Bishop announces Diocesan Financial Concerns, The full text of the statement read at Sunday masses, February 27th in The Victoria Diocese,* March, 2000, p. 5.

Times Colonist, Catholic diocese rocked by debt, Investment losses force sale of assets on Island, court action considered, February 28, 2000, pp. A1-2; *Financial crisis worries Catholics,* Tuesday, February 29, 2000, page C1.

Todd, Douglas, *Vancouver Sun, Successor named for Catholic leader,* February 24, 1999; *Island Catholic church sells land to pay millions in debts,* Monday, February 28, 2000, pp. A1-2; *Ex-bishop admits role in money woes, Remi De Roo has acknowledged a 'major problem' occurred during his Island tenure,* Tuesday, February 29, 2000, page A3; *Fast horses, big deal linked to island Catholic money woes,* Wednesday, March 1, 2000, pp. A1-2; *Probe not personal, Catholic bishop says,* Friday, March 3, 2000, page A3.

Vallis, Mary, *The Province, Church cash woes unfold,* Thursday, March 2, 2000, p. A12; *Bishop probes mystery loans,* Friday, March 3, 2000, p. A16.

Westad, Kim, *Times Colonist, Church took risk on U.S. land, bad investments leave Island diocese in debt,* Wednesday, March 1, 2000, page A1-3; *Church official says bishop approved loan,* Thursday, March 2, 2000, page one; *Secret deals astonished new bishop,* Friday, March 3, 2000, pp. A1-2; *Church debt opens old wounds, financial woes revive touchy political divide,* Sunday, March 5, 2000, pp. A1,6, 7; *Court slaps foreclosure order on church-owned land,* Saturday, March 18, 2000, pp. A1-2; *Commission probes diocese's finances,* Wednesday, March 22, 2000, p. C3; *Church report rips into De Roo, Commission says if former bishop had not retired already, he would have faced papal action for damages that will last generations,* Friday, June 30, 2000, pp A1-3.

Wilson, Carla, *Times Colonist, De Roo admits blame on debt, Former Victoria bishop says sorry, 'acted in good faith',* Saturday, May 20, 2000, pp. A1-2; *Debt Crisis – Catholics dig deep for ailing diocese,* Tuesday, June 27, 2000, p. C1.

Young, Gerard, *Times Colonist, Diocese asks parishioners for millions,* May 14, 2000, page one; *Bishop pledges closer scrutiny of church funds,* Wednesday,

May 24, 2000. pp. A1-2; *Roman Catholics demand answers, the word forgive is far from parishioners' lips,* Thursday, May 25, 2000, pp. A1; *Catholic Diocese in crisis – Landowner in no hurry to help church sell up,* Friday, May 26, 2000, page C1; *Ex-bishop gambled assets from convent, De Roo chased losses and had two sets of books, concludes Roman Catholic Church commission,* Saturday, May 27, 2000, pp. A1,4; *Catholics in Crisis – Mystery Man,* pp. A1-2; *The Promised Land,* C4; *Key Players,* C5; *Money For Horses,* C5, Sunday, June 4, 2000; *Church offered deal to ease debt,* Monday, June 12, 2000, pp. A1-2; *Catholics ease burden of mortgage,* Tuesday, September 19, 2000, pp. A1-2; *Offer to purchase land eases church debt woes,* Tuesday, July 24, 2001, pp. A1-2; *Church deal falls through, Seattle company backs out of deal that would have rid Victoria's Roman Catholic diocese of land in Washington,* Tuesday, August 28, 2001, pp. B1-2.

Totals: *Times Colonist* front page – 19 times between March 1 & September 1, 2000; other section lead page ten times; number of different reporters – eight.

Bibliography

Cirlot, J.E., *A Dictionary of Symbols*, Routledge & Kegan Paul, 1962.

Clarke, Tony, *Behind The Mitre, The Moral Leadership Crisis in The Canadian Catholic Church*, Harper, 1995; *Silent Coup-Confronting the Big Business Takeover of Canada*, Lorimer, 1999.

Daly, Bernard M., *Remembering for Tomorrow, A History of the Canadian Conference of Catholic Bishops, 1943-1993*, CCCB, 1994.

De Roo, Remi Joseph, *Cries of Victims, Voice of God*, Forward by Hon. Thomas R. Berger, edited by Bede Hubbard, Novalis, 1986; *Even Greater Things, Hope and Challenge after Vatican II*, with Bernard and Mae Daly, Novalis, Ottawa, 1999; *Forward In The Spirit, Challenge of The People's Synod*, Preface by Remi J. De Roo, edited by Grant Maxwell & Pearl Gervais, Diocese of Victoria, 1991; *In the Eye of the Catholic Storm, The Church Since Vatican II*, with Mary Jo Leddy and Douglas Roche, edited with an introduction by Michael Creal, Harper, 1992; *Man to Man, A frank talk between layman and bishop*, with Douglas Roche, edited with an introduction by Gary MacEoin, Bruce Publishing, Milwaukee, 1969; *Of Justice, Revolutions, and Human Rights ... Notes on a trip to Central America*, Diocese of Victoria, April 1980; *The Diocesan Synod as a Means to Develop Doctrine*, ICN Publishing, 2000.

Jamieson, Patrick, *Victoria: Demers to De Roo, 150 Years of Catholic History on Vancouver Island*, Ekstasis Editions, 1997. *In The Avant Garde – The Prophetic Catholicism of Remi De Roo and Politics Within the Catholic Church*. Ekstasis Editions Canada Ltd. 2002.

Ward-Harris, E.D., *A Nun Goes to the Dogs, A biography of Mother Cecilia Mary, OSB*, Sono Nis, 1977.

Index